Sacred Architecture of London

First published 2012
by Aeon Books
London NW3

www.aeonbooks.co.uk

British Library Cataloguing in Publication Data

A C.I.P. is available for this book from the British Library

ISBN-13: 978-190465-862-7

Sacred Architecture of London

Nigel Pennick

Aeon Books

CONTENTS

Introduction 1

St Mary Le Strand silhouetted, looking east.

Introduction

In the year 1666, between the second and the sixth of September, the greater part of the city of London was destroyed by an unstoppable conflagration, which soon became known as the Great Fire of London. *The Tablet of Memory*, published, in London, by J. Bew in 1774 tells us that it "burnt down 113,000 houses, the city-gates, guildhall &c. 86 churches, among which was St. Paul's cathedral, and 400 streets; the ruins were 436 acres…". After the catastrophes of the Civil War, the tyranny of Cromwell, the plague of 1665, and the maritime wars against Holland, the fire came as yet another ordeal for the city's inhabitants. But instead of destroying their will to continue, the reconstruction that followed this major disaster resulted in an unprecedented outburst of creativity. From the period after the fire come the most remarkable sacred buildings erected in England since the reformation, churches built according to ancient classical principles. The main creative period was around 1670 to 1750, but the tradition continued until 1792. The churches built after the Great Fire of London express a spiritual dimension of religion that goes beyond sectarian belief. They can be seen to be epitomes of all the cosmos, and of divine creation.

In parallel with fundamentalist interpretation of any particular religion as exclusively and unquestionably true (depending, of course, on which particular religion and sect the true believer belongs to), there is always another parallel current of understanding that tells of an eternal tradition, manifesting in characteristic form in that religion but not bound to its particular doctrines. This universal current is therefore embodied in any sacred building that is constructed according to true principles, whatever deity the building is dedicated to. Although it is used by various religions as a means of expressing the infinite according to the particular interpretation of each cult, sect or faith, this tradition is transcendent of religious doctrine. For it is based on universal symbols rather than the ever-changing revisions and interpretations of scripture imposed upon functional religions by external events and politics. This eternal, universal tradition appears historically in interlinked ways in Pagan, Jewish, Christian and Islamic places of worship and sepulture. As Sir Christopher Wren (1632-1723) notes of the ancients: "Not only their Altars and Sacrifices were mystical, but the very Forms of their Temples".[1]

Hence, in the West, the temple archetype has been used by most sects of the Pagan, Jewish, Christian and Muslim religions as the appropriate form for what are viewed as vessels of the divine light, which is timeless and transcendent, Sir Christopher Wren's "attribute of Eternal".[2] This does not mean, as is frequently suggested, that there is some kind of secret apostolic succession of the esoteric, hidden in an unbroken form from antiquity to the present day, (as manifested in eighteenth century Masonic writings, nineteenth century theosophical texts, and some twentieth century 'Rosicrucian' and wiccan ones). Rather, it indicates that universal symbols and ideas, as well as practical knowledge, reappear when the conditions are right. In human perception, the spiritual is the timeless, universal quality of being. Naturally, there has always been continuity between succeeding generations, together with interchange between creative individuals, both through personal contact and distant media, but this has never been art of a rigid system. Rather, it is free and opportunistic.

As with all cultural manifestations of the spirit, past and present, the spiritual works of post-Great Fire London were pluralistic, crystallizing in a certain way suited to the era. The many sources and currents that came together then were the

---

1 Sir Christopher Wren, in Christopher Wren Jr. (ed.): *Parentalia, or, Memoirs of the Family of the Wrens*, London, 1750, *Tract IV*.

2 Ibid. 261.

result of various parallel developments and cross-influences, a living, growing, changing and developing set of ideas, beliefs, techniques and practices that were not fixed, but open to new insights and creative interpretations. Things made by human hands to embody the universal laws of the cosmos can reconcile our transient mundane existence with the transcendent. Through the presence of such meaningful elements in material culture, we can perceive the essential nature of our being. Only an ensouled artefact can embody this spirit in a palpable form. It has the power to reach outside itself towards humans, who can perceive it not only as an embodiment of the culture from which it has emerged, but also as a particular instance of the universal.

The complete meaningful body of work of the London churches of this period is not just restricted to those relatively few that still exist in the twenty-first century. The totality of the work is relevant: the architects' researches, sketches, plans, preliminary or unbuilt projects and written descriptions as well as the constructed buildings. Of those built, not only the extant ones are significant, but also those that have been altered, destroyed or demolished and those that remain as fragments or ruins. Subsequent oral lore, writings and books about them are equally part of their total cultural meaning. They include later maps, measured plans, artwork and photographs; subsequent history, customs and usages, stories, poems, legends, theories, superstitions and fictional writings. The existing buildings are just the physical core of a much greater and generally unrecognized reality.

These London churches are part of a then emergent Deist current that was instrumental in the formation of Masonic doctrine, with God being viewed non-sectarianly as the Great Architect of the Universe whose principles take material form through number and geometry. This symbolism appears in a poem by George Herbert (1593-1633), *The Church Floore*, which envisages religious values in architectural terms, with the final lines:

> Blest be the *Architect*, whose art
> Could build so strong in a weak heart![3]

In the nineteenth century, the Arts and Crafts architect and teacher William Richard Lethaby, in his *Architecture, Mysticism and Myth* (1892), wrote: "The main purpose and burthen of sacred architecture – and all architecture, temple, tomb, or palace, was sacred in the early days – is thus inextricably bound up with a people's thoughts about God and the universe".[4] It is from this perspective that the London churches built after the Great Fire can be best understood. From surviving materials, it is clear that the architects of these churches saw their work in this light. They examined the meaning, geometry, symbolism and structure of antique temples, both the ancient Jewish one in Jerusalem and those of classical Paganism. In them they saw the common threads of sacredness, reinforced by the repeated acknowledgement of the sacred in ancient Jewish, Pagan and Christian scriptures. The spiritual values embodied in the Temple of Diana at Ephesus and the Temple of Mars in Rome were seen as essentially the same as those expressed by Solomon's Temple and early Christian buildings. Hence the world image, as perceived by God, was brought into physical form in London as it had been in Ephesus, Jerusalem and Rome, as a timeless vision of unity.

Nigel Campbell Pennick

Cambridge, Royal Oak Day, the twenty-ninth of May, 2005,

(revised 2012).

---

3 W.S. Scott: *The Fantasticks: Donne, Herbert, Crashaw, Vaughan*, John Westhouse, London, 1945, 66.

4 William Richard Lethaby: *Architecture, Mysticism and Myth*, London, 1892, 2.

Chapter 1

Legend, Precepts and Principles

My Streets are my Ideas of Imagination
Awake Albion, awake! And let us awake up together.

William Blake

The London Legendarium

Legendary history is the foundation of all ancient traditions. It forms the mythological basis for all religions, as well as national stories throughout the world. Each land, each faith, has its own particular foundation myth and particular named individuals associated with it. Mythic ancestral parental couples like Bor and Bestla, Beli and Anna, Askr and Embla or Adam and Eve vie for priority with more individualized characters such as Aeneas, Brutus, Einiged, Woden, Noah, Romulus and Remus, Hengest and Horsa. Along with sagas, lays, genealogies, legendary chronicles, myths and histories, these characters and stories make up the spiritual basis for individual cultures, the particular legendarium that defines a faith, a nation or a people.

London's classical tradition is an expression of the city's legendarium,[5] a component of what William Blake called "The Acts of Albion" (otherwise 'The Matter of Britain'). The basic elements of the legendarium come through ancient writings that, when they were written, had the authority of having been handed down from what was even then great antiquity, rooted in the eldritch world. These myths tell us about our cultural roots, expressing no less than the character and inner principles of

---

5 On the meaning of *legendaria* and the spirit of place, see Nigel Pennick: *Cambridge – Spirit of Place*, Old England House, Cambridge, 2004, 1–4. For London, Nigel Pennick: 'Legends of London' in John Matthews & Chesca Potter (eds.): *The Aquarian Guide to Legendary London*, Aquarian Press, Wellingborough, 1990, 21-34.

The battered and soot-blackened sculpture of King Lud which once graced Ludgate, kept in the porch of St Dunstan-in-the-West, Fleet Street.

British identity. British legendary history was recorded chiefly by Geoffrey of Monmouth (1136), Matthew of Westminster (1307) and Matthew Paris, who used earlier sources including the writings of Gildas and ancient Welsh redactions of

Brut. Thus medieval writers acknowledged the pre-Christian
origin of the British nation. Later it was re-framed by Raphael
Holinshed in his *Chronicles of England, Scotland, and Ireland* and
features in the inspired works of William Shakespeare, Ben
Jonson, John Milton and William Blake.

The legendarium tells us that London was founded as the
result of a sacred act of the Elder Faith, the invocation of the
goddess Diana. As with every place whose roots were set in
archaic times, London has a legendary founder. He is Brutus,
who was a refugee from the destroyed city of Troy. On his
wanderings by ship with some of the survivors in search of
a new homeland, he came across a temple dedicated to Diana
on the uninhabited island of Leogetia (called Leogicia by
Matthew of Westminster),[6] which had been laid waste in old
times. Matthew of Westminster tells of the solemn rite enacted
by Brutus at Diana's fane: he "stood before the altar of the
goddess, holding in his right hand a sacrificial vessel full of
wine and the blood of a white doe, and broke the silence with
these words:

> Queen of the groves, of all wild beasts the foe,
> You, who through heaven and shades below can roam;
> Reveal, I pray, the future fates, and show
> What land shall give us a safe, lasting home.
> Where I may kindle you a sacred fire,
> And build a temple for your virgin choir.

When he had repeated this nine times, he walked round the
altar four times, and poured forth the blood and wine which he
held on the altar, and lay down on the skin of the doe, which
he had stretched before the altar, and thus, having invited
slumber, he fell asleep. It was then about the third hour of
the night, when mortals are sunk in most pleasant sleep; then

---

6 Matthew of Westminster (trans. C.D.Yonge): *The Flowers of History*,
1307. Henry G. Bohn, London, 1853, Book II, *The Third Age of the
World*, Chapter XXI.

it appeared to him that the goddess was standing before him, and addressing him in this manner:

> In the far west, beyond the Gallic shore,
> A seagirt isle in that vast ocean lies;
> A seagirt isle, which whilome giants bore,
> Now desolate, invites your hand's emprise.
> Seek that, for it shall be your lasting home,
> Your flag shall on a second Troy be unfurl'd... .[7]

Brutus followed these oracular instructions and sailed to Britain. After many adventures, he "came at length to the River Thames, walked up and down its banks, and chose a location suited to his purpose. There then he built a city and called it Troia Nova. For long ages afterwards, it was known by this name, but finally, by a corruption it came to be called Trinovantum".[8]

Later, early forms of the present name London emerged through its connexion with a later King of Britain called Lud. He renewed and rebuilt the city "in such a style that no other city in the most distant kingdoms could boast of palaces more fair".[9] The site of his western gate, Ludgate, and the street-name Ludgate Hill, are memories of the noble King Lud. The battered remains of Lud's statue, removed from the later Ludgate when it was demolished in the eighteenth century, remains in the porch of St Dunstan's-in-the-West in Fleet Street. Lud's name was recalled much later by conservative activists who opposed the use of machinery and the resulting unemployment brought by it. They called themselves the

---

7 Ibid.

8 Gaufridus Monemutensis (Geoffrey of Monmouth): *History of the Kings of Britain*, i, 17. The scene of Brutus offering to Diana was illustrated by Matthew Paris in the thirteenth century in the *Corpus Cambridge* MS 26, 7.

9 First called Kaerlud, then Kaerlundein. Gaufridus, op cit., iii, 20. The Welsh name for London is Llundain, alternatively Caerludd.

Luddites. When the Romans incorporated Britain into their empire, Lud's city was again renewed as Londinium. A medieval lyric, *In Honour of the City of London*, acknowledges the city as New Troy:

> Gladdeth anon, thou lusty Troynovant.
> City that some time cleped was New Troy;
> In all the earth, imperial as thou stant,
> Princess of towns, of pleasure and of joy,
> A richer resteth under no Christian roy,
> For manly power, with craftès natural,
> Formeth non fairer sith the flood of Noy:
> London, thou art the flower of Cities all.[10]

From medieval times onward, this London legendarium was acknowledged in traditional lore, images on buildings and city gates, in craftsmen's guild pageants and the Lord Mayor's

The Torhalle at Lorch, Germany, Carolingian Classical Architecture, late eighth century.

10 From *Early English Lyrics*, ed. A.T. Quiller-Couch, Clarendon Press, Oxford, n.d. c. 1910, 21-22.

procession, as well as in coronations, royal weddings and funerals. The Lord Mayor's procession, held annually, is the oldest unbroken annual mayoral inauguration in the world. At the coronation of King James I on Thursday the fifteenth of March 1603, among the symbolic features welcoming the new king to London was a temporary ceremonial gateway inscribed with the legend LONDINIVM. Ben Jonson's scenography for this 'king's entertainment' included the figure of the *Genius Urbis*, the spirit of the city of London, who emerged from a Temple of Janus which had an altar dedicated to the new king as *Imp. Jacobus Max. Caesar. Augustus* ("The Emperor James the Great, August Caesar", the form of dedication of Roman altars to the *cultus* of the Pagan emperors' *numen*).[11] The guiser personating the Genius Urbis was "crowned with a wreath of plane-tree, which is said to be *arbor genialis*".[12] The London Plane remains the characteristic tree of the city.

Even if not true by present-day criteria of history – what religion or mythical belief is? – this legendarium, with its fascinating place-specific tales, is an integral part of the nature of London and meaningful to those who have any feeling for the continuity of the spirit of place. As with religions, it is not the historical accuracy of the stories that is inspiring, but the ethical principles that underly them, and how they can be used as guides to action in the present.

The Classical Renaissance

The London legendarium speaks of the origin of British civilization in the classical tradition of which Greece and Rome are also part. In the west, this tradition was broken by the collapse of Roman power and the fragmentation of the empire. It

---

11 Jonson, ibid., 455.

12 Ben Jonson: *The Works of Ben Jonson*, 9 vols, London, 1816, Vol. 6, 430.

was drawn together again in a reduced form by Charlemagne when he founded the Holy Roman Empire in 800 CE, but there was not the socioeconomic base to recreate the finest buildings that had existed in antiquity. The Carolingian empire was under continuous attack by Viking incursions from the north, and Islamic invaders from the south, necessitating a large 'defence budget'. A later incursion from the east by the Magyars as far west as central France was catastrophic. The finest Carolingian buildings were based upon the architecture of the still-thriving Byzantine Roman Empire in the east, whose most splendid city was Constantinople. The eastern Roman Empire effectively ceased to exist when Constantinople was conquered by Turkish forces in 1453 and became the capital of the Ottoman Empire, the present-day Istanbul. However, the Carolingian empire was not just a pale reflection of Byzantium. Important technical innovations such as improved steel weaponry and stained glass windows were invented in the west at that time.

A Roman geometrical mosaic in the ruins of the second century CE Villa Adriano, the Emperor Hadrian's palace at Tivoli, Italy.

Later, in the twelfth century, a new form of architecture arose, now called the Gothic, and viewed as an exclusively Christian architecture. At its inception, it was called just "modern", or outside France, *Opus Francigenium* – work in the French form. The name 'Gothic' is a pejorative term given by sixteenth and seventeenth century commentators such as Sir Henry Wotton who admired the classical and (wrongly) considered the Gothic barbaric, but it has stuck and is used universally. The Gothic was based on Roman sacred geometry, but did not follow ancient canons, for it was progressive in nature with an unprecedented form-language and structural system. New forms arose continually, building on earlier experience, as master masons experimented with ever more daring innovations. The finest buildings of the medieval period were made according to Gothic principles.

The Roman author Marcus Vitruvius Pollio, who lived in the first century BCE, wrote an architectural treatise that survives to this day. Known today as *The Ten Books on Architecture*, it is a manual of architecture that deals with practical aspects of building: materials, location, orientation, geometry, design and proportions. There is evidence that it was always available in some form to architects in the west after the fall of the empire. But during the Renaissance it took on the cachet of the definitive work on classical architecture because it was the only work to survive intact from the reign of the first emperor, Octavian (Augustus).

The unification of the pluralistic elements within western civilization, in the shape of the form-language of classical architecture, took place in Italy in the fifteenth century under the influence of Vitruvius. In 1453, Leon Battista Alberti was able to state publicly the bald fact that the basilica, that is, the basic church form, is a particular type of ancient temple. Most Gothic churches, too, are derived from the basilica, though greatly developed beyond it. The basilica is noted by Gabriel

Leroux as being derived from the sanctuaries used by Roman adherents of oriental cults, such as Mithraism.[13] By exposing the ancient Pagan origin of all sacred buildings, and the essential spiritual continuity that this implies, their physical presence could be honoured, rather than being viewed as superseded remains that ought to be shunned. Now, again, their physical presence could be honoured as a vital and noble part of the continuum of traditional architecture. The influential work in this process was Alberti's *De re aedificatoria (On Architecture)*.

Chapter III of Book VII of *De re aedificatoria* (finally published in 1485) is titled "With how much Thought, Care and Diligence we ought to lay out and adorn our Temples; to what Gods and in what Places we should build them, and of the various kinds of Sacrifices".[14] The next chapter has the title "Of the Parts, Forms and Figures of Temples and their Chapels, and how these latter should be distributed". In this section he discusses the forms and sacred geometry of temples. From Alberti onwards, the eternal tradition present in the architecture of the temples of the Elder Faith, occasionally used before, was applied generally to churches. The oneness of temple and church was a recognition of this.

Another seemingly significant work in this process of validation of antique symbolism is Francesco Colonna's book, *Hypnerotomachia Poliphili (The Strife of Love in a Dream)*. Published in Italian in 1499, it describes the author's pursuit of love in the form of a dream.[15] Set in a classical Pagan landscape, it details the architecture of temples with their accompanying sacrifices, rites and ceremonies in honour of the gods, without Christian apologetics. The landscape elements are reminiscent of the

---

13 Gabriel Leroux cited by Gordon J. Laing: *Survivals of Roman Religion*, Harrap, London, 1931, 188-189.

14 Leon Battista Alberti (trans. Giacomo Leoni): *The Ten Books of Architecture (De re aedificatoria)*, London, 1755.

15 English translation by Jocelyn Godwin, Thames & Hudson, 2003.

grounds of the Emperor Hadrian's Villa at Tivoli, emulated throughout the renaissance by popes, princes and prelates, replete with temples, groves, fountains and altars to the *genius loci*.[16] Colonna's temple descriptions are closely related in form and spirit to the work of Alberti that was so influential in church design, and the later studies of ancient Pagan monuments by Sebastiano Serlio and Giovanni Battista Montano.

Classical Essentials Renewed

The London churches of the period 1670-1790 incorporate influences from a number of monumental buildings of antiquity. They include Solomon's Temple in Jerusalem, Egyptian obelisks, the Mausoleum at Halicarnassus, the Temple of Diana at Ephesus, the Tower of the Winds at Athens, the temples of

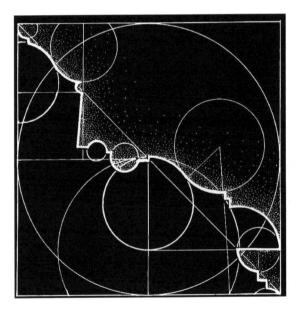

The geometrical principle of a classical moulding.

---

16 See William L. Macdonald & John A. Pinto: *Hadrian's Villa and Its Legacy*, Yale University Press, New Haven & London, 1995.

Bacchus, Jupiter and Venus at Baalbek, the tomb of Porsena, the temples of Vesta, Mars Ultor and Peace in Rome, Roman triumphal columns and arches, and various antique Roman tombs.

In certain periods since the fall of the Roman Empire in the west, architects have made intensive studies of the buildings of antiquity, both from written accounts and actual remains.

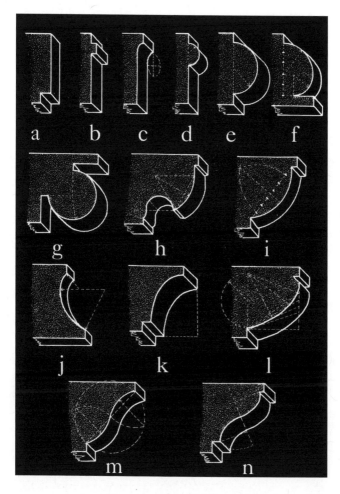

The various standard forms of classical moulding.

As major examples of sacred geometry, proportion, artistry and craftsmanship, the temples, places and mausolea of the ancients have served both as example and inspiration for new works. Constructed according to true principles, using sacred geometry and related harmonic proportion, these examples of ancient skills and wisdom served as the prototypes for architects of the fifteenth century Renaissance and their successors who brought Classical techniques back into general use and extended their possibilities into new forms.

The sacred buildings of antiquity were embodiments of an eternal tradition. The most celebrated buildings of ancient times were talked of as the Seven Wonders of the World. Described by contemporary authors whose works survive, they were the Pyramids of Egypt; the Hanging Gardens of Babylon; the Temple of Artemis (Diana) at Ephesus; the Colossus of Rhodes; the Pharos (lighthouse) of Alexandria; the Hanging Gardens of Babylon; the Temple of Zeus (Jupiter) at Olympus; and the Mausoleum.

Ancient Skills and Wisdom: True Principles in Spiritual Artistry and Craftsmanship

The rubric 'ancient skills and wisdom', coined in Cambridge in 1969 by John Nicholson, describes the knowledge, abilities and the spiritual understanding of how to do things according to true principles. The ability to practise these ancient skills and wisdom requires an understanding of one's personal place in the continuity of one's culture over thousands of years. It necessitates being present in one's own tradition, based upon place and the accumulated knowledge and skills of countless ancestral generations, but also being open to new things and how they can be harmonized with the old. Ancient skills and wisdom are timeless because they are based on universal principles, and these basic essentials of existence and of human nature do not change. Things that are made that respect these essential principles are in themselves also timeless. As Sir

Christopher Wren observed, "Building certainly ought to have the attribute of Eternal".[17]

An understanding of these true principles is a fundamental tenet of the European Tradition. It can be found in the writings of Plotinus (third century CE), most especially his

Radiate wrought-iron window grille in the chapel of the Royal Naval Hospital, Greenwich, designed by Sir Christopher Wren.

Enneads, where he explains that the arts are not an imitation of Nature, but human-mediated expressions of the spiritual source of which Nature is only the outward manifestation. "If anyone thinks meanly of the arts, on the ground that they only mimic Nature", Plotinus writes, "there is a threefold answer. Firstly, we must note that all Nature is itself an imitation of some other thing. Secondly, we are not to imagine that the arts

17 Sir Christopher Wren, in *Parentalia*, op.cit., 261.

merely imitate the seen thing: they go back to the principles of form out of which Nature is generated. Thirdly, in many of their creations, they go beyond imitation".

This understanding of true principles has informed the traditional arts and crafts of England through their most creative periods. It has been present both in the formal, courtly arts of aristocratic and commercial patronage, as well as the everyday handicrafts of the working class. Throughout time, most people have worked diligently at their profession, producing artefacts that have satisfied the needs and aspirations of their place and time, whilst allowing plenty of scope for personal creativity and innovation. Because artefacts speak for themselves, few ancient masters have felt the need to leave writings that express the inner principles that can be seen in their surviving works. From the nineteenth century onwards, however, there are some notable insights provided by the great masters who recognized the proper balance between tradition and innovation. The French master sculptor Auguste Rodin observed that "An art that has life does not restore the works of the past: it continues them", while in the next century the Catalan master architect Antoni Gaudí noted, "Originality consists of a return to the origin".[18] Using true principles means that we do not make passive reproductions, but renew life.

All visible and invisible manifestations of existence come ultimately out of these universal principles; when we consciously recognize them and strive to apply them in our lives and work, then we are in harmony with the deepest roots of our being. Without a sound knowledge and application of true principles to all aspects of life, the individual is morally and spiritually directionless, and vulnerable to arbitrary authoritarian power. A social order that emanates from true principles has the ability and willingness to act kindly, mercifully and

---

18 Antoni Gaudí (1852-1926), 'Originality III', in Maria Antonietta Crippa: *Living Gaudí*, Rizzoli, New York, 2002, 105.

virtuously, valuing the individual. It is a culture totally different
from extravagant materialism. Rather, it is informed by human
dignity, for true principles are formed of the same stuff out of
which each human individual comes.

Every human culture has to deal with the same fundamental
constraints, dealing with them by means of their own characteristic social forms, which exist in accordance with its own
place and time. Thus, the outward forms of spiritually-created
artefacts vary according to culture, place and time. Embedded
within any individual traditional artefact lies generations of
expertise in the use of local materials, constructional principles and usages, cultural meaning, aesthetics and spirituality.
Excepting the spiritual dimension, this even applies to moder-
nity, which is the result of gradual human progress in technol-
ogy over generations. The elegance of construction of traditional European timber frame buildings, for example, lies in
the carpenters' use of no other materials but wood, arranged
according to the geometrical 'art of line'. This 'art of line',
though expressed within the local tradition, is a direct continuance of the symbolic spiritual principles that goes back to
Pythagoras, and beyond to the builders of the archaic timber
structures of Old Europe, Egyptian temples and the megalithic circles of the British Isles.[19] It is present in more sophisticated form in the classical churches of London.

Timelessness and Temporality

In the Middle Ages, the mainstream apologists of Christianity
taught that the timeless was separate from the here-and-now,
existing in the outer beyond, the realm of God that the religion
claimed was accessible only through belief in its doctrines. The
earlier concepts, which these doctrines attempted to suppress,
were expressed most cogently by Aristotle, who perceived the

---

19 See Nigel Pennick: *Sacred Geometry* (1980, 1994); Gordon Strachan:
Chartres: Sacred Geometry, Sacred Space, Floris, Edinburgh, 2003.

timeless within the temporal. In his cosmology, the cycles of the seasons and the eras on Earth reflect the inner workings of the cosmos. Physical objects decay in time but their meaning does not disintegrate with them. The separation taught by a certain current of thought within the Christian religion emphasised an otherness of humans from the organic processes of Nature, describing the human being not by the physical reality of biological being, but in relation to an abstract external and non-material upperworld. According to this theory, the temporal was considered worthless, and the beyond the only true reality. But in practical terms, this was not taken literally. If it had been, then the great cathedrals, built according to true physical principles, would not have come into being.

When the ancient temples were re-evaluated by Alberti, their spiritual principles of rootedness, both in the presence of the earth and in the transcendent, also re-emerged into the European mainstream. The eternal was expressed by the ancient temple builders through the language of classical architecture. Like the seasons, the weather, the tides and other visible processes of Nature, the temples also partook of these elemental forces, expressing them in a particular cultural form that has proved very persistent. Eternal values are encapsulated within classical design. They may be understood through the particular instances of the built and surviving temples of the ancients.

Type, Style and Fashion

Type is a paradigm. Type is a changeless symbol. When it takes physical reality, it is in the form of something that embodies that type; it is not the type *per se*. Classical architecture is a type, not a style; the same is the case with the Gothic. The idea of style is a relatively modern projection back upon already-existent things in order to classify them. Historians of art and architecture have delved into the visible changes of artefacts over time, and perceive them as a progression of one form to the next, sometimes with major breaks and the emergence of new forms. With the emergence of the commercially oriented world-view that sees the principle of fashion as a means to make money (and also, of course, as a form of artistic expression), the concepts of type have been overshadowed. Type is not fashion. For example, trousers are a type: the material, cut, colour, pattern, etc. of any individual pair of trousers is style, and fashion is its particular reference to the prevailing desires of the time. When the perception of what is fashionable changes with time, as it must, then something is deemed "old fashioned" and considered passé. Type can never be passé.

Craftsmanship and Creativity

Craftsmanship taught according to the traditional European guild system, where ancient skills and wisdom is handed on directly from master to apprentice, is not separated from the spiritual dimension of life. In ancient Europe, craftwork was made mindfully of the Gods, who symbolize the inner principles and uses of the work in hand, and the Divine Harmony of the Cosmos that is their expression. Later, under Christianity, it was made in honour of the single Creator and His divine harmony, essentially the same thing with a different ideological interpretation. And later still, in a more pluralistic age, abstract Theosophical ideas and Lethaby's cosmic principles have been similarly expressed. What has remained important throughout time is the system of values, not what dogmas are outwardly professed. Whichever deity or guiding ethos is kept in mind, the inner universal principles, the dynamic interplay of elemental forces, remain the same. Furthermore, the things produced in this way are primarily for use, instruction or delight, made with a loving and respectful spirit for the service of the community.

Creation of anything physical requires the resolution of three principles. The beginning of the work is in the creative imagination. This is the boundless realm of possibilities that is seen as the divine spark in the human being. As the spiritual artist

Johannes L.M. Lauweriks pointed out in 1919,[20] the creative act is a transposition from the realm of the spiritual to the sensory, or the fixing in visible form of something that previously did not exist. What prevent anything being possible are the physical constraints. These begin with the technical limitations of the laws of Nature, and include the restrictions of custom and tradition, social, political and economic factors. The third factor that actually enables the products of the imagination to be brought into physical existence is that of understanding what is possible and what is not, and what balance can be struck between them. Knowing the boundaries of what can be done and the means of doing what is necessary is essential to creative success. The moral philosophy inherent in the spiritual arts and crafts means that the worker is ever aware that the work has a wider dimension than the pursuit of profit or fame. The work is "not for himself, but for the public good" (part of the epitaph of Sir Christopher Wren on his tomb in St Paul's Cathedral). As the notable twentieth century Lancashire Arts and Crafts architect Edgar Wood commented, "Who works not for his fellows starves his soul. His thoughts grow poor and dwindle and his heart grudges each beat, as misers do the dole".[21]

In order to attain something of the eternal, traditional guild craftsmen follow the *Five Precepts*.[22] These are: 1. Suitability for

20 Johannes Ludovicus Mathieu Lauweriks (1864-1932): 'Het Titanische in de Kunst', *Wendingen* 2 Nr. 4, 1919, 5.

21 Text of the carved stone inscription at the monumental stairs designed by Edgar Wood (1860-1935) leading to the place of contemplation in Jubilee Park, Middleton, Lancashire (now Greater Manchester), 1889. Tellingly, the steps and inscription are heavily neglected and vandalized in the early 21st century. Wood was the founder of the Northern Art Workers' Guild (1896). His most celebrated house, Upmeads, Newport Road, Stafford (1908), is named after the home of the hero of the 1896 visionary work, 'The Well At The World's End' (by William Morris (1834-1896).

22 Nigel Pennick, *Masterworks*, Heart of Albion Press, Wymeswold 2002, 4.

purpose; 2. Convenience in use; 3. Proper use of materials; 4. Soundness of construction; 5. Subordination of decoration to the four preceding rules. The spiritual dimension of making is ever-present throughout the processes of making holy spaces and sacred artefacts. Making things in this way is a two-way process, a form of personal spiritual development and a manifestation of the divine power present in all being. The spiritual arts and crafts seek to realize spiritual ideals materially through a process that itself is the craftsperson's spiritual journey.[23] The architects, artists and craftspeople who made the churches of post-Great Fire London (and the Bevis Marks synagogue) certainly brought spiritual principles into a physical form that continues to resonate three centuries later.

Post-Great Fire Workers and Organization

Workplace reforms and new techniques were necessitated by the need to rebuild London rapidly after the catastrophic Great Fire. In the year before the fire, there was a serious skills loss owing to the plague that ravaged London.[24] In order to recruit sufficient skilled workers, the old restrictions on the building trade, limiting the right to work to Freemen of the City, were lifted. Any members of the building trade, including those not from London, were permitted to work there until reconstruction was complete. If such a worker worked for seven years in London, he earned the right to continue to work there.[25] It appears that to fill vacancies some women entered the workforce in hitherto exclusively male crafts. Tradeswomen recorded in churchwardens' accounts are Sarah Freeman, plumber at St James Garlickhythe; Widow Pearce, a painter at St Magnus Martyr,

---

23 Nigel Pennick, *On The Spiritual Arts and Crafts*, Old England House, Cambridge 2004.

24 1665. For an impression of the plague, see Daniel Defoe: *A Journal of the Plague Year* (1721).

25 Bernard E. Jones, *Freemasons' Guide and Compendium*, Harrap, London, 1963, 76.

and Widow Cleer, a joiner at All-Hallows, Lombard Street. The woman blacksmith Ann Brooks worked at St Michael Royal, and "Widdow Baxter, Smith" at St Mary-le-Bow.[26]

However, although it had lost control of the workforce, the London Company of Masons, the trade guild representing builders, was granted the right by Royal Charter to have regulatory powers over all stones used in building "within seven miles of the Cities of London and Westminster" with power of search "in order to see that such be of proper measure and truly wrought".[27] Thus the London guild retained control, whilst 'foreign' builders brought in their various skills to take matters forward. This loss of control and the need for a massive building program led to the use of inferior materials in many cases. Hurriedly made low-grade bricks were a particular problem. In 1711, Sir Christopher Wren commented, "the mighty demand for the hasty works of thousands of

Steps and a radial metalwork grille at St Paul's Cathedral.

26 Gerald Cobb, *The Old Churches of London*, London, 1948, 47, 49.

27 Royal Charter of Incorporation, King Charles II, 1677.

houses at once, after the fire of London, and the frauds of those who built by the great, have so devalued the value of materials".[28] But in most cases, only the best materials and proper craftsmanship were employed to build the churches. The survival of several towers in World War II, though the adjoining church building was burnt or blasted by bombing, attests to the soundness of the materials and the durability of the workmanship. In May 1941, for example, the tower of the blitzed St Clement Danes became a chimney of fire, recorded in a dramatic night photograph. The steeple did not fall, but stands today, in the twenty-first century.

The church architects and surveyors[29] were conscious of their links to eternal principles as expressed in previous buildings transmitted by multiple means: the local legendarium; craftsmen's traditions; published works of theory and new techniques; illustrations of built structures, and the results of investigations of ancient remains. They were ever aware of the local legendarium of each location, remembering that it was an ancient Classical city that formed the basis for contemporary London. This city had its temples and public buildings, the sites of many of which were retained in local knowledge. It was the craftsmen, living exponents of a continuing tradition, who translated the architects' drawings and concepts into physical form.[30]

---

28 Wren, op.cit., 'Letter of Recommendations to a Friend on the Commission for Building Fifty New Churches', *Parentalia*, 319, Point No. 5.

29 At this period, c.1670–c.1740, Wren, Vanbrugh, Hawksmoor, Gibbs, Archer, James, Flitcroft and Dickinson. Several later eighteenth century churches, such as St James', Clerkenwell (James Carr, 1788-1792), have towers that follow on from the later practitioners like Gibbs and Flitcroft.

30 For the philosophical background, see Nigel Pennick, *On the Spiritual Arts and Crafts*, op.cit.

CHAPTER 2

SPIRITUAL PRINCIPLES: PLACE, TIMES AND FORM

Matter takes on actual being by acquiring a form.

Thomas Aquinas, *Summa Theologica*, Ia, lxxv. 6.

Geomancy: The Science of Location

The sacred buildings erected in London after the Great Fire followed the classical tradition as renewed by Leon Battista Alberti. They were not made with the literalism employed by later neoclassical architects,[31] but were the result of the intelligent creative use of themes, geometries and forms from ancient buildings that had been studied by Italian antiquarians and leading architects including Alberti, Serlio and Montano. These architects recognized that the eternal tradition manifests in particular form in any place and time where true principles are applied. The precepts of this tradition are embodied in any sacred building that is constructed according to these true principles and located accordingly. Sir Christopher Wren recognized this when he wrote of the ancients, "Not only their Altars and Sacrifices were mystical, but the very Forms of their Temples". In addition to the classical orders, proportion and measure, these new London temples also incorporated geometrical principles developed by the masters of the medieval Gothic, especially in their towers and steeples. Christopher Wren and Nicholas Hawksmoor designed new Gothic buildings where stylistic considerations were demanded.[32]

The location of buildings, especially those sacred to the *genius loci* (The spirit of the place, frequently acknowledged

---

31 Nigel Pennick: *The Mysteries of St Martin's: Sacred Geometry and the Symmetry of Order*, Sacred Land, Cambridge, 2005.

32 As acknowledged by James Gibbs, *A Book of Architecture containing Desgns of Buildings and Ornaments,* London 1728, VIII.

on Roman altars) and the gods, was a matter of great importance in antiquity. The technique of location was a branch of
augury, derived from the archaic Etruscan Discipline, in which
omens and ostenta were observed in certain landscapes to
determine the spiritual suitability of the place for sacred rites,
altars, temples and mausolea. Members of the Roman College
of Augurs were the masters of this ancient Etruscan art, and
the practical field-surveyors, the Agrimensores, were tutored
in the arts of reading the landscape for its numinous as well
as its physical characteristics. Every Roman temple was thus
located according to the geomantic principles of the Etruscan
Discipline, not according to the price of land or other materialistic considerations that are universal to-day.

The locations on which several post-Great Fire churches
were reconstructed were known to the London legendarium
as the places of former Pagan temples. Over the centuries,
many Roman altars and divine images have been discovered
during building works in the city. Jupiter, Diana, Maponos,
Mars Cocidius, the Deae Matres, the Dioscuri, Bacchus, Isis,
Serapis and Mithras are among the deities commemorated.
The legendarium records that St Paul's Cathedral stands
where the temple of Diana once was, in a sacred temenos.
"Some have imagined a temple of Diana stood here", William
Camden wrote in his *Itinerarium Curiosum*, "and their conjec-
tures are not unsupported. The neighbouring old buildings
are called in the church records, *Camera Diana*" (the chamber
or enclosure of Diana). An altar of Diana was excavated near
to St Paul's on the site of Goldsmiths' Hall in Foster Lane. It is
now in the Museum of London. St Martin's within Ludgate is
on the site of the burial-place of the kings of Britain, where,
according to several traditional chroniclers, King Lud was
interred. In Roman times, there was a cemetery just outside
Londinium's western city gate, Ludgate. St Mary-le-Bow and
St Bride's were found to be on Roman sites when the new

foundations were dug, and St Mary Woolnoth occupies the site of an ancient fane. According to George Godwin the elder, "… a temple, probably that which was dedicated to Concord, at one time occupied the site".[33] Wren's new church of St Mary-le-Bow was patterned on the Temple of Peace in Rome.[34] St Stephen's Walbrook replaced a church of 1428 which itself replaced a church built on the site of the Temple of Mithras.[35]

The architects of the rebuilt Trinovantum affirmed continuity in their new buildings, which had replaced the earlier ones, now burnt. Traditioners all, these architects of this resurgent city followed the rules of the philosophic discipline in emulation of their predecessors.[36] In so doing, they did not make copies of the past, but undertook a masterful expansion and development of tradition, as had the Gothic masters before them, always remaining mindful of the necessary nobility and dignity apparent in ancient temples: "the Reverend look of a Temple it self: which shou'd ever have the most Solemn and Awfull Appearance both within and without", not ostentatious, but "in a plain but Just and Noble Stile".[37] Each new church, or Temple as Sir John Vanbrugh, following Italian renaissance tradition, called them, re-created the genius of the ancient Pagan temple that, as the legendarium tells, once stood at the same place. Continuity was thereby ensured, linking the

33 George Godwin & John Britton, *The Churches of London* …, 2 vols., London, 1839, Vol. 2. P.2 of section on St Mary Woolnoth.

34 Geoffrey Beard: *The Work of Christopher Wren*, Bloomsbury, London, 1982, 21. Actually the Basilica of Maxentius and Constantine, but in his time believed to be a Temple of Peace.

35 Kerry Downes, *A Thousand years of the Church of St Stephen Walbrook*, church leaflet n.d. (c. 2000) 2.

36 See Nigel Pennick, *New Troy Resurgent: Continuity and Renewal through the Eternal Tradition*, Spiritual Land, Cambridge, 2005.

37 John Vanbrugh: *Mr Van-Brugg's Proposals about Building ye New Churches* (c.1711), Bodleian Library, Bod MS Rawlinson B.376, fol. 351-352.

present with the past instead of severing the connection, as happened in modern times.

Orientation

Since archaic times, significant buildings have been orientated with regard to the cardinal directions. Over four thousand years ago, Stonehenge was orientated towards midsummer sunrise. Vitruvius writes that Roman temples faced towards the west so that the devotee standing before the altar would face eastwards.[38] The three earliest Christian basilicas in Rome, founded in the fourth century, S. Pietro in Vaticano (St Peter's, founded 322 CE),[39] S. Giovanni Laterano (324), Sta. Maria Maggiore (358) (St John Lateran and St Mary Major), are all orientated westwards in the Pagan tradition. St Peter's is due east-west, genuinely 'foursquare', and this orientation has been retained exactly throughout all its rebuildings. In the late fourth century, orientation towards the east became the norm. Christian burials were generally orientated east-west with the head to the west, though by the seventeenth century, Sir Thomas Browne wrote, "Christians dispute how their bodies should lie in the grave".[40]

In northern Europe, before the dominance of Christianity, the direction of prayer was to the north.[41] Northern farmhouses, hofs and royal halls were orientated so that the high seat on the northern long wall faced the sun's high point in the south. (A hof is a manor house used for worship in the religion of the north. Temples also existed at important places). A sacred image and 'the gods' nail' were carved on the high

38 Vitruvius, IV, 5.

39 Jocelyn Toynbee and John Ward Perkins, *The Shrine of St Peter*, London, 1956.

40 Sir Thomas Browne, *Hydrotaphia*, in *Religio Medici and Other Essays*. E. Grant Richards, London, n.d., 151.

41 Otto Sigfrid Reuter (1936), trans. Michael Behrend: *Skylore of the North*, The Library of the European Tradition, Cambridge, 1999, 6.

seat pillar on the northern wall.[42] In northern Europe, the hof orientation was combined with church practice. The seating in the choir of such churches and the location of bishops' thrones on the north side of the chancel reproduced the Northern Tradition orientation of royal halls combined with the eastern altar of Christianity. In 990 CE, a Saxon monk of Winchester, Wolstan, notes that a church built by Bishop Ethelwold was orientated eastwards.[43]

In the thirteenth century, Guilielmus Durandus noted that while "contemplating", worshippers must face east, and the exact direction must be observed at the equinoxes.[44] Medieval churches in general were orientated with the altar at the eastern end, though great variations exist, and the custom was not challenged in principle until the reformation and even then only by those who would now be called fundamentalists. In 1584, the Puritan Sir Walter Mildmay obtained the remains of the Dominican Priory in Cambridge, closed in 1538, and founded Emmanuel College there.[45] To wipe out Roman Catholic continuity, he made the chapel into a hall, and converted the north-south hall into a chapel, deliberately defying orientation. This was disapproved of by his contemporaries and successors, and the chapel was never consecrated. Between 1668 and 1673, a new chapel, properly orientated and consecrated, was built to the designs of Christopher Wren. In 1648, in *His Noble Numbers*, Robert Herrick published the poem North and South that records a reason of spiritual purity for orientation:

> The Jewes their beds, and offices of ease,
> Plac'd North and South, for these clean purposes;

---

42 Reuter, op. cit., 5.

43 D. Rock, *The Church of Our Fathers*, London, 1903, I, 172-176.

44 Guilielmus Durandus (William Durand), trans. J.M. Neale and B. Webb, *Rationale Divinorum Officiorum*, London 1843, 216.

45 Royal Commission on Historic Monuments, *City of Cambridge*, 2 vols., London, 1959, I, 61.

That man's uncomely froth might not molest
Gods wayes and walks, which lie still East and West.[46]

The church of St Edmund, King and Martyr, Lombard Street (1670-1707), viewed from the north, showing aberrant orientation towards the north, the only church rebuilt in this way. Later, in 1711, Sir Christopher Wren recommended that all new London churches must face the east. This stricture was abandoned in the nineteenth century.

46 Robert Herrick, *The Poems of Robert Herrick*, Grant Richards, London, 1902, 363.

Antiquarian interest in orientation was also present in the seventeenth century. After the Civil War, Silas Taylor (also known as Silas Domville),[47] a captain in Cromwell's army, devoted himself to antiquarianism that included investigations into church orientation. His military exploits in the Parliamentary forces included his unit's pillaging and looting of the cathedral libraries at Hereford and Worcester. His manuscripts, sold at his death in 1678, contained a text he wrote on orientation: "In days of yore, when a church was to be built, they watched and prayed on the vigil of the dedication, and took that point of the horizon where the sun arose from the east, which makes that variation so that few stand true, except those built between the two equinoxes. I have experimented some churches, and have found the line to point to that part of the horizon where the sun arises on the day of that Saint to whom the church is dedicated."[48]

Orientation played a significant role in all building in pre-industrial days. In addition to the liturgical necessity of eastern altars in churches, secular buildings were located according to prevailing winds and more esoteric considerations, now recognized as geomantic. Most medieval collegiate libraries in England faced "east and west". Willis and Clark note sixteen in Cambridge and Oxford.[49] The majority of sixteenth and early seventeenth century libraries faced "north and south". After the Restoration (1660), Willis and Clark note ten college libraries built with the older orientation, dating between 1663 and 1875.[50]

---

47 Walter Johnson: *Byways in British Archaeology*, University Press, Cambridge, 1912, 225.

48 Taylor, recorded by John Aubrey, citied in Brand, *Popular Antiquities*, II, 6–7, and Johnson, op.cit., 225.

49 Robert Willis & John Willis Clark, *The Architectural History of the University of Cambridge*, 3 vols., Cambridge, 1886, III, 414-415.

50 Ibid., III, 415-416.

In the seventeenth century, the lore of the directions, their corresponding winds and ruling spirits was discussed in a number of texts and used in magical and medical procedures. Robert Fludd's great spiritual work, *Utriusque Cosmi Maioris*[51] has several circular diagrams expounding the occult constitution of man and the world as well as the relationships to the winds, health and sickness. All are orientated, different aspects relating to one of the four quarters of the earth and the heavens. An example of seventeenth century secular orientation for esoteric purposes appears in Ben Jonson's comedy *The Alchemist*. First performed in 1610,[52] a scene in the play depicts a tobacconist, Abel Drugger, enquiring of Subtle, the devious alchemist of the title, how he should arrange his new shop. It is clear that Drugger is asking for the proper orientation of the shop and the correct location of its fittings according to occult principles so that his business will be a success. Drugger asks Subtle for help:

> I am a young beginner, and am building
> Of a new shop, an't like your worship, just
> At corner of a street: Here's the plot [ground plan or
> map – N.P.] on't -
> And I would know by art, sir, of your worship,
> Which way I should make my door, by necromancy,
> And where my shelves; and which should be for boxes,
> And which for pots. I would be glad to thrive, sir ....[53]

After further banter, Subtle finally examines the plot, asks "This is the west, and this the south?" and gives the following geomantic diagnosis:

---

51 Robert Fludd, *Utriusque Cosmi Maioris scilicet et Minoris Metaphysica, Physica atque Technica Historia*, 2 vols., Oppenheim, 1617.

52 Published in the 1616 folio edition of his works, reproduced in W. Gifford (ed.), *The Works of Ben Jonson*, Vol. 4, London 1816, 5–192.

53 Act 1, ibid., 37, 41.

Make me your door, then, south; your broad side, west:
And on the east side of your shop, aloft,
Write Mathlai, Tarmiel and Baraborat;
Upon the north part, Rael, Velel, Thiel.
They are the names of those Mercurial spirits,
That do fright flies from boxes.[54]

Although used for comic effect, Jonson's detail of the spirits' names came, like all of Jonson's magical references and procedures, from a real source, for they appear in Pietro D'Albano's *Heptameron, seu Elementa Magica* (c.1567). The spirits are among those ascribed to Wednesday, the day of Mercury, and thus auspicious for business. Jonson's masques, which also contain Pagan rites, mythology, folk-lore and witchcraft, are backed up by copious notes and references to authors, both classical and contemporary.

Emergent speculative freemasonry, which came out of the same milieu, was formalized in the early eighteenth century. It conducted its rituals in lodges orientated east-west, and still does. The master's presence was in the east, just as the priest stands in the east at the altar of an orientated church. At the time of the Great Fire, the vast majority of London's churches, including St Paul's cathedral, which mostly dated from the medieval period, were properly orientated. A surviving drawing of the ground plan of St Clement Dane's, from the office of Wren, shows the original medieval walls with the plan of the new church superimposed upon it.[55]

At St Clement's, the medieval orientation a few degrees north of east was retained in the new building. At St Paul's, Wren altered the orientation by a few degrees from that of the old medieval cathedral, but retained the altar in the east.

54 Act 1, ibid., 41.

55 Pierre de la Ruffinière du Prey, *Hawksmoor's London Churches, Architecture and Theology*, University of Chicago Press, Chicago, 2000, fig. 33, p. 72.

The majority of Wren's churches were orientated somewhat south of east. St Paul's, St Bride's, St Augustine and St Michael, Cornhill (mainly by Hawksmoor) all stand a few degrees north of due east. In Westminster, St James, Piccadilly, is aligned almost north-east, south-west. The unique oval-polygonal St Benet, Fink, demolished 1846, was due east-west. There was only one post-Great Fire church that blatantly defied orientation. It is St Edmund, Lombard Street, built between 1670 and 1679, designed by Robert Hooke,[56] and aligned north-south with the altar in the north. In his later life, as a Commissioner for the fifty new churches of 1711, Wren wrote a letter of recommendations for the desirable qualities of new churches which had the comment, "Nor are we, I think, too nicely to observe east or west in the position, unless if falls out properly".[57] But the Commissioners as a body seem to have thought differently from his pragmatic suggestions, and all of the churches built by them were properly orientated. At least one proposal (by Sir John Vanbrugh) for a northern orientation of St George's Bloomsbury, which was to be built on a site longer on the north-south axis than the east-west, was finally rejected, and an east-west solution found. The church was duly orientated to the true cardinal directions.

Building on the Right Lines

Shortly after the Great Fire finally burnt itself out, Christopher Wren drew up a plan for reconstructing the city. In place of the medieval lanes and alleys, London was to have straight avenues linking fine classical buildings. The Romans were famed for their straight roads that ran across the empire, and they remained the main road system of Great Britain in the seventeenth century. The British legendarium ascribed them to the ancient British king Belinus, who had ordered the 'Royal

56 Margaret Whinney: *Wren*, Thames & Hudson, London, 1971, 64.
57 Wren, 1711, op. cit., *Parentalia*, 319.

Roads of Britain' to be constructed.[58] Straight streets punctuated by obelisks, fountains, monuments and churches were driven through Rome by architects under the pontificates of Popes Sixtus V (1585-1590)[59] and Alexander VII (1655-1667). Aligned upon prominent characteristic structures, these axial 'right lines' give a structural and spiritual coherence to the city. Wren argued that in London churches should be located on insular sites not hemmed in by other buildings, serving as sacred landmarks linked by straight streets. But political, economic and legal circumstances did not allow Wren's grand unifying vision to prevail, and only a few churches were built in this way. Wren's plan survives as a 'what might have been'. There would have been two separate alignments of five churches, another line of three, two churches flanking the west front of St Paul's, and two facing one another across a piazza. The effect on other cities in Great Britain if this plan had gone ahead can only be imagined.

Despite the fame of his abortive plan, there have been few artistic attempts to reconstruct what Wren's London would have looked like from the street. One impression was made by the twentieth century Baroque artist Rex Whistler (1905-1944), who painted a fanciful reconstruction of this London that never was as the drop curtain for productions of *The Rake's Progress* by the Sadler's Wells Ballet Company (designed in 1935 and last used in 1942, destroyed). It shows a perspective view of a Wrenian straight street, punctuated by a royal statue in Roman garb, beside which are Baroque spires resembling those of the churches of Christopher Wren and James Gibbs.[60]

58 Gaufridus, op. cit., III, 5.

59 Giovanni Bordino, *De Rebus Praeclare Gestis a Sixto V Pont. Max*, Rome, 1588.

60 Rex Whistler: 'Designs for the Theatre' (part 2). *The Masque* No.4, 1947, 8.

Although Wren's plan came to nothing, a few examples of the principle were built after 1711 under the Commission whose function was to select and acquire sites, procure designs, and fund and build fifty new churches in and around the cities of London and Westminster.[61] Nicholas Hawksmoor's never-built design for "a Basilica after the Primitive Christians" (1711) puts it within a rectilinear street plan, with straight approaches on three sides. It was intended for a site in Bethnal Green, which was never used.[62] The tower of St Anne's, Limehouse (1712-1724), one of the churches located and designed by Hawksmoor, is directly on the central north-

south axis of the Greenwich Hospital across the river (the cardo of the Etruscan Discipline, on which this plan is based).[63] This line of sight is now blocked by the Docklands skyscrapers around Canary Wharf. Another of his churches, St Alfege, Greenwich (1712-1730, a rebuild of an earlier church), was to be approached by a new straight road laid out at right angles to this axis.[64] This line is the decumanus in the Etruscan Discipline. The existing later streets, Romney

The axial alignment of a street on the west façade and tower of St Anne, Limehouse (1712-1714).

---

61 Act of Parliament, *Statute at Large*, IX Anne, c.22, 1711.

62 Kerry Downes: *Hawksmoor*, Thames & Hudson, London, 1970, 100.

63 J.H.V. Davies, 'Nicholas Hawksmoor', *Royal Institute of British Architects Journal*, Vol.69, No.10, October 1962, 376.

64 Vaughan Hart, *Nicholas Hawksmoor*, Yale University Press, New Haven & London, 2002, 178.

Road and its continuation, Nelson Road, were not constructed exactly on Hawksmoor's intended alignment. Standing four-square on an 'insular site' at the intersection of four straight streets in Westminster, not far from the Abbey and Houses of Parliament, Thomas Archer's church of St John, Smith Square (built 1714-1728) has four identical towers at the four intercardinal corners.

Along with Nicholas Hawksmoor, James Gibbs (1682-1754) was appointed as Surveyor to the 1711 Commissioners. His first church built for the Commissioners was St Mary-le-Strand, replacing the 134 feet high maypole that stood in the middle of the Strand.[65] Its foundation stone laid on the twenty-fifth of February 1714, the structure was completed in 1717 and it was consecrated in 1723.[66] Close to the church, and on its axis, a tall column bearing a statue of Queen Anne was planned, but never constructed. Both Gibbs and Hawksmoor were admirers of such 'right lines' as they were called. Hawksmoor drew up plans for rebuilding Cambridge along right lines, with a major axis from King's College Chapel to the gatehouse of Christ's College, but it was never implemented.

In London there is a line-of-sight along the Strand between St Mary-le-Strand and Wren's church of St Clement Danes, which has a steeple by Gibbs. This is certainly deliberate. Alfred Watkins (1855-1935) noted it as being in alignment with Gibbs's church of St Martin's-in-the-Fields. According to his thesis, this is the result of ancient pre-Christian alignments being preserved through site-continuity.[67] The new city of Karlsruhe in Baden (Germany), contemporary with the work

65 Nigel Pennick, 'Historic Lines of Britain and Europe', in Nigel Pennick & Paul Devereux, *Lines on the Landscape*, Robert Hale, London, 1989, 154-156.

66 Smith, *The Streets of London*, 212.

67 Alfred Watkins, *Early British Trackways*, Hereford & London, 1922, 22; *The Old Straight Track*, Methuen, London, 1925, 124.

of Gibbs and Hawksmoor, is the most perfect manifestation
of the system. Its foundation stone was laid at the centre on
the twenty-eighth of January, 1715. It had thirty-two straight

*The meridional alignment at Karlsruhe, Germany (1715), looking
south from the central tower which stands at the centre of conceptual
lines, straight city streets and roads radiating far out into the
countryside. This principle of 'right (i.e. straight) lines' appears in
British planning of the same era.*

roads radiating from the ducal palace tower at its centre, and churches on insular sites, and the layout remains to this day.[68]

Punctual Times - Electional Astrology

Foundation laying marks the important moment when a building begins to come into physical reality. Traditionally, it is conducted with memorable rites and ceremonies at a particular time, and some kind of foundation deposit is left as a token of the act.[69] In the post-fire period, rites and ceremonies were performed at every foundation. The foundation stone of St Martin-in-the-Fields, for example, was laid on the nineteenth of March 1721 "with full religious and Masonic rites".[70] On the twentieth of June in the same year, General Steuart laid the foundation stone of St George, Hanover Square, striking it with a mallet, and pouring a libation of wine with the invocation, "The Lord God of Heaven, preserve this church of St George".[71]

Since early times, the horoscope of the instant of foundation has been deemed indicative of the future of the building or enterprise.[72] The art of electional astrology seeks to find the most auspicious configuration of the heavens to determine the precise time to lay the first stone of a building. A horoscope is drawn up in advance, and the foundation stone laid at the precise moment indicated. To the building, this is the instant of birth, equivalent to the natal time in human astrology. In post-Reformation England, electional astrology was used in

---

68 Nigel Pennick, *Beginnings: Geomancy, Builders' Rites and Electional Astrology in the European Tradition*, Capall Bann, Chieveley, 1999, 224, 226-241.

69 Generally coins and sometimes documents.

70 J. McMaster, *A Short History of St Martin's in the Fields*, London, 1916, 75.

71 William Atkins, *A History of St George, Hanover Square*, London, 1976.

72 See Nigel Pennick, *Beginnings: Geomancy, Builders' Rites and Electional Astrology in the European Tradition*, Capall Bann, Chieveley, 1999, 248-271.

the foundation of colleges, institutions and churches. Unusual and precise times of stone laying, known as the 'punctual time', attests to elections. For example, the foundation of the west range of Caius Court of Gonville and Caius College in Cambridge was laid by Dr John Caius at 4.00 am on the fifth of May 1565.[73] Patrick McFadzean has calculated that Caius was founded with Mercury rising. Seemingly emphasising this, the college had a structure called 'The Sacred Tower', demolished in 1717. It had a statue of the god Mercury on its apex.

Accurate computational astrology emerged in England under Cromwell's republic and continued at the Restoration with the work of several almanac-makers who were also astrological commentators.[74] Influential English astrological works of the period include *Merlinus Anglicus* and *Christian Astrology* by William Lilly (1644 and 1647); Jeremy Shakerley's *Tabulae Britannicae* (1653), *Genethlialogia; or, the Doctrine of Nativities* and *Collectio Geniturarum* by John Gadbury (1658 and 1662); Thomas Streete's *Astronomia Carolina* (1661) and almanacs by Vincent Wing, who was a professional land-surveyor. The milieu of astrology was universal in London at the time when the new churches were being located, planned and founded. So it was natural that electional astrology was employed for major buildings erected after the Great Fire.

John Flamsteed, Astronomer Royal to King Charles II, calculated the inceptional horoscope for the Royal Exchange (the twenty-third of October 1667), and the Royal Observatory at

---

73 Robert Willis & John Willis Clark, *The Architectural History of the University of Cambridge*, Cambridge University Press, Cambridge, 1886, Vol. I, 171. Caius was founded with Mercury rising, Patrick McFadzean, personal communication. The college had 'The Sacred Tower' which had a statue of the god Mercury on its apex (demolished 1717).

74 J.T. Kelly: *Practical Astronomy during the Seventeenth Century: A Study of Almanac-makers in America and England*, Ph.D. thesis, Harvard, 1977; ch. 2 passim, 240 – 241.

Greenwich (3.14 pm on the tenth of August 1675). The Royal Observatory election has the Sun in the ninth house, appropriate for the philosophical and scientific pursuit of astronomy. The rising sign is Sagittarius, which is the natural ruler of the ninth house, and the beneficent planet Jupiter, the ruler of Sagittarius, is in that sign, almost exactly at the position of its rising.[75] The early speculative freemason, Elias Ashmole, records the exact time of the foundation-stone laying of St Paul's Cathedral, at 6.30 am on the twenty-sixth of June, 1675 in the south-eastern corner facing sunrise.[76] In 1723, its architect, Sir Christopher Wren, was buried at this south-eastern corner. The foundation of the Royal Naval Hospital at Greenwich was laid by Wren and John Evelyn at exactly five o'clock in the afternoon on the thirtieth of June 1696. Flamsteed indicated the exact instant through direct observation with his instruments.[77]

---

75 Patrick McFadzean, *Astrological Geomancy: An Introduction*, Limited edition of 40, Northern Earth Mysteries, York, 1985, 4. For modern interpretations of the basic principles of electional astrology, see V.E. Robson, *Electional Astrology*, New York, 1972, and Gregory Szänto, *Perfect Timing, The Art of Electional Astrology*, Wellingborough, 1989.

76 Elias Ashmole (ed. C.H. Josten), *Elias Ashmole (1617-1692), His Autobiographical and Historical Notes*, Vol. 4 (1966), 1432.

77 John Evelyn (ed. E.S. de Beer), *Diary*, V, 249.

The alignment of St Martin-in-the-Fields, St Mary-le-Strand and St Clement Dane's churches with The Strand was surveyed by Nicholas Hawksmoor and James Gibbs. The latter two churches were depicted on the cover of the famous 19th century Strand Magazine in which the original Sherlock Holmes stories appeared.

A church whose date of foundation-stone laying is recorded is St George, Hanover Square (1712–1724), elevation. Drawing by Nigel Pennick.

CHAPTER 3

NUMBER, MEASURE AND HARMONY

> As from the power of sacred lays
> The spheres began to move,
> And sung the great creator's praise
> To all the blessed above.

John Dryden, *A Song for St Cecilia's Day.*

The Eternal Tradition

The underlying principles of spiritual architecture are sacred geometry and number. The principle of number was discussed by Renaissance architectural theorists and applied in their building design. Often seen as the basis of proportion, and hence classical beauty, the actual virtues of numbers *per se* also appears as a significant principle. The Pythagorean qualities of number, known since antiquity, are not the abstract numbers of modern mathematics, but entities in their own right. In this view, number and geometry are not distinctly different, but aspects of the holistic understanding of space. As Jacopo de'Barbari explained, "There is no proportion without number, and no form without geometry".[78]

The sacred art of geometry embodies the abstract realities expressed in geometrical forms that are visible expressions of the innermost truths of the world's being, acting in accordance with the course of Nature.[79] Sir Christopher Wren's motto was *Numero, Pondera et Mensura*, 'By Number, Weight and Measure'. This saying is ascribed to Solomon, and taken from the Vulgate *Book of Wisdom* (xi, 21). Order is brought out of chaos through

---

78 Jacopo de' Barbari, letter to Frederick, Elector of Saxony; P. Barocchi (ed.), *Scritti d'arte del Cinquecento*, Milan 1971, 67.

79 See Nigel Pennick, *Sacred Geometry* (1980), Capall Bann Publishing, Chieveley 1994; Nigel Pennick & Professor M. Gout, *Sacrale Geometri: Verborgen Lijnen in de Bouwkunst*, Uitgeverij Synthese, The Hague 2004.

the proper use of number, weight and measure. Then life is brought into harmony with the spiritual ideal. Such architecture manifests a spirituality that transcends religious doctrines, in the creation of an ennobling presence. True order can exist only in harmony with Nature, when human life is in accordance with the spiritual ideal. Until recently, Wren's ceremonial measuring rod was on display in the crypt of St Paul's Cathedral. Wren's manuscript note on Hawksmoor's drawing of the Mausoleum states: "The Fabrick was in the Age of Pythagoras and his School, when the World began to be fond of Geometry, and Arithmetick". Elsewhere, he wrote, "Geometrical Figures are naturally more beautiful than other irregular; in this all consent as to a Law of Nature".[80]

Sacred geometry and the proportions relating to geometry and musical harmony are indispensable to spiritual architecture. Because these elements reflect the eternal structure of the Cosmos, and hence, in Judaeo-Christian cosmology, God's Creation, they produce beautiful and harmonious ensouled structures. Traditional building uses true principles, integrating the spiritual with the material dimension. "Building certainly ought to have the Attribute of eternal"[81] wrote Sir Christopher Wren, and this meant not only proper constructional techniques, but also the embodiment of eternal values. Emerging from the symbolic side of medieval sacred geometry, especially among the alchemists, in the new illustrated books of the seventeenth century sacred diagrams became a means of expressing the inner spiritual workings of the cosmos. They appear in philosophical works published both in Great Britain and what is now Germany. These diagrams, frequently copied, are today little regarded by historians of architecture. One important diagram, originating with the late fifteenth century Bristol alchemist, Thomas Norton, was significant enough

---

80 Wren, *Parentalia*, op. cit., *Tract* I, 351.

81 Wren, *Parentalia*, op. cit., 261.

Thomas Norton's alchemical diagram from Cooper's Philosophical
Epitaph *(1673). The geometrical arrangement ascending from the
underworld to the upperworld is a symbolic model for the London
church steeples of Wren and his followers.*

to appear in several versions. This is the *Signaculum Mundi Pythagoricum*, a diagram associated with his *Ordinall of Alchemy* (1477) published in Britain in 1653. This diagram appears in Norton's *Tractatus chymicus*, (Frankfurt, 1616); Elias Ashmole's *Theatrum chymicum Britannicum* (London, 1652) and W. Cooper's *The Philosophical Epitaph*, (London, 1673). The Bristol legendarium tells how Norton made the red elixir, which then being stolen, was used to build the church of St Mary Redcliffe in that city.

Other examples of geometric cosmic diagrams published in the seventeenth century, with titles such as *The Hermetic Scheme of the Universe*, include those by Robert Fludd,[82] and Michael Maier.[83] They appear as the *Keys* of Basilius Valentinus[84] and in the works of Athanasius Kircher.[85] Kircher's symbolic approach was used by Jesuit church designers, who, in turn, were one of the influences upon the London designs. For example, the tower of St Magnus Martyr near London Bridge is patterned on the tower and turrets of the Jesuit church of Carolus Borromeus in Antwerp, attributed to Pieter Huyssens and Peter Paul Rubens, and built in 1621. The towers of these London churches are particularly notable as examples of geometrical ingenuity that embody and express the principles depicted in published Hermetic diagrams. Later Masonic diagrams of the eighteenth century also make use of some of these philosophical motifs, which are present in some of the surviving fittings of post-Great Fire London churches, such as the pulpit in St Mary Woolnoth.

---

82 Robert Fludd, *Utriusque Cosmi Majoris scilicet et Minoris Metaphysica …* Johann Theodor de Bry, Oppenheim, 1617.

83 Michael Maier, *Atalanta fugiens*, Oppenheim, 1618.

84 D. Stolcius von Stolcenberg, *Viridarium chymicum*, Frankfurt, 1624.

85 E.g. Athanasius Kircher, *Obeliscus Pamphilius*, Rome, 1650; *Musurgia universalis*, Rome, 1650; *Ars magna lucis*, Rome, 1665.

Pythagorean Philosophy

The principle of number was discussed by renaissance architectural theorists and applied in their practical building design. Often seen as the basis of proportion, and hence classical beauty, the actual virtue of numbers *per se* appears as a significant independent principle. The Pythagorean qualities of number, preserved from antiquity, are not the abstract numbers of modern mathematics, but entities in their own right. In this view, number and geometry are not distinctly different, but aspects of the holistic understanding of space. In the sixth century BCE Pythagoras had taught that number was the first principle of all things.

The Pythagorean world-view, upon which London classical buildings are ultimately patterned, describes in simple terms the principles inherent in existence. Process is usually described as having a threefold nature, most simply apparent in the sequence: beginning – continuance – end. Existent realities, such as matter and planar space, are understood in a fourfold way. Material is explicable in terms of the four elements; four directions divide the plane of the Earth's surface; whilst the four seasons divide the year. Pythagoras taught the importance of the divine numerical series: 1, 2, 3, 4 as the creative power of the cosmos. Pythagoreans described existence by means of the Tetraktys, put in visible form as a triangle composed of ten points, arranged from the top down, 1, 2, 3, 4. Of the various forms of Tetraktys, the fourth composes the four elements, and the eighth, the Intelligible Tetraktys, the four faculties of the human being: intelligence and mind; knowledge; opinion; and sensation.

The four elements are a symbolic description of the nature of the material world. They are hypothetical qualities that combine to make particulars. Confusingly, the same word is used in modern chemistry to describe the basic characteristic elements in the periodic table. The two are quite distinct, and the ancient meaning is not a primitive forerunner of

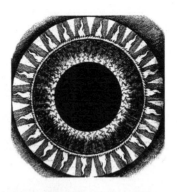

Above: The divine emanation diagram from Robert Fludd, Utriusque cosmi... *(1617).*
Below: marquetry panel of the same symbol on the pulpit of St Mary Woolnoth.

the modern, but a quite different symbolic system. The four elements have their being within the framework of the physical structure of the world, the dimensions, which Pythagoras classified into four parts: the seed or starting-point (the Cosmic Egg), height, depth; and thickness or solidity. This tetrad is the archetype of all growing things, and things that are made by means of the human arts and crafts. The fourfold model of existence is found throughout the European tradition from the earliest times. Thus the geomantic division of towns and cities into four quarters (hence the word 'quarter' for a district) goes back to the Etruscan Discipline, the mantic art of the Augurs of Etruria in the first years of the first millennium BCE.

The oldest surviving description of the tetrad of principles known as the four elements comes from Empedocles in his text *On Nature* (c. 445 BCE). The division of the matter of the world into these four symbolic qualities is the basis for the traditional western understanding of the subtle nature of material existence. Within the cosmos, the individual natures of things, both non-living and living, can be described by means of these four fundamental principles, Earth, Water, Air and Fire. There is sometimes confusion over the use of the word 'Earth' to describe both the place where we live, and one of the four elements whose virtues are components of this place. When we refer to Earth as one of the four elements, this means the densest form of material existence. When Earth refers to the place that gave us birth and sustains our being, this is viewed as the interaction between of all four forms of matter: solid Earth; liquid Water; gaseous Air, and plasmatic Fire. Within them, wholly part of all four and yet transcendent of them is the subtle 'fifth element', the Quintessence.

When these elements are combined in certain ways, they produce four natures. Aristotle stated that fire is the result of heat and dryness; air, heat and wetness; water, cold and wetness; and earth, cold and dryness. The four elements are thus a description of the nature of the material world. This tetrad is the archetype of all growing things, and things that are made by means of the human arts and crafts. All is in constant motion, constant change. Pythagoreanism was of interest to the intellectuals of the seventeenth century, and the fixity of number and the dimensions as contrasted with the transience of physical existence was a particular concern, then as now. In his poem, *Of The Pythagorean Philosophy*, the Poet Laureate John Dryden (1631-1700) wrote:

> This let me further add, that Nature knows
> No steadfast station, but, or ebbs or flows;
> Ever in motion; she destroys her old,
> And casts new figures in another mould.
> E'en times are in perpetual flux, and run
> Like rivers from their fountain rolling on....[86]

> .....Then to be born, is to begin to be
> Some other thing we were not formerly:
> And what we call to die, is not to appear,
> Or be the thing that formerly we were.
> Those very elements which we partake
> Alive, when dead some other bodies make:
> Translated grow, have sense, or can discourse,
> But death on deathless substance has no force.[87]

The Sacred Science of Number

Pythagorean precepts viewed the mystic virtues of numbers as the source of all geometrical figures. In Book V of his *De Harmonia Mundi* (1521) Francesco Giorgi writes: "According to the writings of Pythagoras it was believed that the fabric of the soul and the entire world was arranged and perfected in these numbers and proportions. And from the odd as from the male, and from the even as from the female; everything is

---

86 John Dryden, *On the Pythagorean Philosophy*, lines 262-267.

87 Ibid., lines 390-397.

generated from these powers combined".[88] The Pythagorean numbers are:

One: the Monad, a single point, the essential, primal, indivisible beginning and source of all numbers, perfection and goodness.

Two: the Dyad. Departure from unity, doubling, loss of singleness, excess and the beginning of imperfection in duality. The line joining two points.

Three: the Triad. The first real number with a beginning, a middle and an end.[89] It signifies the restoration of harmony through the triangular balance of forces, the planar surface.

Four: the Tetrad. Foursquare stability as expressed in the square and the cross. Solid matter. The first feminine square, two times two; the elements, the humours, the virtues and the seasons, the archetype of wholeness.

Five: the Pentad. The pentagram, uniting the first female number, two with the first male, three, in mystic union. It is the origin of the Golden Section, the number of regular polyhedral 'Platonic Solids' and in 'incorruptible' number because multiples always end in five.

The Hebrew name of God at the centre of the domed ceiling of St Mary Abchurch.

Six: the Hexad. The first perfect number. Six is the

---

88 Francesco Giorgi, *De Harmonia Mundi totius*, Venice, 1525, fol. 81 verso.

89 "Trinitas numerorum prima", Marsilio Ficino, commentary on Plato's *Timaeus*.

perfect number because it is the sum of one plus two plus three, and the product of the multiplication of the first feminine and masculine numbers, two times three. In square measure, it is the area of the triangle with sides of three, four and five units.

Seven: the Heptad. This is the virgin number, for seven has neither factors, nor is it a product. It was also considered significant because a circle could not be divided geometrically into seven parts in ancient times. A simple geometric construction of the heptagon was discovered as late as the seventeenth century by Count Carlo Renaldini (1615-1698).

Eight: the Octad. This is the first cube, the product of two times two times two.

Nine: the Nonad. This is the first masculine square, three times three, an 'incorruptible' number that, however multiplied, reproduces itself (e.g. $2 \times 9 = 18$; $1 + 8 = 9$ etc.).

Ten: the Decad. This contains all the archeypal numbers, one plus two plus three plus four as the Tetraktys. It is an 'incorruptible' sacred number, 'the Mother of the Cosmos'.

Twenty-seven is the first masculine cube, threefold three.

Twenty-eight is the second perfect number, the sum of $1 + 2 + 3 + 4 + 5 + 6 + 7$.

Thirty-five is the sum of the first feminine and the first masculine cube: eight plus twenty-seven.

Thirty-six is the product of the first square numbers, four times nine; the sum of the first three cubes $1 + 8 + 27$; and, as the sum of the first eight numbers, $1 + 2 + 3 + 4 + 5 + 6 + 7 + 8$, and the square of the first one six times six, is the third perfect number.

Leon Battista Alberti, whose recognition that churches were temples was so important in the adoption of classical architecture by later architects, was a follower of Pythagorean number-theory. Three, viewed as the first real number,[90] Alberti notes, "Thus all the philosophers affirm, that Nature herself consists in a ternary principle".[91] Three is of significance in the Christian tradition as the number of the Trinity, whose doctrine teaches the unity of three in one. Divine presence is often depicted as an equilateral triangle from which emerge rays of light. In the Baroque, the Hebrew Tetragrammaton appears within the triangle, and in Masonic emblems, the eye of God. Four is another divine number, for "…some philosophers teach that the number four is dedicated to the Deity, and for this reason it was used in the taking of the most solemn oaths, which were repeated four times".[92] Equally, Alberti stated, "and so the number five must be allowed to be divine in its nature, and worthily dedicated to the Gods of the Arts, and particularly Mercury";[93] "…. they tell us, that even among the most excellent numbers, that of six is the most perfect, or consisting of all its own entire parts, for example: $1 + 1 + 1 + 1 + 1 + 1 = 6$; $1 + 2 + 3 = 6$; $1 + 5 = 6$; $2 + 2 + 2 = 6$; $2 + 4 = 6$; $3 + 3 = 6$".[94] Finally, for the number 10, "*Aristotle* was of the opinion, that the number ten was the most perfect of all which was probably because its square is composed of four continued cubes put together".[95]

Ratio and Harmony

Musical ratios are another integral part of the Pythagorean philosophy that underlies classical architectural design,

---

90 Aristotle, *De Coelo*, I, 1 268a; Plutarch, *Symposium*, IX quest. 3.

91 Leon Battista Alberti, *De re aedificatoria*, IX, V, Giacomo Leoni's translation, London, 1755, 196.

92 Ibid.

93 Ibid.

94 Ibid. arithmetical notation modernized.

95 Ibid.

demonstrating the hidden harmony that pervades the cosmos. The anonymous Greek author of the alchemical text *Anonymus* places the origin of the four elements in the Cosmic Egg, which is the image of the world itself. The author notes that the four elements are also present in music, because there are four main harmonies, and the tetrachord, the basic row, is composed of four elemental tones. Theon of Smyrna, who wrote in the second century CE, tells how the four main harmonies of the diatonic scale, the preserve of the Muses, combine the numbers 1, 2, 3, and 4 as the Musical Tetraktys. These four harmonies are the fourth, 4:3; the fifth, 3:2; the octave, 2:1; and the double octave, 4:1. There are six possible tetrachords called Aëchos, Isos, Katharos, Kentros, Paraëchos and Plagios. Three are ascending scales, and three descending (Aëchos, Isos and Plagios). Combined, these make twenty-four distinct musical elements. By combining these in proper ways, all forms of music, the benedictions, hymns and other parts of divine science, can be made. There are limitless possibilities of combination.

To summarize, this ancient Greek system, incorporated in Pythagorean teachings, taught by Franchino Gafurio and used by Alberti and later renaissance architects in building design, is based upon the progression 1:2:3:4, producing the intervals of the octave, the fourth and the fifth. The following three simple ratios are considered harmonious:

8:16; 2:1 Octave, Diapason.

4:6; 2:3 Fifth, Diapente

9:12; 3:4 Fourth, Diatessaron

There are also two composite consonances:

1:2:3 octave and a fifth

1:2:4 double octave

The 3, 4, 5 triangle is Pythagorean because it creates a right

angle with sides with whole-number ratios. Three ratios are
present in the 3, 4, 5 triangle; 4:3; 5:4 and 5:3. Its area is 6
square units, the perfect number. Plato taught that the harmony
of the cosmos is present in the seven numbers 1, 2, 3, 4, 8, 9
and 27.[96] They form two geometrical progressions, 1, 2, 3, 4,
8 and 1, 3, 9, 27. Conventionally, these are depicted on two
lines diverging from a single point like a pair of compasses. It
takes is name *lambda* because of its resemblance to the Greek
alphabetic character. In the renaissance, following Pythagoras,
harmony was not perceived as the bringing together of similar
things, but the union of opposites. The Pythagorean philosopher Philolaus defined harmony as the unification of the
composed manifold and the accordance of the discordance.[97]

An important disseminator of Pythagorean harmonic principles was Franchino Gafurio. In two books, *Theoria musice
(1492) and De Harmonia musicorum instrumentorum* (1518), he
described musical consonances and harmonies in numerical terms. His 1492 book has a fourfold illustration depicting
Pythagoras, Philolaos and Jubal or Tubal Cain. In the first illustration, Jubal presides over six smiths using hammers of different weight to hit a piece of metal on an anvil. In the second,
Pythagoras is shown twice, striking six suspended bells, and
six water-filled tumblers. Each sequence is numbered 4, 6,
8, 9, 12, and 16, the same as the relative weights of Tubal's
hammers. The third picture shows Pythagoras again, with a
plectrum in each hand, playing a 6-stringed dulcimer whose
strings are tensioned by weights bearing the same sequence of
numbers. The fourth pictures shows Pythagoras and Philolaus.
Each plays a whistle and holds two others. They are numbered
in the same sequence as bells, tumblers and dulcimer weights.

96 Taylor, A.E., *A Commentary on Plato's Timaeus*, London, 1928, 116ff.;
  Cornford, F.M.: *Plato's Cosmology*, London, 1937, 49, 66ff.

97 H. Diels, *Die Fragmente der Vorsokratiker*, Berlin, 1934, I, 410, fragment
  10.

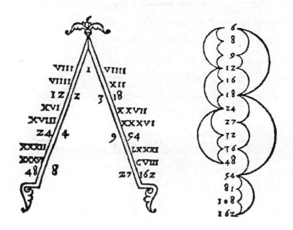

Diagram of the lambda and harmonic ratios by Francesco Giorgi, De Harmonia Mundi *(1521). The Library of the European Tradition.*

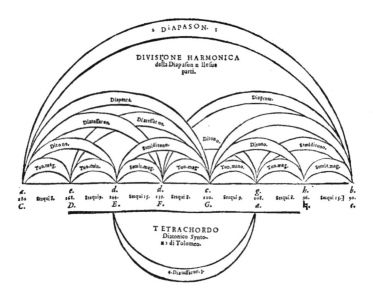

Harmonic ratios from Gioseffo Zarlino da Chioggia, Istitutioni harmoniche *(1573).*

The harmonic mean division of the octave is shown in a frontispiece engraving illustrating Gafurio's 1518 work. The illustration depicts the professor lecturing his students. To Gafurio's right are three unequal organ pipes with the numbers 3, 4 and 6. To his left are three lines, also marked 3, 4 and 5. Beneath the lines is a pair of dividers, open, reminiscent of the *lambda*. From Gafurio's mouth emerges a scroll with the words, "Harmonia est discordia concors" – "Harmony is discordant concordance". Harmony is not brought about by the consonance of two tones, but from two unequal consonances taken from dissimilar proportions. Raphael's painting in the Vatican, *The School of Athens*, shows the Pythagorean musical doctrine in diagrammatic form. The divine harmony, in reflecting the structure of the cosmos, has the power to enchant. John Dryden's *A Song for St Cecilia's Day*, performed on the twenty-second of November, 1687, also refers to the myth of Jubal:

> What passion cannot music raise and quell?
> When Jubal struck the corded shell,
> His listening brethren stood around
> And wondering, on their faces fell
> To worship that celestial sound:
> Less than a God they thought there could not dwell
> Within the hollow of that shell
> That spoke so sweetly and so well
> What passion cannot music raise and quell?[98]

Architectural Harmonics

The music of the spheres, in all its complexity of endless realignments, changing relationships and new harmonies, thus reflects the limitless combinations of the elements that allow the multiplicities of the existent world to have their being. These musical numbers also produce harmony when applied to architectural proportion, symbolically relating the structure

---

98 John Dryden, *A Song for St Cecilia's Day*, II, lines 16-24.

to the inner workings of the cosmos. Some musical theorists of the renaissance were actually involved in architectural
design. In 1490, Franchino Gafurio went to Mantua to discuss
the building of a tower at Milan Cathedral with the architect
Luca Fancelli.[99] Leon Battista Alberti commented:

> the truth of Pythagoras's saying, that Nature is certain
> to act consistently….. I conclude that the same numbers
> by means of which the agreement of sounds affects our
> ears with delight are the very same which please our eyes
> and our minds…. We shall therefore borrow our rules
> for the finishing our proportions, from the musicians,
> who are the greatest masters of this sort of numbers,
> and from those particular things wherein nature shows
> herself most excellent and complete.[100] …..We have
> already observed, that harmony is an agreement of
> several tones, delightful to the ears …. This harmony
> the ancients gathered from interchangeable concords
> of the tones, by means of certain determinate numbers;
> the names of which concords are as follows: *Diapente*,
> or the fifth, which is also called *Sesquialtera; Diapason*, or
> the eighth, also called the double tone, and *Disdiapason*,
> the fifteenth or *Quadruple*. To these was added the Tonus,
> which was also called the *Sesquioctave*. These several
> concords, compared with the strings themselves [of the
> musical instruments producing the tones – N.P.], bore
> the following proportions. The *Sesquialtera* was so called,
> because the string which produced it bore the same
> proportion to that which it is compared, and one and
> a half does to one; which was the meaning of the word
> *Sesqui*, among the ancients. In the *Sesquialtera* therefore
> the longer string must be allowed three, and the shorter,

99 Rudolf Wittkower, *Architectural Principles in the Age of Humanism*,
   London, 1998, 119.

100 Alberti, op.cit., 197.

two. The *Sesquitertia* is where the longer string contains the shorter one and one third more; the longer must be as four, and the shorter as three. But in that concord which was called *Diapason*, the numbers answer to one another in a double proportion, as two to one, or the whole to the half; and in the *Triple* they answer as three to one, or as the whole to one third of itself. In the *Quadruple*, the proportions are as four to one, or as the whole to its fourth part... Of all these numbers the architects made very convenient use, taking them sometimes two by two, as in planning out their squares and open areas... sometimes taking them three by three ..... wherein as the length was to bear a proportion to the breadth, so they made the height in a certain harmonious proportion to them both.[101]

The Three Means

We are now to say something of the rules of these proportions (wrote Alberti), which are not derived from harmony or the natural proportions of bodies, but are borrowed elsewhere for determining the three relations of an apartment ... These the philosophers call *Mediocrates* or *Means*, and the rules for them are many and various. But there are three particularly which are most esteemed; of all which the purpose is, that the two extremes being given, the middle mean or number may correspond with them in a certain determined manner, or to use such an expression, with a regular affinity. ... consider three terms, whereof the two most remote are one the greatest, and the other the least; the third or mean number must answer to these other two in just relation or proportionate interval. Which interval is the relative distance which this number stands from the other

---

101 Alberti, op. cit., 197.

two.[102] The arithmetical mean is determined by "Taking the two extreme numbers, as for instance, eight for the greatest, and four for the least, you add them together, which produce twelve, which twelve being divided in two equal parts, gives us six. This number six, as the arithmeticians say, is the mean, which standing between four and eight, is at an equal distance from each of them.[103] The geometrical mean is calculated as follows: "let the smallest number, for example, four, be multiplied by the greatest, which we shall suppose to be nine; the multiplication will produce 36: the root of which sum as it is called, or the number of its side being mutliplied by itself must also produce 36. The root therefore will be six, which multiplied by itself is 36, and this number six is the mean. This geometrical mean is very difficult to find by numbers, but it is very clear by lines....[104]

Finally, Alberti describes the musical mean:

The third mean, which is called musical, is somewhat more difficult to work out that the arithmetical; but, however, may be very well performed by numbers. In this the proportion between the least term and the greatest, must be the same as the distance between the least and the mean, and between the mean and the greatest ... Of the two given numbers, let the least be thirty, and the greatest sixty, which is just the double of the other. ... I then divide the whole interval ... into three parts, each of which parts therefore will be ten, and one of these three parts I add to the least number, which will make it forty, and this will be the musical mean desired. And this mean number forty will be distant from the greatest number just double the interval which the number of the mean

102 Ibid., 197-8.

103 Ibid., 199-200.

104 Ibid., 200.

is distant from the least number; and the condition was that the greatest number should bear that portion to the least".[105] By the help of these mediocrites the architects have discovered many excellent things, as well as with relation to the whole structure, as to its several parts.[106]

Whole Number Ratios in the Eternal Tradition

Francis C. Penrose, who studied the proportions and orientation of ancient Greek temples as well as Wren's St Stephen's Walbook, wrote in 1890, "Although it may not be so absolutely demonstrable in architecture as it is in music, that commensurability of adjacent parts in a scale of low numbers is a necessary element of perfection, it at least rises to a very high degree of probability that it is so; and that this quality prevails in the work of Sir Christopher Wren will be seen …".[107]

The means of determining whole number ratios geometrically is by the diagram known as the helikon. This was described by Ptolemy in antiquity as "a device made by students of mathematics to display concordant ratios". It is named after Mount Helikon, the abode of the nine Muses in ancient Greek cosmology, as, among other things, it governs the intervals of traditional music.[108] In 1545, Sebastiano Serlio (1475-1553) published the use of the helikon in the design of architectural features, such as the location and dimensions of doors and windows, so it is also referred to as 'Serlio's construction'. Although Serlio published sporadically, he was highly influential. In 1611, his collected works were published posthumously in London as an English translation called *The Five Books of*

---

105 Ibid.

106 Ibid.

107 Francis C. Penrose, 'St Stephen's Walbook', *Royal Institute of British Architects Transactions* N.S. VI, 1890, 245.

108 See Nigel Pennick & Helen Field: *Muses and Fates*, Capall Bann, Milverton, 2004, 33-38, 65-68.

Architecture, and a major Italian edition came out in Venice in 1619, *Tutte l'opere d'architettura et prospettiva di Sebastiano Serlio bolognese*. The arrangement of arches known as the Serliana and his geometrical designs for urns and similar finials were adopted by almost all the major British architects working in London after the Great Fire. The Serliana is sometimes called the 'Venetian window' and was used for the east windows of churches without an apse, such as St George, Hanover Square; St Martin-in-the-Fields, the Vere Street Chapel and St Giles's as well as in other, more novel ways on facades and towers by Nicholas Hawksmoor. At St Martin-in-the-Fields, James Gibbs used the helikon not only for the overall proportional system of width to length to height, but also as the guiding geometry for the portico façade.

This most elegant geometrical diagram is essentially a square divided by four diagonals. Two connect opposite corners of the square, and the other two from corners to the centre of the opposite side. The intersection-points of the lines of the helikon produce whole number proportional ratios through similar triangles. The sacred geometry inherent in the helikon is the essence of classical architecture, epitomized in the writings of the first century BCE Roman architect Vitruvius, who taught integrated design techniques, emphasising the construction of the whole work in perfect geometrical and proportional correspondence with the individual components.[109] Sacred geometry and its inherent proportions are the indispensable ground base of sacred architecture. Because the interrelation of elements reflects the mathematical structure of the cosmos and hence, in Classical tradition, expresses the Divine Harmony (in Judaeo-Christian cosmology, God's Creation and in Masonic terms, the work of the Great Architect of the Universe), the building is not only internally harmonious, but also an ensouled manifestation of the eternal tradition.

---

109 Marcus Vitruvius Pollio: *De Architectura*, I, 2, 2.

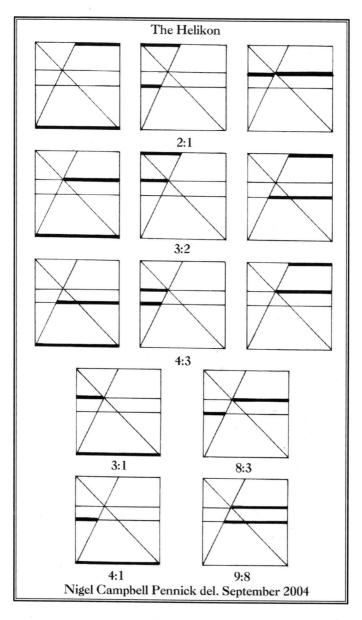

The Helikon

2:1

3:2

4:3

3:1   8:3

4:1   9:8

Nigel Campbell Pennick del. September 2004

The Helikon diagram and whole-number ratios.

General Principles of Classical Architecture

The aim of classical design is to appropriately relate the building to the location and the various elements of the building to one another in such a way that harmony is the result. There are several technical terms to describe the various means by which this harmony can be achieved: Taxis, Concinnitas, Finitio and Collocatio. Vitruvius defined taxis as the "balanced adjustment of a work separately, and as the whole, the arrangement of the proportion with a view to a symetrical result.[110] Leon Battista Alberti taught that the objective of concinnitas is to use a precise rule to compose naturally separate components of a building into a harmonious whole. The principle of concinnitas exists in nature, which accounts for the absolute perfection of natural things. "That the beauty of all edifices arises principally from three things, namely, the number, figure and collocation of the several members".[111] Beauty comes from the sympathetic consonance of the parts of any work, according to numerus, finitio and collocatio (definite number, outline and position),[112] organized by concinnitas, the absolute and fundamental rule of nature.[113] Numerus, finitio and collocatio have been seen as relating to the Aristotelian principles of quantity, quality and relation.[114]

The term *Finitio* has been the subject of much interpretation. In the English edition of *De re aedificatoria*, 1726 (and in the two following editions of 1739 and 1755), Giacomo Leoni translated *finitio* as 'finishing'. "By the finishing I understand a certain mutual correspondence of those several lines, by which the proportions are measured, whereof one is the length, the

---

110 Vitruvius, op. cit., I, II, para.2.

111 Alberti, op. cit., IX, V.

112 The Latin *numerus, finitio* and *collocatio*.

113 Alberti, IX, V.

114 Flemming, W., *Die Begründung der modernen Aesthetik und Kunstwissenschaft durch L.B. Alberti*, Berlin/Leipzig, 1916, 33.

other the breadth, and the other the height",[115] wrote Alberti. In Roman surveying, the specialist called a *finitor* established and measured boundaries within a *limitatio* (surveyed area). Alberti uses the word *finitorium* that renaissance sculptors used to determine relative position and scale.[116] It appears that *finitio* means general definition: delimitation, outline, edge, boundary, contour, surface or form in the sense of outward limits; the measured outlines of the building as a spatial object as determined by solid geometry.

The arrangement of every part of a structure ensuring that each is in its appropriate location, according to the harmonious principles of nature, is called *collocatio*.[117] This can mean position, location or placement in the sense of composition, arranging the work so that it is complete and well-formed. Precision is an important element in this work, for without accurate measurement and construction the most harmonious of designs will not be brought into being, a principle well understood by Sir Christopher Wren in his motto: *Numero, Pondera et Mensura.*

Techniques Ancient and Modern – Wren's 'Tracts'
Sir Christopher Wren's interest in the inner nature of antique Classical architecture led him to work upon paper reconstructions of some of the famous sacred buildings of antiquity, recorded in ancient texts. "Architecture aims at Eternity", wrote Wren "and therefore is the only Thing uncapable of Modes and Fashions in its Principals".[118] By recovering the essence of antiquity through these researches, he was able to embody it in his modern buildings. Wren's few writings

115 Alberti, op.cit., IX, V, 196.

116 Gadol, J., *Leon Battista Alberti: Universal Man of the Early Renaissance*, Chicago/London, 1969, 108-117.

117 Vagnetti, L., 'Concinnitas. Riflessioni sus significato di un termine Albertiano', *Studie decoumenti de architettura*, II, 1973, 139-161.

118 Wren, *Parentalia,* op. cit., *Tract I*, 351.

Corinthian capital, geometrical analysis of plan.

Corinthian capital elevation drawing.

about ancient monuments were edited by his son, Christopher Wren Jr. (1675-1747), and published by his grandson Stephen Wren in *Parentalia* (London, 1750). They appear in an appendix titled *Of Architecture; and Observations on Antique Temples, &c.*, part of what is known as *Tract* IV. The temples described in this *Tract* are the Temple of Artemis (Diana) at Ephesus, the Temple of Mars Ultor and the Temple of Peace, both at Rome. (The Roman building known as the Temple of Peace in Wren's day was later identified as the Basilica of Maxentius and Constantine). Two of the buildings described – the Temple of Diana and the Mausoleum – were of the celebrated Seven Wonders of the World. Wren's writings on the Mausoleum are titled *Of the Sepulchre of Mausolus King of Caria*, and are of interest because they served as the model for part of the church of St George, Bloomsbury. As a mathematician, astronomer and architect, Wren's interest in number and dimension is clear.

The original Mausoleum stood at Halicarnassus in Caria, on the Aegean coast, (now Bodrum in Turkey). Ephesus, locus of the Temple of Artemis, is further north in the same country. This magnificent royal tomb, which gave us the generic name, 'mausoleum', was constructed on the orders of his wife, Artemisia, for the provincial king Mausolus, who died in 353 BCE.[119] It stood for over one thousand six hundred years until it collapsed in an earthquake in 1304. Subsequently its ruins were utilized as a source of building material, and dispersed. Fragments of it were rediscovered later and are preserved in the British Museum. Pliny's detailed description of it survives in his *Natural History*.[120] It is the source of later attempts to recover its form and structure that found physical form in an eighteenth century church tower in London. Wren wrote in

---

119 "… *obiit Olympiadis CVII anno secundo*" – died in the second year of the 107th Olympiad. Pliny, *Natural History*, 36.4.30.

120 ibid, 36.4. 30-32.

the *Parentalia* (his text has the original capitalization, italics and spelling used):

> The Sepulchre of *Mausolus* is so well described by *Pliny*, that I have attempted to design it accordingly, and also very open, conformable to the Description in

Corinthian capital by Wren, St Mary Abchurch (1681-1686).

Martial. The skill of four famous Artists, *Scopas, Briaxes, Timotheus* and *Leochares,* all of the School of *Praxiteles,* occasioned this Monument to be esteemed one of the seven Wonders of the World [the sculptures of Scopas were on the east side; Bryaxis the north; Timotheus the south – N.P.[121]]. These Architects living before the Time of *Alexander*, and before the Beginning of the Temple of *Diana* at Ephesus ... I conclude this Work must be the exactest Form of the Dorick. It appeared from the City *Halicarnassus* to the Sea, that is North and South, 64 Feet, and so much every way; for, each Artificer took his Side; and being hexastyle, contained in all 36 Pillars; that is to say, 20 for the four Fronts, and 16 within, which supported the *Pteron* .....

Supposing then in the Order, which *Vitruvius* calls *Systyle,* (where the Inter-column is double the Diameter of the Column) if the Column is 4 Feet in Diameter, and the Inter-column 8 Feet, the whole Facade will be 64 Feet. The Heighth of the Columns of 7½ Diameter will be 30 Feet, and with the *Dorick* Entablature of a fourth Part of the Column, will make 37½ Feet, which is just 25 Cubits; as *Pliny* makes the Heighth of the first Story; above the *Cyma* of the Cornice must be a *Zocle* of 2½ Feet, for fixing the Statues, which will make in all 40 Feet from the Floor. Upon the 16 inward Columns rose the *Pteron* .... the Pilasters whereof, that they might be visible, were supported on a Substructure, or Pedestal, of 20 Feet, so elevated to be seen above the Statues of 7 Feet, and being 14 Feet behind the *Cyma* of the outward Columns, could not be lower. The Pilasters then of the *Pteron* being 24 Feet, made with their Cornice 30 Feet more; and upon this the Stone Covering rising 24 Feet more ... made the whole *Pteron* 74 Feet. Now, if round about the lower

---

121 Pliny, 34.4.31.

Colonade is added an Ascent in Steps of 10 Feet, (the third of the Pillar) there will be to the Platform on the Top 124 Feet, upon which stood the triumphal Chariot of *Mausolus*, in Marble, 16 Feet high; so the whole Heighth will be 140 Feet, as by *Pliny*. – The whole Circumference I have computed 416 Feet .....

I have computed by just Proportions, which indeed are very fine. First, the Ascent in Heighth is a third Part of the Pillar; then the Column with the Architrave being 32, will be half the Facade 64, and the Face of the *Pteron* and Pedestal, will have the Appearance of being as high as broad over the Heads of the Statues ... The Breadth at the lower Steps to the whole Heighth, is as 3 to 4, which is the Sides of *Pythagorick* rectangular Triangles. The Ordinance of the Whole falls out so wonderfully, and the Artists being contemporary with the School of *Plato*, I known not but they might have something to practise from thence, in this harmonick Disposition. I have joined the 16 inward Pillars into four Solids, and continued the same to the Top; opening also the middle Inter-column to the *Pteron*, that Solid may be upon Solid, and Void upon Void; so all is firm, yet airy."

Clearly, Sir Christopher Wren put a great deal of thought into the architectural meaning of the ancient descriptions by Martial and Pliny and came up with a workable building containing consonant proportions which could have been constructed if needed. The elements of its elevation are interrelated by a series of whole-number ratios, based upon a ten-foot module: 1:3:3:3:4; 1:4:5:4; 4:3:3:4; 5:5:4; 7:7; 10:4. The proportion of width to height is 16:31 for the structure and 16:35 including the crowning sculpture. Wren naturally used the English Statute Foot that dates from 1305 (12 inches: 304·8 mm), but Pliny's measurements naturally referred to an ancient foot, perhaps the local Aegina Foot of 315 mm, or the Common Greek Foot of 316·25 mm.[122]

Whether or not it is an historically accurate reconstruction of this ancient wonder, this Tract records Wren's method of working, and gives us an insight into the numerical and proportional systems still apparent in the extant classical churches of London built after the Great Fire. An illustrative

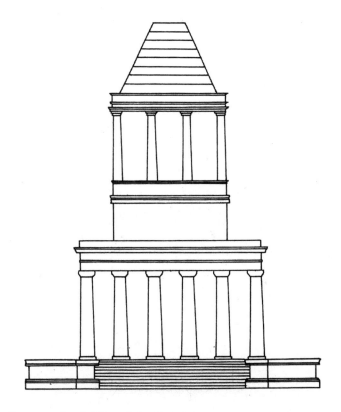

Reconstruction by Wren of the Mausoleum at Halicarnassus. Drawing by Nigel Pennick after Nicholas Hawksmoor.

---

122 F.G. Skinner: *Weights and Measures*, London, Her Majesty's Stationery Office, 1967, 60.

drawing, which was not engraved for *Parentalia*, was made by his then assistant, Nicholas Hawksmoor, according to Wren's dimensions. It was omitted from the book, "on account of the Drawing being imperfect" (it is only diagrammatic). The original drawing survives in the British Architectural Library of the Royal Institute of British Architects. It is clearly the origin of the stepped pyramid on a pedimented columnar base that Hawksmoor later built in Bloomsbury. By then he was no longer Wren's assistant, but Surveyor-General of Westminster Abbey and one of the surveyors to the Commissioners of the Fifty.

In 1721, in Vienna, the Austrian architect Johann Bernhard Fischer von Erlach (1656-1723), who visited England in 1704, published a book of engravings titled *Entwurff Einer Historischen Architektur.* This was intended to be "a history of architecture with illustrations of famous buildings of antiquity and foreign countries". As well as Solomon's Temple in Jerusalem, it detailed the Seven Wonders of the World and other notable ancient buildings. His version of the Mausoleum is reproduced here. Shortly after this publication, the tower of St George's, Bloomsbury, was built, based upon this reconstruction. The actual site of the Mausoleum and its dimensions remained unknown until Sir Charles Newton rediscovered it in 1856.[123]

123 James Fergusson, *A History of Architecture in All Countries*, John Murray, London, 1893, 282.

CHAPTER 4

THE SACRED ART OF GEOMETRY IN ACTION

It is in the public interest to learn and practise the art of geometry.

Justinian's *Compendium of Civil Law.*

Geometric Possibilities

The basics of geometry do not change, neither does the symbolism. Geometry is the underlying continuity in sacred art, which has been known and developed from the time of megalithic Europe and the ancient Egyptians, and added to by the analytical work of the Greek philosophers Archimedes and Euclid. A key work in western geometry is Euclid's *The Thirteen Books of the Elements*, written originally in ancient Greek, but transmitted to later times through Arabic and then Latin versions. In the twelfth century, the Italian Gerard of Cremona, and the English scholar Aethelhard, produced Latin translations, and in the thirteenth century, Johannes Campanus of Novaro made a version that was influential until the renaissance.[124] Euclid's work contains definitions, postulates, propositions and proofs of various geometical problems that have formed the basis of teaching 'Euclidean geometry' to this day.

However, the most influential architectural theorist of the renaissance, Leon Battista Alberti, does not mention Euclid, but was a follower of Archimedes. In addition to the known written sources of antiquity, Archimedes, Euclid and Vitruvius being among the most significant, there is a parallel transmission through craftsmanship, generally kept as trade secrets. By the mid-seventeenth century, all the various ancient works were published and available to architects, as well as the

---

124 T.L. Heath, *Euclid: The Thirteen Books of the Elements*, Cambridge University Press, Cambridge, 1926, 91-113.

now-divulged trade secrets of the masons and carpenters, who had formerly not given them to anyone who was not a fellow practitioner. In addition, there was continuous research and progress brought about through new insights and discoveries. It is because of the integration of these multiple sources in the seventeenth century that the unique buildings erected after the Great Fire of London took the form they did.

The Circle

The circle is a most basic form, visible in the sky in the roundness of the sun and the full moon, on Earth in the circle of the horizon; in the patterns made by raindrops in standing water, and in the stems, branches and trunks of plants. Archaic buildings, too, were circular, whether the bender-tents of nomads, the stone-and-wood huts of the ancient Britons or the traditional makeshift shelters of forest charcoal-burners erected until the middle of the twentieth century. The oldest structures by far in Great Britain are the stone circles. To the Etruscans, from whom the western geomantic tradition largely comes, via Rome, circular temples were dedicated to a single deity, whilst the rectangular served three gods.[125]

The circle is often taken to symbolize eternity, continuous, never beginning and without end, and, like all non-verbal forms, it is ever open to rediscovery. In the fifteenth century, Leon Battista Alberti wrote that the circle was an Egyptian symbol for time.[126] In 1648, in *Love, What It Is*, Robert Herrick wrote:

> Love is a circle that does restless move
> In the same sweet eternity of love.

In sacred geometry, the circle is sometimes depicted containing a figure of the ideal man, whose bodily proportions related to geometric figures. With the straightedge and compasses, all

---

125 Fergusson, op.cit., 292.
126 Alberti, op.cit., VIII, 169.

the major geometric figures can be drawn without measurement. Deriving from the circle, the vesica piscis, the equilateral triangle, the square, the hexagon, pentagon and other polygons all have direct and fixed relationships with one another. As the alchemical text, *The Seventh Key* of Basil Valentine states, "My son, take the simple and round body and do not take the triangle or quadrangle, but take the round body, for the round body is more related to simplicity than the triangle. Also it should be noted that the simple body has no angles, since it is the first and the last among the planets just as the sun is among the stars".[127] By the seventeenth century, however, the model of 'Vitruvian Man' was on the decline, and building appeared in a more symbolic light, where the classical forms were made to express the inner essences of the cosmos rather than as a reflection of the human body.

Ad Quadratum

Perhaps the most ancient form of sacred geometry, after the circle, is the square and its derivatives, the octagon and the octagram. The Egyptian pyramids, square in plan and accurately orientated to face the four cardinal directions, were emblematical of the stability of the world, symbolizing the transition-point between the earth and the celestial spheres above. Geometrically, the square is unique. The geometrician can divide it precisely into two and multiples of two by drawing without measurement. It is divided into four squares by making a cross connecting the centre of opposite sides. This also defines the exact centre of the square. It can be again divided into four triangles by drawing straight lines connecting opposite corners. This also defines the exact centre. When all eight lines are drawn, they form the eightfold division of space, to the cardinal and intercardinal directions. These

---

127 Valentine, Basil, *Artis auriferae quam chemiam vocant*, 3 vols., Basel, 1610, II, 207-208.

are the directions of the eight winds known to the ancient Macedonians and Athenians.

The basis of Ad Quadratum (Latin for 'to' or 'on the square') is the subdivision of the square by connecting the middle of adjacent sides. This creates a smaller square oriented at 45° from the original one. The diagonal of the smaller square is the length of the side of the larger one. This ratio also appears when a square is drawn from the diagonal of the larger square. By repeated creation of squares derived from one another, larger or smaller, a series of related ratios, and hence dimensions, appear, and, put in its most basic form, this is the secret of the proportional system of Gothic architecture. When two equal squares are superimposed at 45 degrees from one another, the octagram is created. Its internal figure is the octagon. This is the most frequently used geometric form in Roman architecture and the forms later derived from it: Byzantine, Romanesque, Islamic, Gothic and later classical buildings.

In the late middle ages, the sacred art of geometry as applied to building was still a closely-guarded trade secret. This can be seen by the records of a meeting of operative masons from various provinces of the Holy Roman Empire that was held at Regensburg in 1459.[128] There, the delegates agreed a text for new statutes ruling the craftsmen's local administrative bodies, known as lodges. Paragraph 13 states that the technique of how "to take an elevation from the plan" should not be shown to anyone who is not "of our handicraft".

In 1486, Matthäus Roriczer, a delegate at the conference who had not signed the final resolution, broke this agreement. He issued a small handbook titled *Das Büchlein von der Fialen Gerechtigkeit*. This is a key work in the understanding of Ad

---

128 Frankl, Paul, 'The Secret of the Medieval Masons', *The Art Bulletin*, XXVII, 1945, 46-64; Swaan, Wim, *The Gothic Cathedral*, London, 1969, 100.

Quadratum sacred geometry. "With God's help, I have undertaken to explain something of the art of geometry, and from the beginning of the draughted stonework, to explain how, and in what proportions, from geometrical principles, by division with compasses, it should be determined and brought to the correct dimensions".[129]

According to Roriczer, the geometrical ordination of a pinnacle begins with a square of the dimensions of the pinnacle's base. The centre points of the four sides are joined, making a smaller square, the fundamental diagram of Ad Quadratum. The area of the smaller square is half that of the larger. This subdivision by squares progresses until the requisite number of smaller components is achieved. Then, the lengths of the proportionate squares are used to determine the significant vertical dimensions of the pinnacle in whole-number multiples. The diminishing dimensions of the squares are the cross-sections of the pinnacle at various heights.

The publication of these principles was a major breach of professional secrecy that paralleled the contemporary publication of classical principles in Italy by Leon Battista Alberti.[130] No longer were the techniques of sacred geometry available only to the few craftsmen, but to anyone who could read and gain access to one of the new printed books. The profession of the architect as a man who was not necessarily a member of the building trade was now able to emerge as something distinct in its own right.

The Cube

The cubic form, having three straight axes at right angles to one another, is the square projected into three dimensions, and the fundamental basis of building in brick and stone. There is

---

129 Roriczer, Matthäus, *Das Büchlein von der Fialen Gerechtigkeit*, Regensburg, 1486, introduction.

130 E.g. *De re Aedificatoria*, Florence, 1485.

only one way of making a cubic stone properly: every angle must be right, each edge straight and each surface perfectly flat. Any errors are immediately apparent, and the stone is unfit for its purpose. Thus the cube is the symbolic embodiment of virtue, an image of perfection. Vitruvius wrote of the cube: "Pythagoras and those who came after him in his school thought it proper to employ the principles of the cube

Ad quadratum ground plan of the church of Our Lady at Trier, Germany.

in composing books on their doctrines".[131] In the thirteenth century, Pierre de Roissy wrote, "Squared stones signify the squareness of the virtues of the saints. These are Temperance, Justice, Fortitude and Prudence".[132] These four Cardinal Virtues, with their origin in classical Pagan philosophy, were, before the rise of amoral modernist theories of politics, known to be essential to the harmonious functioning of society. The cubic stone or 'perfect ashlar' is a central symbol in speculative freemasonry, expressing this virtuous meaning.

The cube was used as the elemental form in seventeenth century classicism in the Netherlands, employed by the leading architects of the time, Jacob van Campen, Hendrick de Keijser,

A medieval mason's geometrical drawing preserved by L'Oeuvre de Notre-Dame, Strasbourg, France. The few surviving parchments demonstrate the primacy of drawing as an art; without first making the drawings, there would be no architecture.

131 Vitruvius, op. cit., Book V, introduction.
132 Cited by Bernard E. Jones, op. cit., 410.

*The projection of plane geometry into three-dimensional vaulting,
Gloucester Cathedral (1337–1357). Drawing by Nigel Pennick after
Cyril E. Power, 1923.*

Jacob Lois, Pieter Post and Philips Vingboons.[133] Vingboons's 1648 architecture book, *Afbeelsels der voornaemste Geobouwen*, took the cube as the basic form for building the ideal house.[134] Subsequently, the cubic form was used frequently for small buildings in England, often in the form of a cube for the inhabitable structure and another cube above it that defined the cupola or other roof form (e.g. James Gibbs's 'Boycott Pavilions' at Stowe, 1726). Several commentators have noted that the body of the church of St Mary Woolnoth takes the general form of a cube, with its close associations with Pythagorean, Judaic and Masonic symbolism, though they have not explained why this particular church should take this form.[135] Nicholas Hawksmoor's St Mary Woolnoth is unusual because this cubic principle, generally employed in secular buildings, was applied to a church. But its position in the legendarium as the successor of the Temple of Concord, and as the Lord Mayor's church, clearly necessitated a special form. "Of all forms, the cube and the hemisphere are the most sacred", William Richard Lethaby later wrote, "the first was that of the Sanctuary at Jerusalem, and that chosen by St John as the type of the Holy City; 'its length, breadth and height were equal'".[136]

The Vesica Piscis and Ad Triangulum

The vesica piscis (Latin for 'fish-bladder') is a form produced when two equal-sized circles are drawn through each others' centres. A symbol in its own right, it is encountered frequently in Gothic art and architecture. It appears as the mandorla enclosing Our Lady or the Christ, as well as in certain forms of arch and window tracery. By drawing a straight line between the two

---

133 K.A. Ottenheym, 'Mathematische uitgangspunten van de Hollandse bouwkunst in de 17de eeuw', *De zeventiende eeuw*, 7, 1, 1991, 17-35.

134 Ibid., 22.

135 Du Prey, op. cit.,106, Vaughan Hart, *Nicholas Hawksmoor*, New Haven, 2002, 98.

136 Lethaby, op. cit., 65.

circles' centres, and then straight lines from these points to the apices, two equilateral triangles are produced, base-to-base. This is one means of drawing the equilateral triangle. The other is using the property of the radius of the circle to its circumference, where the radius measures of exactly six divisions. By connecting opposite points with straight lines, the hexagram, composed of two interlinked equilateral triangles, is formed. If the six points are joined by straight lines to adjacent points, then a hexagon is produced. Thus the circle and the vesica are the origin of triangular geometry, traditionally called Ad Triangulum. The relationship between the vesica and the pointed arch is apparent, and Ad Triangulum was indeed a favoured technique in the Gothic era (e.g. the ground-plan of King's College Chapel, Cambridge, designed in 1446 by Reginald Ely).

Geometrical analysis of the plan of a pillar in Milan Cathedral, Italy, after Caesare Caesariano, 1521.

Because of the nature of building, and the difficulty of making accurate 60 degree angles, triangular structures are rare. Some triangular structures were built during the Roman imperial era. But they were uncommon, and the reason for

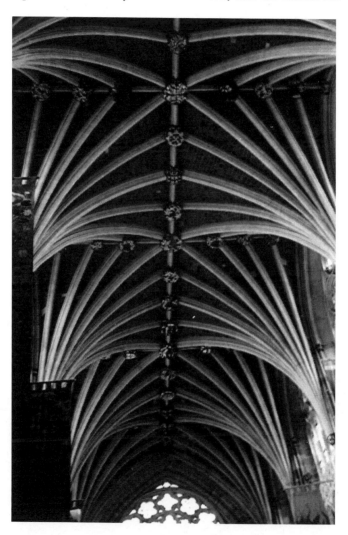

Vaulting of the nave of Exeter Cathedral, mid-fourteenth century.

their triangularity in the existing survivors is unclear. Serlio and Montano illustrated several antique Roman buildings that were based on the equilateral triangle. They were probably small temples and tombs. The tomb of the Curii at Aquilea has an upper part supported by three pillars.

The most overtly symbolic triangular building in England is Sir Thomas Tresham's triangular lodge at Rushden in Northamptonshire, built in 1593. Representing the Christian trinity, it is designed emblematically and symbolically. The ground-plan is an equilateral triangle measuring 33 feet 4 inches along each side, making the three sides together exactly 100 feet. There are three floors, with three windows on each storey on each side, each window divided into three. Each side has a Latin inscription of thirty-three characters. The internal rooms are hexagonal.

Clearly, Tresham's triangular lodge is unique and in no way characteristic of English buildings of the time, except in architectural style, the national form of mannerism. But it is an unequivocal sign that symbolic geometry and numerology were understood and sufficiently valued to be used in at least some buildings of that time. In the post-Great Fire era, Thomas Archer's rectory at Deptford, built at the same time as his church of St Paul, is considered one of the great losses of English baroque architecture.[137] Completed in 1731, it was demolished in 1883. From the reconstructed plan,[138] it was basically triangular, with octagonal rooms at the apices and semicircular rooms forming the sides of the triangle. James Gibbs's Temple of Liberty in the landscaped gardens of Lord Cobham's country house at Stowe, north of Buckingham (1739), is also basically triangular. This Gothic building has a very unusual geometry. The inner room is a circle in an

---

137 See Paul Jeffery, 'Thomas Archer's Deptford rectory; a reconstruction', *The Georgian Group Journal*, 1993, 32-42.

138 Ibid., 37.

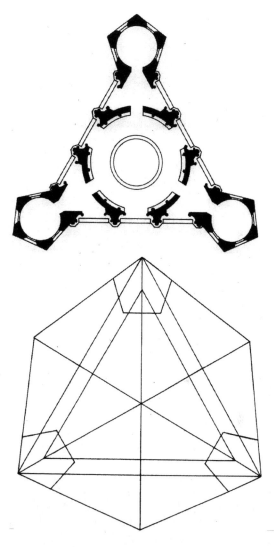

Plan and geometric analysis of the Temple of Liberty at Stowe, Buckinghamshire, England, showing the triangle-hexagon-pentagon relationship designed by James Gibbs in 1739. The plan is re-drawn by Nigel Pennick after James Gibbs, geometrical analysis by Nigel Pennick.

equilateral triangle, at the apices of which are two pentagonal turrets and one pentagonal tower. Dedicated "To the Liberty of our Ancestors", it was surrounded by statues of the seven Saxon gods: Sunna, Se Mona, Tiw, Wodn, Thuner, Frig and Satern, carved by John Michael Rysbrack with their names written in Anglo-Saxon runes.[139] No triangular churches were built in Great Britain at this time.

The multigeometric Perron at Liége, Belgium.

---

139 Ibid., 159.

The Fivefold and the Golden Section

The fivefold division of the circle, the pentagon and pentagram, is the starting-point for the proportion known as the
Golden Section or Golden Cut. This is a proportion that exists
between two measurable quantities of any sort when the ratio
between the larger and smaller one is equal to the ratio between
the sum of the two and the larger one. Geometrically, it is the
ratio in the pentagram between the side of the inner pentagon and its extension into the pentagram, a ratio of 1:1·618.
Conventionally it is symbolized by the Greek character Φ. In
any increasing progression or series of terms with Φ as the
ratio between two successive terms, each term is equal to the
sum of the two preceding ones. Numerically, this proportion
appears in the numerical series named after Leonardo Bigollo
Fibonacci (1170-c.1240), the Fibonacci Series. The series is
constructed additively, i.e. 1, 2, 3, 5, 8, 13, 21, 34, 55, 89, 144,
and so on. Organic growth is patterned on this system.

Much has been written about the Golden Section and
its application to art and architecture. In his *Timaeus*, Plato
discussed it as the key to cosmic physics, and in the renaissance, *De Divina Proportione* (1509) by Luca Pacioli (c.1445-1517)
was, and remains, influential in the realm of sacred geometry.
Many twentieth century writers detected it everywhere in
ancient remains (e.g. Matila Ghyka, *Esthétique des proportions
dans la Nature et dans les Arts* (1933)). One of the most influential architects of modernism, Le Corbusier (1887-1965),
used the Golden Section as the foundation of his own system
of proportional measurement, the Modulor. Few five-sided
buildings have emerged from this current, though a design by
Serlio survives. There are no pentagonal churches of the post-
Great Fire era in London. Giovanni Santini's chapel at Zd'ár in
Moravia is a notable baroque exercise in the fivefold that was
actually built. The most notable of all fivefold buildings is the
Pentagon in Washington, a twentieth century manifestation of

masonic symbolism present throughout United States federal imagery.

The Sevenfold

Leon Battista Alberti asserted: "It is certain, that almighty God himself, the creator of all things, takes particular delight in the number seven, having placed seven planets in the skies, and having been pleased to ordain with regard to Man, the glory of his creation, that conception, growth, maturity and the like, should all be reducible to this number seven".[140] To the Pythagoreans, seven was also special, being a 'virgin number' because a circle could not be divided geometrically into seven equal parts in ancient times. In medieval Christianity, the sevenfold was identified with the seven gifts of the Holy Spirit, depicted in stained glass work as a circle surrounded by six other circles, which is not a sevenfold division of the circle, but a sevenfold emanation of it.

The renaissance association of the heptagon or sevenfold with a goddess was made by Francesco Colonna in his *Hypnerotomachia Poliphili* (1499). His description of Venus's Fountain in the centre of a theatre (circular, divided into four sections, each subdivided into eight) may have been the inspiration for Sir Christopher Wren's later reconstruction on paper of Diana's Temple. In *Hypnerotomachia Poliphili* "The mysterious fountain

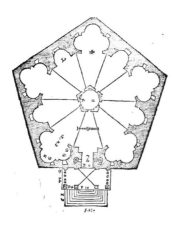

Design for a pentagonal building. Sebastiano Serlio from The Five Books of Architecture, *London, 1611.*

---

140 Alberti, op. cit., IX, V, 196.

of the Divine Mother" is described as a heptagonal building supported on seven pillars and topped with a cupola
surmounted by a cosmic egg (see below). Geometrically, to
divide a circle into seven with any accuracy is difficult. The
medieval rule-of-thumb method of laying out one seventh
part of a circle was by the so-called Druid's Cord. This is a
cord or rope divided into thirteen equal sections by twelve
knots. It can be used to produce a 3, 4, 5 triangle, and hence
the right angle, and also the 5, 4, 4 triangle, whose angle
is an approximation for one-seventh part of a circle.[141] In
Hypnerotomachia Poliphili, Francesco Colonna describes the
geometrical way to make a heptagon: within a circle, draw an
equilateral triangle on its radius, then make a line from the
centre through the middle of the side adjacent to the circumference. That length gives the sevenfold division of the

circle. In the next century,
Albrecht Dürer gave two
ways to make a heptagon.
One is drawn using an equilateral triangle, the method
described by Colonna, whilst
the other is derived from the
construction of the pentagon. Neither is accurate, but
as rule-of thumb approxi-
mations, both work well.

A more accurate geometri-
cal way to divide the circle
into seven equal parts was
discovered in the seventeenth
century by Count Carlo
Renaldini (1615-1698), who
wrote a number of books

*A sixfold Roman building on the
Appian Way near Rome recorded
by Giovanni Battista Montano
(1534–1621).*

141 Nigel Pennick, *Sacred Geometry*, op. cit., 45.

on algebra, geometry and general mathematics. His technique for drawing equal polygons of any number of sides within a circle was an elegant solution to this significant problem. It is achieved by first drawing a line across the circle's diameter. Divide this into the number of equal parts equivalent to the number of sides of the intended polygon. Then draw a pair of arcs whose radius is the diameter of the circle, starting at each end of the line. Draw a line from the intersection of the arcs to the second division point on the line across the circle, and extend it to meet the circle. The length between the end of the line across the circle, nearest to the new line, and the intersection point is the length of the polygon's side. Setting this length on the compasses, then mark off the other points and complete the polygon. This is the best approximation. A

A late seventeeth century pulpit sounding-board in the church of St Michael Paternoster Royal, with sixfold geometrical marquetry (damaged by a cut-out made in the 20th century to install electric light).

heptagon cannot be drawn accurately with just straightedge and compasses, as was proven by Carl Friedrich Gauss in 1796.

With progress in geometry and surveying techniques, sevenfold planned towns came into being in the late sixteenth century. The Italian military engineer Marchi, who went to the Netherlands in 1559, appears to have introduced the geometrical fortress to the flatlands of northern Europe. Several still exist.[142] The fortified town of Coevorden was laid out by

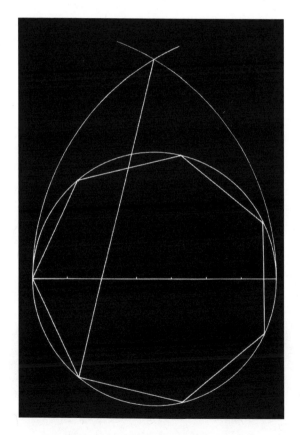

Renaldini's method of drawing regular polygons.

---

142 Ian V. Hogg, *Fortress*, London, 1975, 44.

Johann Rijswijk in 1597, Scherpenheuvel in 1603 and the cita-
del at Mannheim in 1606. All were seven sided. Describing the
basic method of fortification used at this era, Lord Sydenham
wrote, "Draw a polygon round the area to be defended; make
of each side a bastioned front, obtain saliency and crossfire
over the front by ravelins …".[143]

At the same time that the military engineers were creating
heptagonal defences, alchemists and self-styled Rosicrucians

The seven-sided military defences of Coevorden, the Netherlands.

143 Major G. Sydenham Clarke (Lord Sydenham (1893)), cited by Hogg,
op.cit., 58-61.

were writing about the symbolism of the sevenfold. Alchemical symbolism expresses the sevenfold in the *stella perfectionis*, the 'star of perfection',[144] the figure of perfect conjunction,[145] depicted as a seven-pointed star, each point having the attributes of the seven planets. Another literary source for a mystic sevenfold structure comes from the *Fama Fraternitatis*, a text about the life and teachings of the mysterious Brother R.C. (Christian Rosenkreuz), published several times between 1614 and 1617.[146] The *Fama Fraternitatis* described the rediscovery of his tomb: "In the morning following, we opened the door, and there appeared to our sight a vault of seven sides and seven corners, every side five foot broad, and the height of eight foot. Although the sun never shined in this vault, nevertheless, it was enlighted with another sun, and was situated in the upper part of the ceiling. In the midst, instead of a tombstone, was a round altar…".[147]

Sir Christopher Wren's investigations into ancient architecture produced one sevenfold structure. In the appendix to Christopher Wren Junior's *Parentalia* "Of Architecture: and observations on Antique Temples &c." there is a plate of the Temple of Diana at Ephesus, reconstructed by Sir Christopher.[148] An engraving showing the temple[149] was drawn by Henry Flitcroft (1697-1769) and engraved by Gerard Vandergrucht (1696-1776). Wren wrote that the Temple of Diana "two hundred and twenty year in building" introduced the "*Ionick* Order". In length, the temple measured 425 feet,

144 Franciscus Kieser, *Cabala chymica*, Mühlhausen, 1606, 128.

145 *The Crowne of Nature*, 15.

146 Arthur Edward Waite, *The Real History of the Rosicrucians*, London, 1887, 64.

147 Ibid., 77.

148 Lydia M. Soo, *Wren's 'tracts' on Architecture and Other Writings*, Cambridge, Cambridge University Press, 1998, 14.

149 Plate following page 361.

in breadth 220. Wren calculated the disposition of its pillars from the number 127 as decastyle-dipteron. This form leaves seven columns over, which Wren allocates to a "Tabernacle, or Shrine", situated in the middle of the *cella*, containing the colossal image of Diana Multimammaea. Henry Flitcroft's *Plan of the Temple of Diana at Ephesus with the Shrine* shows this seven-pillared structure at the centre of building. Diana Multimammaea is the many-breasted goddess who appears as the personification of Nature in alchemical prints and the emblematic sculpture by Caius Gabriel Cibber on the pedestal of the Monument to the Great Fire of London, built 1671-1677.

A further engraving depicts an elevation of the temple front and the sevenfold shrine. This is composed of a circular plinth with seven steps, rising between the bases of Ionic columns that support a circular entablature, above which rise three receding circular fascias supporting a circular dome. "*Diana Artemis* was the Moon" Wren explains, "her Solemnities were by Night: the nineteen Pillars in the Ailes represented her Period; the seven Pillars in the Chapel in the Middle of the *Cella*, the Quarter of her menstrual Course". In envisaging this sevenfold tabernacle of Venus, Wren may have been following the sevenfold structure of what was believed to have been the temple of Venus at Baalbek (second century CE). In Wren's time the Roman temples at Baalbek (then in the Levant province of the Ottoman Empire, now Lebanon) were much studied. In 1660, a series of seventeen views of Baalbek by Jean Marot was published in France. Baalbek was visited also by Jacob Spon and George Wheler during their architectural travels in Croatia, Greece and Asia Minor in 1675 and 1676, and published in detail in a book that circulated widely in France, the Netherlands and Great Britain.[150]

---

150 Jacob Spon & George Wheler, *Voyage d'Italie, de Dalmatie, de Grèce, et du Levant faix aux années 1675 et 1676*, 2 vols., Lyon, 1678; Amsterdam, 1679; London, 1682.

Because of the constructional difficulty of making seven-fold buildings in physical reality, very few have ever come into being. One that was actually constructed was the altar to the Saxon gods in the grounds of the stately home at Stowe in Buckinghamshire. This altar was a circular plinth with seven niches, at the centre of which was a column surmounted by a near-spherical garlanded urn topped by a pine-apple.[151] Taken away in 1921, it was associated with James Gibbs's triangular Temple of Liberty, which still stands. Sir Christopher Wren constructed no sevenfold buildings. But in his church of St Stephen Walbrook (designed before 1672), whose cupola reflects the conjectural shrine of Diana in Flitcroft's drawing, Wren used a proportional system which had the number seven as the predominant figure. The sevenfold proportions detected by Francis Penrose at St Stephen's are: 2:7; 7:5; 7:8; 7:9; 3:7; 7:15; 7:18; 7:20.[152] The 2:7 ratio was also used by James Gibbs at St Martin-in-the-Fields. Another of Wren's domed churches, St Swithun, Cannon Street (built 1677–1681, destroyed 1941), had an octagonal dome, supported by one full column and seven half-columns. When rebuilding the city churches was finished, there were seven churches with domes, but this is not necessarily of any significance.

The Eightfold

The square of every odd number above the monad is a multiple of eight plus the monad. All squares of odd numbers above the monad differ from one another by a multiple of eight, e.g. $72 - 52 = 49 - 25 = 24 = 3 \times 8$. The eight- and sixteen-fold division of the horizon was used by the augurs to interpret the appearance of ostenta and to search for portents, and is best known through the Etruscan Discipline. It thereby

---

151 John Martin Robinson, *Temples of delight: Stowe Landscape Gardens*, The National Trust/Pitkin, London/Andover, 1990, 158.

152 Francis C. Penrose, 'St Stephen's Walbook', *Royal Institute of British Architects Transactions* N.S. VI, London, 1890, 246-247.

symbolizes the order of the world. The octagon and octagram
are significant elements in European traditional architecture.
They are the basis of the geometrical principle known as Ad
Quadratum, which was the basis for most Roman, Byzantine,
Carolingian, Romanesque and Gothic buildings. In addition
to its geometric properties, the Ad Quadratum figures of the
octagon and the octagram embody symbolic principles. The
octagram appears in ancient Greece as Aristotle's *tetrasomia*
principle. Here, the emanations of the four elements - earth,
water, air and fire – are expressed in two pairs of opposites:
hot – cold, and dry – moist. They are depicted as the corners
of two interpenetrating squares, an octagram. Hot is placed
between air and fire; dry between fire and earth; cold between
earth and water; and moist between water and air. As a ground
plan, it was used frequently by Roman mosaic designers.

The Tower of the Winds at Athens, designed by the
Macedonian architect Andronikos Cyrrhestes around 50 BCE,
is an octagon whose sides face towards the cardinal and intercardinal directions. Each side bears a relief of the corresponding wind. Whichever wind was blowing was indicated by a
pointer held by a bronze triton weather vane on top of the
building. The symbolism of this tower seems to have influenced later church builders, both Gothic and classical. Antique
tombs, too, were frequently octagonal. Derived from Roman
models, the form was used in the design of mosques and
mausolea throughout medieval Islam, an early instance being
The Dome of the Rock in Jerusalem, and a much later manifestation in the Taj Mahal (1632-1652).[153] In medieval Europe,
monastic chapter houses, together with the bases of perrons,
crosses, and market halls, frequently took the octagonal form.

The octagon was most favoured for the design of water-
sources in the form of public fountains. In the days before
water was piped to houses, the public fountain was the only

153 Agra, India.

source of water, and thus its reliability was a matter of life and death. Located at the centre of streets and market-places, public fountains reflected the ancient symbol of the four rivers of the world springing up in the central Paradise and watering the four quarters of the Earth. The early Christians adopted the octagonal fountain form for their baptisteries, in which new candidates of the religion were received into the church through the rite of baptism. In Rome, the baptistery of San Giovanni Laterano (St John Lateran, Rome, 432-440 CE) was one of the earliest of this form. At the baptistery of St Thecla's church in Milan is a quotation ascribed to St Ambrose:[154]

> With eight niches the temple rises for sacred use
> The fountain is eight-sided, worthy of the gift.
> The house of holy baptism must arise in the number eight.

In Italy especially, free-standing octagonal baptisteria were built close to cathedrals. In association with Sir Christopher Wren's cathedral, Nicholas Hawksmoor designed a free-standing octagonal baptistery to be built in front of St Paul's at the entrance to the temenos. It was never constructed.

The Oval

In the renaissance, the oval form, scarcely ever used in Gothic building, became a practical form in architecture. It is possible that what is now called the 'gardeners' method' was an early means of drawing an ellipse. This uses two pins or pegs at the foci of the ellipse and a string or rope to define the marker's path when the string is held in tension by it. It is a version of the 'Druid's cord'.[155] However, it is relatively inaccurate, because it depends on keeping the string at equal tension at all times and the drawing instrument at a standard angle.

---

154 337-339 ce. Heinz Götze, *Castel Del Monte: Geometric Marvel of the Middle Ages.* Munich – New York, Prestel 1998, 117.

155 Pennick, Nigel, *Sacred Geometry*, op.cit., 45.

In his *Quinto Libri d'Architettura* (1537-1575), Sebastiano Serlio (1473–?1553) gave four geometric techniques for constructing ovals from arcs drawn from the basic geometric figures, circle, triangle and square. In his *Scielta de Varii Tempietti Antichi* (1636), Giovanni Battista Montano (1534–1621) illustrated numerous smaller antique Roman buildings that survived in his day – tombs, mausolea and lesser temples, many of which have now disappeared. Some were based upon the

Ovals in wrought iron above a door of St Anne, Soho (1680-1686).

oval form. Some of his engravings illustrate the same ancient buildings that Serlio described earlier. Inspired by the work of Montano and Serlio, later the leading Baroque architects,

Geometric construction of ovals, by Borromini (1599–1667), redrawn by Nigel Pennick.

including Gianlorenzo Bernini, Francesco Borromini, Carlo Fontana and Guarino Guarini, created buildings in which the oval played a major role.

In London, Sir Christopher Wren designed a few churches with oval domes. His unrealized plan for the New London after the fire included an oval church near Holborn Bridge. The most notable constructed churches, both now destroyed, were St Benet, Fink (built 1670–1681, demolished 1846), and St Antholin, Watling Street (1678–1683, demolished 1875). St Benet's was a church in the form of an irregular decagon with an oval dome and lantern supported on six columns. Its ten-sided form was deceptive, because it was the rationalization into straight lines of an oval. This oval was formed by four arcs taken from the corners of a square, which, because St Benet was orientated to true east-west, faced the intercardinal directions. The north and south walls were not curved, but each was composed of four sections of a fourteen-sided

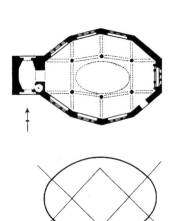

regular polygon. St Antholin, Watling Street had a six-sided inner ground-plan. Internally it had eight columns supporting an oval dome. Again a rationalization of an oval, St Antholin's western section was based upon angles derived from the fivefold division of the circle. Wren used the more conventional circular domes at St Mary Abchurch, St Mildred Bread Street, St Swithun, St Stephen Walbrook and St Paul's Cathedral. Some designs for churches after 1711 had oval

St Benet Fink (1670-1681, demolished 1846) ground plan and geometric analysis of oval.

forms, but none were constructed, probably because of financial strictures (e.g. Nicholas Hawksmoor's first, unbuilt design for St George's, Bloomsbury).

CHAPTER 5

PRACTICAL GEOMETRY TECHNIQUES

Form is a revelation of essence.

Meister Eckhart (c.1260-1328)

The Arts of Line

There are several basic ways of applying geometry to building. Measurements can be taken either from the edge of solid material, as in the craft of carpentry, or from the centre of the wall, as in bricklaying and masonry. The masons' line runs plumb centre, and the carpenters' line runs along surfaces. These two different 'arts of line' stem from the characteristics of the material used. Stonemasons mark out the centre, from which the edges and surfaces are created, whilst carpenters mark out a face edge, from which the other surfaces are derived. Only in wood turning do the two principles coincide, though the centre may be derived from a face edge, as in balustrades which have a square component. The art of making timber-frame buildings measures out the sacred geometry along edges, not through the centre-lines of the main posts. Corresponding stone pillars have their conceptual lines running plumb centre. Overall geometrical schemata can vary, depending upon the emphasis. The geometry of inner spaces is highly significant; more so than the outer shell in Gothic architecture, though geometry is applied to every individual external feature. This is more apparent in the simpler Gothic buildings, such as chapels, chantries and chapter houses, rather than the much more complex cathedrals. In classical architecture, interiors are ruled by lines that define the inner surfaces of the walls, floor and ceiling. Facades are also ruled by lines defining the outer surfaces. This geometry is very apparent in Dutch classicism and in James Gibbs's gable geometry, published in 1732 in his *Rules for the Drawing the Several Parts of Architecture*.

Stone and timber are both natural materials, with their own inner structure depending on type. So both wood and stone must be cut so that the inherent grain of the wood or bedding planes of the stone (if the stone is not freestone) are in an optimal orientation when supporting the finished building. The ability to select the correct materials for a building, and to place them appropriately, is the skill of a master. Melding the two kinds of 'art of line' together where they meet, as at the stone wall/timber roof junction, requires high geometrical acumen. The remaining great Gothic castles, guild-halls and cathedrals are the height of this art. The same techniques continued into the era of classical building in London after the Great Fire. In essence, only the form had been altered.

Westminster: Centre of Sacred Geometry

Westminster Abbey was too far away from the City of London to be affected by the Great Fire. In medieval times, in the absence of a university, it was the major centre of learning nearest to London. The chronicler Matthew of Westminster documented the London legendarium, and the outstanding 'Cosmati Pavement' remains as an example of a medieval concept of the microcosm presented in geometric form. The 'Cosmati Pavement' at Westminster is characteristic of the work of certain Roman master craftsman marble-workers (*marmorari*). More correctly, it is called cosmatesque, because the craftsmen came from two families, the Cosmati and Vassalletto, known as the *Magistri Doctissimi Romani*, Expert Roman Masters. This description is taken from contemporary inscriptions they used to describe themselves.[156] Within their oeuvre, which flourished between the early twelfth and the early fourteenth centuries, are geometric mosaics, usually made of porphyry, serpentine and coloured glass, used as inlays or in pavements in the technique known as opus sectile. The

---

156 Marco Bussagli, *Rome: Art and Architecture*, Königswinter, 2004, 254.

Expert Roman Masters based their designs on classical and late antique Roman models, whose sacred geometry was also the origin-point of the later development of Islamic architectural

Eight-sided fountain in the Great Court at Trinity College, Cambridge, 1600.

geometry. The tesserae of these mosaics are mainly squares and triangles of varying size. In any individual piece of work, they are geometrically related to one another, allowing all sorts of

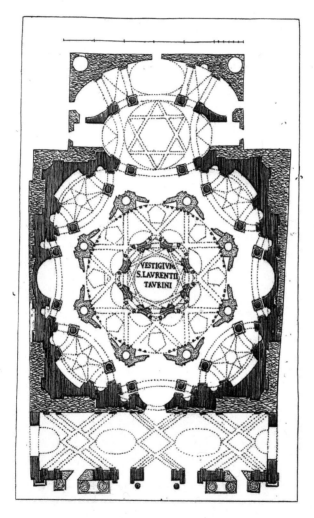

Plan of the church of San Lorenzo (St Laurentius), Turin, Italy, by Guarino Guarini (1624–1683), developing the basic sacred geometry of the earlier, smaller, church in the new one.

geomtrical tesselations to be created. To make such complex geometrical mosaics from hard stones required a high level of geometrical understanding and masterly craftsmanship.

Many cosmatesque pavements are remarkably complex instances of sacred geometry, probably, as at Westminster, with cosmological significance. An opus sectile pavement mosaic of this kind in Anagni Cathedral in Italy, dating from 1104, is claimed to be possibly the oldest extant fractal design. The fractals are the infills of a roundel that has a six-petalled Ad Triangulum geometry based upon the sixfold division of the circle by its radius, with equilateral triangles derived from this division. These subdivided equilateral triangles are known in fractal geometry as Sierpinski gaskets in the fourth order of iteration.[157] Similar, though less developed forms exist in Rome on the late thirteenth century tomb of Vanna Aldobradeschi in the church of Santa Maria in Aracoeli, and in the cloisters of San Giovanni Laterano.

It is clear that Westminster was an important centre of knowledge of sacred geometry, for another significant example remains in the form of the abbey chapter house. During the thirteenth century, a completely new form was developed for monastic chapter houses in England. As places of assembly for the institutional governing body, they were polygonal in form, sacred structures where it was believed that the Holy Spirit descended upon those present.[158] Extant stone vaults of this type exist at Lichfield Cathedral (1239-1249), Westminster Abbey (1246, rebuilt 1866-1873) and Salisbury Cathedral (1263-1284). Geometrically, these vaults have a highly sophisticated construction. They are composed of tri-radials whose ribs radiate from the central column, with the points of their

---

157 Heinz Götze, *Castel de Monte: Geometric Marvel of the Middle Ages*, Munich, 1998, 105.

158 Nussbaum, Norbert, *German Gothic Church Architecture*, New Haven/ London, Yale University Press, 2000, 106-107.

rhomboids divided in half longitudinally. Related forms exist
at Lincoln Cathedral (c.1230-1235), Southwell Minster (1280)
and Wells Cathedral (before 1306), which is a thirty-two-
fold division of the circle, an elaboration of Ad Quadratum.
According to Cyril E. Power, "It was the problem of roofing
these magnificent polygonal halls which prepared the way for
many of the intricate developments of vault design characteristic of the next century".[159]

The octagonal chapter house at Westminster Abbey was
described by Abbot Richard de Ware (abbot 1258–1283, who
also commissioned the 'Cosmati Pavement') as "the work-
shop of the Holy Spirit where the Sons of God assembled".[160]
The central column, supporting the middle of the vault at the
centre of a polygonal building, symbolizes the descent of the
Holy Spirit among Jesus's disciples at Pentecost. Manuscript
illustrations of King Arthur's round table with the Holy Grail
appearing at the centre express a similar miraculous manifestation of the Holy Spirit in the same spatial arrangement as these
monastic chapter houses.

The Westminster legendarium tells that the first church on
this erstwhile triangular holy island of Thorney was built on
the site of a temple of Apollo. "Was it a Temple of Apollo
under the emperor Diocletian, or later, as John Flete implies, in
the fifth or perhaps the sixth centuries when the Pagan Saxons
and Angles over-ran the island?", wrote Gustave Doré and
Blanchard Jerrold,[161] "Or was the story of Apollo merely
a spiteful invention as Wren surmised, got up by the Abbey
monks in rivalry to traditions of Diana at St Paul's? We shall

159 Power, Cyril E., *English Mediaeval Architecture*, 3 vols., London, 1923,
    II, 217. Originally given as a series of lectures at Goldsmith's College,
    London, 1907.

160 Götz, Wolfgang, *Zentralbau und Zentralbautendenz in der gotischen
    Architektur*, Berlin, 1968, 317.

161 Gustave Doré and Blanchard Jerrold, *London: A Pilgrimage*, London,
    1872, ch. XI.

never know, let us fondly trust, whether foundations of a
Pagan shrine lie below the Christian ground". It is said that this
first Westminster church was consecrated, not by Mellitus, the
first Bishop of London in the early seventh century CE, who
duly turned up to perform the rite, but by an apparition of St
Peter accompanied by a host of angels brilliant with celestial
splendour.[162]

Nicholas Hawksmoor's most powerful Gothic structures
are the twin towers at the west end of Westminster Abbey,

*The geometry of the lower section of a gothic supporting pier at
Winchester Cathedral.*

162 Dean Stanley, cited by W.J. Loftie, *A Brief Account of Westminster
Abbey*, Seeley, London, 1894, 21.

completed in 1745. His major Gothic tower in the City of London is St Michael, Cornhill, built 1718–1724, whose turrets are based upon those of King's College Chapel, Cambridge (John Wastell, 1515). Hawksmoor saw the origin of the Gothic in late classical models, and thus recognized the direct continuity between ancient Pagan and Christian structures.[163] Hawksmoor had a clear understanding of the sacred geometry of the abbey, and probably had access to ancient material in

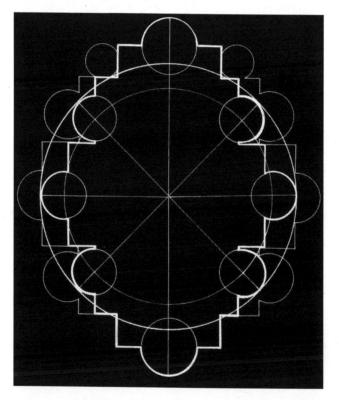

The geometry of the upper section of a supporting pier at Winchester Cathedral.

163 See Vaughan Hart, op. cit., 57, 62–63.

the abbey library and could hardly have ignored the 'Cosmati Pavement' when employing his 'architectonricall method'[164] in the design of the twin towers.

Paramateric Diagrams

Another element in the geometrical design of the post-Great Fire churches appears in the little-known paramateric diagrams of the period. I coined the term 'paramateric diagram' in June 1990 to describe seventeenth and eighteenth century geometrical drawings shown to me by Joy Hancox in her researches into the Byrom Collection, and on re-examining them, I rediscovered their meaning. This collection consists of 516 drawings that apparently once belonged to an eighteenth century Jacobite, masonic or 'Rosicrucian' secret society. They are linked with John Byrom (1692-1763), but contain material from

Inside the operative stonemasons' lodge at Hereford Cathedral during restoration work, 2000, showing cut stone ready for placement.

---

164 Description of his method by Hawksmoor, the third of September 1726; G. Webb (ed.): 'The Letters and Drawings of Nicholas Hawksmoor Relating to the Building of the Mausoleum at Castle Howard 1726-1742', *Walpole Society*, 19 (1930-1931).

the seventeenth century. Among them are certain geometrical diagrams, unlike the usual 'art of line' of contemporary published works. They are not direct guides, as is 'the art of line', but paramateric diagrams. A paramateric diagram is a parameter for a design in graphic form, containing within itself the necessary proportions and sometimes keys to the geometry of a structure. They can be found in certain architectural illustrations, such as a diagram of the section of Milan Cathedral in Cesare Caesariano's 1521 edition of Vitruvius. Similar circles and lines scribed on ancient spire-top balls[165] of churches in the Rhineland are said to contain all the information for rebuilding the church, should it be destroyed.[166] The first description of paramateric diagrams appeared as an appendix by the present author in Hancox's *The Byrom Collection*.[167] In this appendix, the editors inexplicably altered 'paramateric' to 'parametric', which means something different.[168]

These diagrams are a remarkable survival of what might have been just portable working diagrams for architects, carried about for use on site, and then discarded once the building was finished. Byrom diagrams consist of a series of concentric circles at seemingly irregular intervals, with associated dots and straight lines. Some are clearly geometric diagrams in Ad Triangulum and Ad Quadratum form, or relate to the Thibault diagram. From the main body of concentric circles a linear component emerges, with divisions related to the main body, but extending beyond it. They denote the relative dimensions and proportions of components of a classical building. Hancox related some of them

---

165 Usually supporting a weathercock.

166 Private informants, Germany, 1985.

167 Joy Hancox, *The Byrom Collection: Renaissance Thought, The Royal Society and the Building of the Globe Theatre*, Jonathan Cape, London, 1992

168 Nigel Campbell Pennick: 'Parametric Diagrams'(sic), in *The Byrom Collection*, 'Appendix One', op. cit., 291- 292.

to the timber-frame theatres built in London in the time of Shakespeare and Jonson, such as the Globe and the Swan. Others seem to refer to Westminster Abbey[169] and King's College Chapel in Cambridge.[170]

Paramateric diagram, after a drawing in the Byrom Collection.

169 Hancox, op. cit., 268-275.
170 Ibid., 131-139.

The beauty of paramateric diagrams as a means of preserving information is one of elegant economy. Everything necessary for the building is set forth in a single diagram, from which all dimensions, proportions and geometrical constructions may be read. Parameteric diagrams are a traditional way of describing architecture, quite different from the better known plan and elevation method. Orthogonal projection was used first for architectural design by Raphael (1483-1520), Antonio da Sangallo the Younger (1484–1546) and Peruzzi (1481–1536),[171] and it is obvious that other functional systems of design and depiction existed prior to them. Orthogonal projection is based upon a cubic geometry that divides space at right angles with the axes x, y, and z. All modern architecture, industrial design and engineering is described in terms of these three axes, whether graphically or electronically. Paramateric diagrams are analogues of space, not descriptions. They are a glimpse into the holistic skills of the ancients, enabling the classical architect to bring the Vitruvian virtues of order, eurythmy and symmetry into physical form. By using such diagrams, the post-Great Fire architects were able to bring the symmetry of order into their new buildings.

Surveying, the Thibault Diagram and the European Martial Arts.

The seventeenth century saw a great leap forward in mathematical understanding. Ever more accurate instruments and calculations enabled new techniques to be applied in many areas of human endeavour – time-telling, navigation, surveying, mechanics and the arts of war. It was through the necessities of war that many advances came. The advent of artillery warfare (the first use of cannon on the battlefield was by the English army at Crécy, 1346) required geometricians to assist

171 Veronica Biermann, Alexander Grönert, Christoph Jobst & Roswitha Stewering, *Architectural Theory From the Renaissance to the Present*, Taschen, London, 2003, 78.

accurate range-finding and targeting. The study of ballistics greatly expanded geometrical understanding, and led to the development of ever more accurate surveying and measuring instruments. This also assisted general surveying, which was of importance both on the battlefield and for civil purposes, such as road building, mining and architecture.

Treatises on surveying and the use of instruments, many newly invented, began to emerge from the presses in the later part of the sixteenth century. Much of it had a mystical dimension, for the esoteric and exoteric sciences had not separated at that time. Leonard Digges wrote two important books on the subject, *Tectonicon* (1556) and *Pantometria* (1571). *Tectonicon* described two accurate instruments equipped with sights and a plumb-bob, the 'carpenter's ruler' and the 'carpenter's squire'. The latter work describes the 'theodelitus' and the 'geometricall square', which, combined together, was the first described altazimuth theodolite.[172] An instrument derived from the medieval astrolabe and called 'the geographicall plaine sphere' was illustrated by William Cunningham in his *Cosmographical Glasse* (1559).

Early seventeenth century instruments include the 'familiar staffe' of John Blagrave, the 'geodeticall staffe' and 'topographicall glasse' of Arthur Hopton,[173] Philip Danfrie's 'trigonometre', and the 'recipiangle' developed by Leonhard Zubler.[174] In 1616, the most important surveyor's manual of the era emerged from the pen of Aaron Rathborne. Titled *The Surveyor* it was the first truly practical textbook and was not superseded until William Leybourn's *The Compleat Surveyor* appeared in 1653. It was in Leybourn's era that the classical London churches were built and the few constructed alignments laid out. The 'decimal chain' as an accurate measuring

---

172 J.A. Bennett & Olivia Brown, *The Compleat Surveyor*, Whipple Museum of Science, Cambridge, 1982, 4.

173 Arthur Hopton, *Baculum geodaeticum*, London, 1610.

174 Bennett & Brown, op. cit., 3.

device was promoted by Rathborne and used until a more
practical device was devised by Edmund Gunter, Gresham
Professor of Astronomy. Rathborne's 'decimal chain' measures a perch in length (16 feet 6 inches), divided into 100
'seconds'. Gunter's is 22 yards long, divided into 100 'links'.
An acre compries 100 square Gunter chains. It is this chain,
66 feet long with 100 links, which was used in British surveying until the advent of the metric system.

In the sixteenth century, the new geometric understanding
of the dynamics of artillery was applied on a smaller scale to
the hand-to-hand martial arts. The first scientific manual of
fencing was published in 1553 in Italy by the geometrician
and architect Camillo Agrippa. In Spain, Jeronimo Carranza
and Luis Panchero de Navaez furthered Agrippa's geometric

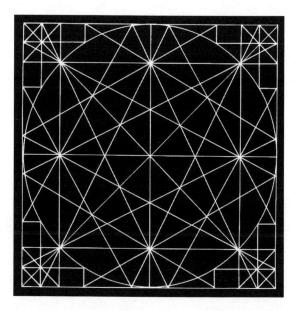

*Gerard Thibault's sacred geometry ground diagram used as a basis for
fencing movements.*

approach.[175] Spanish techniques were taken to the Low Countries, where they were further analyzed and systematized. In 1600, the Professor of Mathematics at the University of Leyden also taught fencing.[176]

Of all the grand masters of sword fighting, Gerard Thibault is undoubtedly the most innovative. Thibault was a polymath,[177] well regarded for his abilities in painting, architecture and medical knowledge. He furthered the basic principles

Gerard Thibault's geometrical diagram with paramateric overlay.

175 Joy Hancox, *The Byrom Collection*, London, Jonathan Cape 1992, 46-47.

176 Ibid., 47.

177 H. de la Fontaine Verwey, 'Gerard Thibault and his 'L'Académie de l'Espeé'. *Quaerendo* VIII, Autumn 1978, 288.

of the Spanish school, and in 1611 entered a prize fight against the best exponents of the martial art. Emerging triumphant, Thibault was summoned to demonstrate his skill to Prince Maurice of Nassau, who was so impressed that he commissioned him to write the definitive work on the subject. Thibault spent fifteen years working on his great fencing manual *L'Académie de l'Espeé*,[178] in which the geometric understanding of the body inherent in Man the Microcosm was applied to the martial arts.

Thibault's principles, tested in the unforgiving world of real combat, expressed the doctrine of Man the Microcosm: that the proportions and geometry of the human body is a particular manifestation of the geometry inherent in the Cosmos. "Man is the most perfect and most excellent of all the creatures in the world" he wrote, " … his body displays an epitome, not only of all that we see here on Earth, but also all that is in heaven itself, expressing everything with such a gentle, beautiful and complete harmony, with such an exact concurrence of number, measure and weight, miraculously related to the virtues of the four elements and the influence of the planets ….. Both ancient and modern architects have been unable to discover anything else in the world which might better serve as a measure according to which they should design the arrangement of their works, than this model, man". Thibault's citing of "number, measure and weight" exactly matches Sir Christopher Wren's *Numero, Pondere et Mensura*.

Thibault's *L'Académie de l'Espeé* contains 46 engravings that illustrate his geometrical principles of fencing. *Tabula II* shows the human body superimposed upon a basal figure that is also the ground-plan for the movements in fencing. I will call this the Thibault Diagram. It is a geometric figure derived from a circle circumscribed within a square whose sides are 14 units in length, a grid of 196 squares. The large square is divided

---

178 Gerard Thibault, *L'Académie de l'Espeé*. Elzevier, Leyden, 1628.

into eight by lines between opposite corners and the centre of opposite sides, and further by other lines that emanate from the edge of the small square at each corner, and points determined by intersections of the grid with the circle. The circle is the compass of the body, defined by the size of the human frame and the weapon wielded. An old English martial arts adage: "Keep within the compass, then you will be sure, to avoid the problems, that others must endure", refers to this defensive compass, keeping the bodily space readily defensible. Keeping within the compass avoids over-reaching oneself, which allows one's opponent to mount an effective counter-attack.

The techniques of geometry applied to sword fighting appear to have been known in England, where some may have viewed it as an unfair departure from traditional English martial arts skills. In *Romeo and Juliet*, William Shakespeare has the dying Mercutio denounce his killer, Tybalt, as "a rogue, a villain, that fights by the book of arithmetic!" (Act III, Scene I. The play is dated to around 1597, though the character Tybalt who kills Mercutio and then is killed in turn by Romeo is clearly a reference to Thibault, who emerged triumphant in 1611). Following his time, the Company of Maisters who taught the English martial arts, and who had probably absorbed Thibault's geometric method into their traditional practices, went out of existence. The twin blows of the 1623 *Monopolies Act* and the banning of public gatherings in 1630 by the Privy Council (on the pretext that they aided the spread of the plague) seem to have caused the Company to wind up.[179] Later, the latter prohibition was extended under Cromwell's fundamentalist rule, when all entertainment was banned in 1644. At the Restoration, stage-gladiators appeared as a form of entertainment, and by the end of the seventeenth century,

179 Terry Brown, *English Martial Arts,* Anglo-Saxon Books, Hockwold-cum-Wilton, 1997, 20–21.

prize fights and public exhibitions were common in Britain.[180]
Books of practical self-defence began to appear,[181] and the
geometric tradition seems to have been marginalized and
forgotten as serious military training focused on other matters
just as architecture also moved away from the Vitruvian model
of the body as emblematic of the building.

Optics and Perspective

From the renaissance, the discovery of the rules of perspective
by Italian artists created a new way of designing artefacts.[182] In
the early sixteenth century, artists created architectural murals
that looked real when viewed from the correct point. In 1515
Baldassare Peruzzi (1481-1536) painted a wall in the Villa
Farnese in Rome with a view to the outside through a double
colonnade of pillars and a balustrade. Trompe l'Oeil figures
began to appear in murals, peeping round apparently open
doors, and down from balconies. Paolo Veronese (1528-1588)
was a master of these effects, which at first were restricted to
secular contexts, such as Veronese's masterpiece balcony with
spiral columns at the Villa Barbaro Giacomelli in Maser.

Several significant architectural authors wrote treatises on
perspective. They include Daniele Barbaro, Vignola, Egnatio
Danti, Lorenzo Sirigatti and Niceron. The key works of this
new school of thought were published in London from 1611
onwards, and played their part in the development of classical building in Great Britain. The earliest investigations into
perspective were made by painters, who devised various techniques to measure and capture the true appearance of objects.
Leon Battista Alberti was reputed to be the inventor of the

---

180 Brown, op. cit., 80.

181 E.g. N. Petter, *Onderrichtinge der Vooreffelicke Worstel-Kunst*,
    Amsterdam, 1674.

182 J.R. Kuhn, 'Measured appearances, Documentation and Design
    in Early Perspective Drawing', *Journal of the Warburg and Courtauld
    Institutes*, LIII, 1990, 114 – 132.

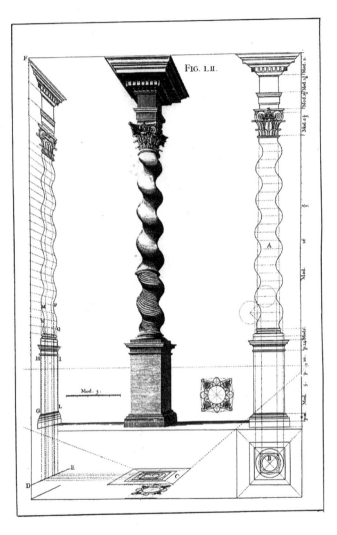

*Drawing a spiral column, from John James's English translation
of Andrea Pozzo's book on architectural perspective, 1707. All
architectural structures began with drawings, and Pozzo's book was
highly influential in the visual treatment of architectural features (see
the following illustrations of features by James and Hawksmoor).*

camera ottica (optical chamber), a device alluded to in his treatise on painting, *De Pictura*. In the *camera ottica*, an object painted in fine detail is observed by means of "well placed crystals" so that it appears as real.[183] The technique of painting optical devices necessitated a working understanding of the principles of perspective. Antonio di Tuccio Manetti, Filippo Brunelleschi's biographer, recounts how the architect made a panel with a painting of the baptistery in Florence. This panel had an eye hole drilled through the back so that a viewer could look through it and see the painting reflected in a mirror. Thus the observer saw it from the proper viewing-point and it appeared as a three-dimensional perspective image.[184]

Sebastiano Serlio's investigations into geometry not only produced the helikon diagram but also applied perspective to architectural design. His nine finished works were published sporadically in various versions from 1537 in Venice, Paris and Lyon. The principles were published as a volume posthumously in 1611 in London as *The Five Books of Architecture*. The use of Serlian motifs by all the London architects after the Great Fire attests to his influence.

With the improvement of lens-making that led to the invention of the telescope, experiments in the alteration and projection of images through lenses and mirrors became possible. Giambatista della Porta, in his 1558 treatise on optics, *Magia naturalis*,[185] claimed to have brought together the secrets of making the *camera ottica* and similar optical devices, and published them for the edification of the public. It described the *camera obscura* for the first time. As *Magia oft de Wonderlicke wercken der*

---

183 G. Tiraboschi, *Storia della letteratura itaiana*, 4 vols., Modena, 1772-1795, vi, I, 322.

184 E. Battisti: *Brunelleschi, the Complete Works,* London, 1981, 103.

185 Giambatista della Porta, *Magia naturalis*, 2 vols., Venice, 1558. For the history of this device see J.H. Hammond, *The Camera Obscura, A Chronicle*, Bristol, 1981.

nature, Porta's book was published in Dutch in Antwerp in 1566. It was influential in the subsequent creation of optical 'toys' in the low countries in the seventeenth century. These were portable boxes with perspectivized and anamorphic achitectural settings that could be viewed by the use of bent and spherical mirrors.[186] In his *Ars magna lucis et umbrae*, published at Rome in 1646, the 'master of a hundred arts', Athanasius Kircher (1602-1680) described his new invention, the projector, or 'magic lantern'. Now images could be projected onto surfaces by light, leading to a greater understanding of the geometric nature of the image itself. Perspectivized 'toys' and the magic lantern were the entertainment end of the serious researches used in navigation, astronomy, warfare, painting and architecture.

Perspectivized, *trompe l'oeil* painting was at its height in the seventeenth century. Dutch masters of the technique worked in London, first Samuel van Hoogstraten (1627-1678), and later, Jan van der Vaart (1647-1721). He came to London in 1674 and painted a much admired false door in Devonshire House that year, totally realistic with a violin apparently hanging from a beribboned knob upon it. Andrea Pozzo (1642-1709), like Athanasius Kircher a member of the Jesuit order, found fame when he used a new perspective technique to paint a cupola on the flat ceiling of the church of St Ignatius in Rome. Painted between October 1684 and July 1685, it caused a sensation when unveiled on the patronal day of St Ignatius (the thirty-first of July), whose transformative vision at La Storta it enshrined. He later taught his techniques to the world in a work titled *Prospettiva de'pittori et architetturi*, published in Rome between 1693 and 1700, which was "meant to assist artists and architects".

In 1707 this ground-breaking work on architectural

---

186 Ria Fabri, ' Perspectiefjes in het spel 'Optische Spielereien' in Antwerpse kunstkasten uit de zeventiende eeuw', *De Zeventiende Eeuw*, 15 (1999), 109 – 117.

perspective was published in English translation by John James. There was no copyright then, and certainly no royalties for the author. Useful and interesting books were translated and produced at will by publishers throughout Western Europe. Although Pozzo was a Jesuit lay brother, there was no mention of this in the English edition, for the Jesuit Order was a proscribed organization in ultra-Protestant Britain, and death was the punishment for any Jesuit caught here. The

Perspectivized corridor by Nicholas Hawksmoor in Christ Church Spitalfields, London (1714).

financing of the English edition came through the pre-
payment of subscribers, who included craftsmen, booksell-
ers, mathematicians and members of the aristocracy. Wren,
Hawksmoor and Vanbrugh gave their approval to *Perspective*,
which was dedicated by the English publisher in Protestant
piety to "Her most Sacred Majesty, Queen Anne".

There are many subtle examples of the art of perspective in London classical churches. John James, as the cham-
pion of Pozzo in England, used perspectivization in the
atrium of St George's Church in Hanover Square. Nicholas
Hawksmoor's use of perspectivized design is apparent in the
three aedicules on the north side of St Mary Woolnoth, the
arches of St George in the East and in the side corridors of
the western entrance of Christchurch, Spitalfields. Here, the
pilasters and mouldings are perspectivized to give an appearance of greater depth. Earlier, Sir Christopher Wren designed

Perspecive effect of internal mouldings in St George Hanover Square.

perspectivized rustication for the entrance of St Mary-le-Bow. The coffering of the apse ceiling of St Clement Danes and parts of the architectonic interior of St Paul's are perspective designs. Tall steeples are a natural field for perspectivization. The most notable are those of St Giles-in-the-Fields, by Henry Flicroft, 1731-1734, and the now demolished Hawksmoor-James columnar steeple of St John, Horselydown. Also at St Paul's is the perspectivized architectural painting of the inside of the dome. Executed by Sir James Thornhill and finished in 1720, it is a more conservative version of Pozzo's illusionistic 'virtual dome' in St Ignatius's in Rome. Elsewhere, Thornhill was more adventurous and emulated Pozzo more closely than at St Paul's.

This principled interaction of apparent and true dimensions is the key to the genius of classical, baroque and rococo design. The true dimensions, derived from the Pythagorean system of proportion, are modified by perspective so that they *look* proportionally correct from the human stand-point. Paradoxically, the canonical dimensions sometimes do not appear correct when foreshortened from the actual angle of view. Although the scientific techniques of working out these visually-pleasing apparent dimensions were discovered in the renaissance, the principle was used in ancient Greece in the entasis of columns and the optical distortion of the platforms upon which temples such as the Parthenon were built.

CHAPTER 6

SYMBOLS AND EMBLEMATA

> Man rashly mounting through the empty Skies
> With wanton Wings shall cross the Seas wel-nigh
> And (doubtles) if the Geometrician finde
> Another World where (to his working Minde)
> To place at pleasure and convenience
> His wondrous Engines and rare Instruments,
> Even (like a little God) in time he may
> To some new place transport this World away.

> **Salluste du Bartas, *His Devine Weekes and Workes,***
> **(translated by J. Sylvester, London 1606).**

The Emblem Books

The influential tradition of emblem books emerged from the renewed interest in the meaning of classical myths, allegories and symbols in fifteenth century Italy. Francesco Colonna's book, *Hypnerotomachia Poliphili*, published in Venice in 1499, provided the influential early emblematicists, Andrea Alciato and Achille Bocci, with some of their motifs. Alciato's *Emblemata*, which first appeared in 1531, ran through 170 known editions. Between 1531 and 1700, it is estimated that over two thousand editions appeared of around one thousand different emblem books, written by six hundred authors.[187] Achille Bocci (1488-1562), who taught in the Faculty of Rhetoric at the University of Bologna from 1508 until 1562, was an important influence upon the development of the emblem book, developing the theory of emblematics in a practical form.[188] His major work, Symbolicae Quaestiones (1555)

---

187 Michael Bath, 'Recent Developments in Emblem Studies', *De Zevientiende Eeuw*, 6-2 (1990), 91-96.

188 Elizabeth See Watson, *Achille Bocci and the Emblem Book as Symbolic Form*, Cambridge University Press, Cambridge, 1993.

used Pagan imagery which gave specific functions for gods
and personifications such as Atlas, Bellerophon, Constantia,
Fortuna, Hercules, Mercury, Minerva, Neptune, Proteus and
Sapientia as well as Socrates' daimon and the triumphal car of
the Gallic Hercules, Ogmios (depicted as binding the ears of
his followers with the chains of eloquence). In addition, Bocci's
emblems employed architectural features such as Temples of
Janus, Fortune and Honour, urns, garlands and obelisks (which
had appeared in *Hypnerotomachia Poliphili* and later in physical
form in the new classical architecture). The classical Pagan
tradition had been explored in both Boccaccio's *Genialogia
degli Dei (Genealogy of the Gods)* and Colonna's *Hypnerotomachia
Poliphili*. Many appear to have been designed according to the
precepts of the art of memory.[189]

After Alciato's *Emblemata*, the *Iconologia* of Cesare Ripa is one
of the most influential of emblem books. First published in
Rome in 1593, *Iconologia* was an encyclopedic work that depicted
abstract and concrete themes in symbolic form. Virtues
and vices, time and the world, senses, emotions and human
pursuits such as art and agriculture were depicted through allegorical figures with emblematic attributes. Originally unillus-
trated, a new edition published in Rome in 1603 added woodcuts that were the inspiration for numerous subsequent and
expanded illustrated editions that appeared after Ripa's death
around 1623.[190] As well as new Italian editions, Ripa's *Iconologia*
appeared in several French, Dutch and German editions
during the seventeenth century. During the period after the
Great Fire of London, there were French editions of 1677,
1681 and 1698; a German edition of 1669-1670; and several

---

189 See Frances A. Yates, *The Art of Memory*, Routlege & Kegan Paul,
London, 1966.

190 Edward A. Maser, introduction to Cesare Ripa, *Baroque and Rococo
Pictorial Images, the 1758-60 Hertel Edition of Ripa's Iconologia*, Dover
Publications, New York, 1971 ix – x.

Dutch editions after 1644.[191] These would have been available to learned people in London before the first English edition was published as *Moral Emblems* in 1709, as would the works discussed below.

In addition to the overt emblem books themselves, the tradition of emblematic symbols was universal by the seventeenth century. Emblematics appeared in contemporary heraldry and Christian devotional engravings, as well as the extensive alchemical and astrological literature of the period. There were no learned persons of the time, including architects, who could not have known and understood emblemata. Relevant to the London architects after the Great Fire are the numerous books of symbolic and sometimes satirical or erotic emblems published in a number of northern European countries which had trading links with England. They include the Dutch works of Roemer Visscher, P.C. Hooft, Jacob Cats, and Jan de Leenheer.[192] There was also a tradition of emblemata in England.[193] Like several others, *Emblemes* by George Wither (1635) drew on earlier Dutch iconography. Withers's book included an oracular system using the four winds as the basis of fifty-six possible readings, linking the tradition of divination with emblems. This is a link with popular emblematic cards, including the Tarot. Motifs from Withers's *Emblemes* were used later by John Wood the Elder in the metopes of the houses in his classical Circus in Bath (begun 1754).

Emblemata and iconological figures were recognized at the time to not be fixed images that have a single reading to be

---

191 Ibid. xi.

192 Roemer Visscher, *Sinnepoppen* (Amsterdam, 1614); P.C. Hooft, *Emblemata Amatoria* (Amsterdam, 1611); Jacob Cats, *Silenus Alcibiadis, sive Proteus* and *Spiegel van den ouden ened nieuwen tijdt* (Middelburg, 1618 and The Hague, 1632); and Jan de Leenheer, *Theatrum Stultorum* (Brussels, 1669).

193 See Mario Praz, *Studies in Seventeenth Century Imagery*, London, 1939; Rosemary Freeman: *English Emblem Books*, London, 1948.

taken literally, but images that positively encourage individual interpretation. In the introduction to his *Sinnepoppen* (1614) the Dutch poet Roemer Visscher points out that the meanings of his illustrations are not fixed, but can be interpreted in various ways. The accompanying printed text is only one of a number of possible 'readings'. This idea of the viewer's 'reading' creating meaning, rather than the author's or artist's intention, popularized as cutting-edge contemporary thought by twentieth century post-modernists, is actually a seventeenth century concept.

The icononological influence upon London classical architects of this period remains little recognized. Symbolic forms abound in the emblem books, as well as classical imagery. Aaron Rathborne's 1616 treatise, *The Surveyor*, has an

The Twin Pillars.
Left: Boaz and Jachin, the symbolic pillars of Solomon's Temple as visualized in a Biblical engraving by John Sturt, London, 1721.
Right: The entrance pillars to Greenwich Hospital, designed by Thomas Ripley, 1751.

emblematical title-page. It is an architectural setting flanked by allegorical female figures of arithmetic and geometry, who stand on circular pedestals or altars in front of pilasters that are topped by a celestial and a terrestrial globe. This became a recognizable symbol in later masonic imagery, and the globe-bearing pillars of the east gate of the Royal Naval Hospital at Greenwich, designed by Thomas Ripley and built in 1751, can still be seen. These elements were used by the London classical architects, and are notable features of their surviving buildings, most especially the Monument, which has the most remarkable surviving public emblem of all. Emblematic figures, such as garlanded circular altars, winged cherubim, death's heads and images of the Last Judgement as well as urns, the cosmic egg and the pine-apple, were employed by the post-Great Fire architects in their buildings. The skyline of Classical architecture of London abounds in urns, pine-apples, egg-like forms, demonic faces, cherubim and skulls. Derived from the Graeco-Roman tradition as renewed in the emblem-books, they have practical and symbolic functions.

The Phoenix

Perhaps the most potent symbol of all after the Great Fire is the Phoenix, the prime symbol of continuity in renewal, "A god-like Bird! Whose endless Round of Years, Out-lasts the Stars, and tires the circling Spheres".[194] This mythic bird lives a thousand years, and then, in its decline, makes a funeral pyre of rare Sabaean herbs, in whose flames, kindled by the Sun, it is cremated. From its own ashes the bird rises again, renewed in full vigour. In 1666, John Evelyn used the image of the city rising again like the Phoenix.[195] The Phoenix is transcendent of time, but it is not immortal, for it dies repeatedly

---

194 Thomas Tickell, in *The Minor Poets, or The Works of the Most Celebrated Authors, Of whose Writings there are but small Remains,* 2 vols., Dublin, 1751, II, 233.

195 John Evelyn, *Diary and Correspondence*, London, 1894, III, 88.

and undergoes eternal renewal. Thomas Tickell's poem, *A Description of the Phoenix: From Claudian*,[196] celebrates this image of transcendent life:

> Thrice happy *Phoenix!* Heav'n's peculiar Care
> Has made thyself thyself's surviving Heir;
> By death thy deathless Vigor is supply'd,
> Which sinks to Ruin all the World beside;
> Thy Age, not thee, assisting *Phoebus* burns,
> And vital Flames light up thy fun'ral Urns.....
> When Nature ceases, thou shalt still remain,
> Nor second *Chaos* bound thy endless Reign;
> Fate's tyrant Laws thy happier Lot shall brave,
> Baffle Destruction, and elude the Grave.

The gable end of the south transept of St Paul's Cathedral has an arched centre that continues the lines of the cherub-headed window below. It is filled with a sculpture, by Caius Gabriel Cibber, of the Phoenix rising anew from its fiery pyre, its resplendent rays radiating forth. The pyre burns on a plinth with the inscription "Resurgam" – 'I shall rise again'. This memorialized an event recounted in *Parentalia*[197] that occurred in the ruins of Old St Paul's when Wren was locating the place where the centre of the dome – the omphalos of the new cathedral – would be. A labourer was ordered to go to a nearby pile of rubble and bring back a flat stone ("such as should first come to Hand") to mark the central point. He brought back a fragment of gravestone. On it was the single word in large capitals; "Resurgam". It is clear that this was viewed as a symbolic ostentum of Providence. The Phoenix who rises again has a special relationship to the sun-god Phoebus, who provdes the spark that lights the pyre. So it is appropriate that at St Paul's, the carving faces the south, the direction of the

---

196 Tickell, op. cit., 236-237.

197 Christopher Wren, *Parentalia*, op. cit., 292.

sun at its midday height, and the direction ascribed to fire in Hermetic diagrams of the four quarters.

The Monument to the Great Fire of London

The greatest symbolic structure of the age is the monument to the Great Fire of London, designed by Christopher Wren and Robert Hooke and built between 1671 and 1677. It followed the ancient Roman tradition of erecting a pillar to the gods as an offering after a catastrophe. This tradition began with the first Jupiter column set up in Rome in 63 BCE after lightning destroyed the images of Jupiter and one of the twins beneath the Roman Wolf on the Capitoline hill.[198] The Roman column and many that followed it in other parts of the empire were topped by equestrian images of Jupiter riding down the destructive storm-demon Typhon, emblematic of order triumphing over chaos.[199] The Great Fire monument is

The carving of a phoenix rising from the flames with the inscription Resurgam *by Caius Gabriel Cibber on the south transept front of St Paul's Cathedral.*

198 Cicero, *De divinatione*, 1, 19ff.

199 Gerhard Bauchhenss, *Jupitergigantensäulen*, Aalen, 1976, 17-19.

an enormous Doric pillar rising from a pedestal emblazoned with sculptures emblematic of the fire and the city's recovery from it. It commemorates both the loss of life and property wrought by the fire, and the heroic effort made to reconstruct the city, phoenix-like, from the ashes.

The column, two hundred and two feet high and fifteen feet thick, known as just 'The Monument', is topped by a gilded brass urn emitting flames. The plinth on which the column stands has the most significant public emblematic work of the period, "Hieroglyphick figures"[200] sculpted by Caius Gabriel Cibber in 1674. The plinth is 28 feet square and 40 feet high, a 7:10 ratio. John Thomas Smith gave this account of it in his 1861 work, *The Streets of London*:

> The west side of the pedestal is adorned with a curious emblem in alt relief, denoting the destruction and restoration of the city. The first female figure represents the city of London, sitting in ruins in a languishing posture, with her head dejected, hair dishevelled, and her hand carelessly lying on her sword. Behind is Time, gradually raising her up; at her side a woman gently touching her with one hand, whilst a winged sceptre in the other directs her to regard the goddesses in the clouds, one with a cornucopia denoting Plenty, the other with a palm-branch, the emblem of Peace. At her feet is a bee-hive, showing that by industry and application the greatest misfortunes are to be overcome. Behind Time, are citizens exulting in his endeavours to restore her; and beneath, in the midst of the ruins, is a dragon, who, as supporter of the city arms, with his paw endeavours to preserve the same. Opposite the city, on an elevated pavement, stands Charles II, in a Roman habit, with a laurel on his head and a truncheon in his hand; and, approaching her, commands three of

200 Jo Darke, *The Monument Guide to England and Wales*, Macdonald, London, 1991, 56.

A Roman Jupiter Column at Stein in Germany.

his attendants to descend to her relief. The first represents the Sciences, with a winged head and circle of
naked boys dancing thereon, and holding Nature in her
hand, with numerous breasts, ready to give assistance to
all; the second is Architecture, with a plan in one hand,
and a square and pair of compasses in the other; and the
third is Liberty, waving a hat in the air, showing her joy
at the prospect of the City's speedy recovery. Behind the
king, stands his brother the Duke of York, with a garland
in one hand to crown the rising city, and a sword in the
other for her defence. And the two figures behind are
Justice and Fortitude; the former with a coronet, and the
latter with a reined lion: and under the royal pavement, in
a vault, lieth Envy, gnawing a heart, incessantly emitting
pestiferous fumes from her envenomend mouth. And
in the upper part of the plinth, the reconstruction of
the city is represented by builders and labourers at work
upon houses".[201]

Temple Bar

On their ceremonial entrances into cities, in emulation of
ancient Roman imperial custom, renaissance grandees were
greeted by sacred images, triumphal gateways, musicians,
emblematical performances and guisers personating Pagan
deities. The fantastic symbolic pageantry of the Holy Roman
Emperor, Maximilian, is recorded in a series of 137 woodcuts
by Hans Burgkmair (1473-1531) and others, and published in
1526.[202] In 1515, the future emperor Charles V was received
in Bruges in a pleasure garden that had a musician guising as

201 John Thomas Smith: *The Streets of London*, Richard Bentley, London,
1861, 412-413.

202 *The Triumph of Maximilian I*, ed. Franz Schestag, Adolf Holzhausen,
Vienna, 1883-1884.

Orpheus playing his harp.[203] Maximilian's *Ehrenpforte* (triumphal arch), published in 1517, is a ten-foot high composite print, made from 92 separate woodcuts designed by Albrecht Dürer and Hans Springinklee. The entry of Charles IX into Paris in 1571 included triumphal arches depicting classical deities and demigods including Juno, Castor and Pollux and Francia, the personification of France.[204] The coronation rites in 1603 of the first king of Great Britain, King James I, included ceremonial gateways and a temporary temple of Janus complete with an altar dedicated to the numen of the new king.[205]

The symbolic ceremonial gateway called Temple Bar was the boundary point between the cities of London and Westminster. It was the formal crossing-point where monarchs visiting the City stopped to be greeted and admitted by the Lord Mayor. A permanent version of the temporary festive gates and triumphal arches common in royal pageantry, Temple Bar was built in stone between 1670 and 1672 by Joshua Marshall and Thomas Knight.[206] It was conceived as a royal monument, and bore four royal statues. On the outer, western, face of the gate were kings Charles I and II, and on the inner Elizabeth I and James I. Iron spikes were provided on the roof for the display of traitors' heads.

In the time of Charles II, after the 'Meal-tub Plot' was thwarted, an anti-Catholic pageant was held on the anniversary of the accession of Queen Elizabeth I, the 17th of November. The grand procession which began at Moorgate ended with

203 Herman Pleij (trans. Diane Webb), *Dreaming of Cockaign: Medieval Fantasies of the Perfect Life*, Columbia University Press, New York, 2001, 218.

204 Bouquet, Simon: *Bref Recueil*, Paris, 1572, passim.

205 Jonson, Ben, 'Part of King James's Entertainment, in Passing to His Coronation' (published 1616), *The Works of Ben Jonson*, 9 vols., London, 1816, Vol. 6, 455.

206 Jo Darke, *The Monument Guide to England and Wales*, Macdonald, London, 1991, 52.

a bonfire at Temple Bar where the Pope was burnt in effi-gy.[207] During this festivity, the statue of Queen Elizabeth I was bedecked with a crown of gilded laurel, and a golden shield with the motto: "The Protestant Religion and Magna Charta". This festival is described at length in a pamphlet of 1679 titled *The Burning of the Pope at Temple Bar in London*. At that time, the Great Fire was still officially stated to be the result of Roman Catholic terrorism. The festival was soon suppressed as a threat to public order, and Guy Fawkes Day became the main November Protestant bonfire celebration.[208]

Temple Bar was taken down in 1878 as a hindrance to traf-fic. Its site is marked in Fleet Street by the memorial erected in

Temple Bar, re-erected 2004 opposite the northern crypt entrance of St Paul's Cathedral.

207 John Thomas Smith, op. cit., 273

208 Ibid., 275. For a historic overview of the fifth of November as a Protestant festival, see Ronald Hutton: *The Stations of the Sun*, Oxford University Press, Oxford, 1996, 393-397.

1880. It is a plinth surmounted by a London dragon, designed by Horace Jones. In 1887, Temple Bar was re-erected at Theobalds Park in Hertfordshire, where it remained, neglected, deteriorating and almost forgotten until the dawning of the twenty-first century. It was dismantled, renovated and reconstructed in 2004 as the gateway between the temenos of St Paul's and Paternoster Square. It is now orientated north-south, with the outer, formerly western, face, on the Paternoster Square side.

Urns and Vessels, The Cosmic Egg, Pyramids and Obelisks, the Pine-apple and the Death's Head

"The treasures of time lie high, in urns, coins, and monuments, scarce below the roots of vegetables"

Sir Thomas Browne (1605–1682), *Hydrotaphia.*

Urns and Vessels

In antiquity, the urn was closely associated with the cult of the dead. It had several meanings, depending on its form and the context in which it was used. Ancient Greek funeral rites involved washings and libations that required ritual vessels for the necessary liquids. Painted representations of tombs show small vessels, sometimes garlanded, placed on tomb surfaces. The Greek custom of bathing a bride-to-be with water from a holy well necessitated a ritual vessel, the loutrophoros. When an unmarried woman died, the same kind of vessel was buried with her. Possibly she was seen as the bride of no man, but of Hades. Stone loutrophorai were made to mark the tombs of unmarried women. A broken stone loutrophoros with fluted lower part and a guilloche border, dated 350-320 BCE, is preserved in the Fitzwilliam Museum in Cambridge.[209]

Along with symbolic items like pomegranates and eggs, real vases and urns were also left as offerings at tombs. Sometimes grave stelai and columns were topped with real vessels, such

---

209 Catalogue number GR.1b.1885.

as a cup, volute krater or kantharos.[210] Other vessels, carved in marble, were also used as grave-markers. The lekythos was a favoured form, sometimes made with a relief carving of the deceased. These stone images of vessels were bedecked with real garlands on sacred festivals of the dead, and would have been echoed by the real vessels left at the tomb in honour of the rites and ceremonies conducted there. Many ancient Greek and Roman tombs, and depictions of them in stone, are based on ways of displaying the ritual urn as the focus of veneration.

Before the Christian religion taught the literal resurrection of the body, and hence the necessity for it to remain in some physical form after death, cremation was the preferred form of bodily disposal in classical religious rites. The body was burnt on a pyre, and the ashes collected together and placed in some kind of casket or urn. If an urn, it was then either buried in a tomb, or occasionally, placed in a prominent location where the memory of the individual could be acknowledged. The

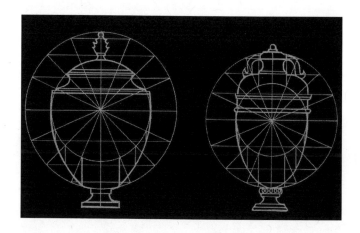

Geometry of urns.

---

210 See A.D. Trendall, *Red Figure Vases of South Italy and Sicily*, Thames & Hudson, London, 1989, fig. 179, where figures are seated on a tomb from which rises a fluted Ionic column bearing a volute krater.

ashes-containing urn was always rarer than the real pottery vessel or the solid, symbolic, tomb urn. From the renaissance onwards, urns became a major feature of the restored classical architecture.

Urns on the steeple of St Bride, designed by Nicholas Hawksmoor.

In his *Quinto Libri d'Architettura* (1537-1575), Sebastiano Serlio gave four geometric techniques for constructing ovals and their derivatives. Serlio's ovals are derived from arcs drawn from basal geometric figures, the circle, triangle and square. He also published diagrams of the geometric construction of urns, to be used as finials with the same functional purpose of Gothic pinnacles, to add weight to assist buttressing. These published designs derive the urns' forms from constructions based on circles, which are subdivided by horizontal lines that determine egg-shapes from which the final urn forms are developed. These were taken up by the London architects and used everywhere.

Along with circular altars, urns were a symbol of ancient religion. In his 1629 poem, *On The Morning of Christ's Nativity*, John Milton associated them with spirits and shades "in urns and altars round".[211] *Hydriotaphia* or *Urn Burial* by Sir Thomas Browne gives the flavour of seventeenth century musings on

Urns designed by James Gibbs.
Left: The Radcliffe Camera, Oxford.
Right: The University Senate House, Cambridge.

---

211 John Milton, *The Poetical Works of John Milton*, Routledge, London, n.d. c. 1880, 335.

cremation as a classical funeral rite: "… From the funeral pyre of Hector, burnt before the gates of Troy; and the burning of Penthesilea the Amazonian queen …. While as low as the reign of Julian, we find that the king of Chionia burnt the body of his son, and interred the ashes in a silver urn. The same practice extended also far west; and, beside Herulians, Getes, and Thracians, was in use with most of the Celtae, Sarmatians, Germans, Gauls, Danes, Swedes, Norwegians… ".[212] Belinus, king of the ancient Britons, was also cremated, so the London legendarium tells us, and his ashes enshrined in a golden urn on the top of the tower he had built at Billingsgate.[213]

Urns as vessels for ablutions, anointings and libations were illustrated frequently in depictions of antique rites and ceremonies. The *Bible* records Hiram of Tyre casting vessels "of bright brass" for the Jerusalem Temple in his foundry on the Plain of Jordan.[214] The Biblical scene of Jacob illustrated here, engraved by John Sturt in London in 1721, has the necessary vessels for his inaugural libation when he set up "a stone for a pillar". English builders' rites and ceremonies sometimes saw vessels buried in foundations, perhaps having been first used in the inaugural rites. Glass vessels have been discovered as foundation deposits in England. St Nicholas's church at South Kilworth in Leicestershire, built between 1390 and 1420, had slim tapering bottles under the foundations.[215] A green glass phial still containing oil, dated around 1400, was found in the foundations of an ancient wall at Whitstable, Kent, in the early twentieth century.[216]

Flaming urns are a feature of some London churches as

212 Sir Thomas Browne, op. cit, 123.

213 Gaufridus, op.cit, III, 10.

214 *The Bible*, 2 Chronicles, 4: 17; 1 Kings, 7: 13, 45-47.

215 *Proceedings of the Society of Antiquaries of Scotland.* Second series IV, 1867-1870, 284.

216 W. A. Thorpe, *English Glass*, Adam & Charles Black, London, 1949, 85, pl. XV (b).

well as the summit of the Monument. The meaning of them is recorded by Sir Thomas Browne: "Some apprehended a purifying virtue in fire, refining the grosser commixture, and firing out the aetherial particles so deeply immersed in it".[217] What we see represented in stone is not fire, but rather the emergent

Jacob setting up his pillow-stone as an altar. A Biblical engraving by John Sturt, London, 1721.

217 Sir Thomas Browne, op. cit, 124.

aether. According to Plutarch, Varro wrote that on the cremation of a father by his sons, on seeing his bones freed from
the flesh they cried out that he was now deified.[218] Ceremonies
were performed at the place enshrining the ancestral ashes
at the festival called Parentalia,[219] and in the *Aenid*, Virgil has
Aeneas say of his father's shade at his tomb, "let us ask him
for fair winds".[220] Requests for the intercession of the ancestral
dead in Paganism became prayer to the saints in the Christian
religion.

The London urns are frequently carved with stone garlands.
The Pagan Romans celebrated the festival of Rosaria in May,
when tombs and funeral urns were lavishly bedecked with
roses.[221] All Souls' Day carried on some of the features of
the Rosaria, with the bedecking of graves, which continues
in Roman Catholic tradition. Stone urns apparently draped
in mourning were at one time fashionable as grave monuments in Christian cemeteries, especially in the eighteenth and
nineteenth centuries. In classical tradition, groups of urns
in an architectural setting, such as in niches, could serve as a
pantheon of the dead, or the relics of solemn rites and ceremonies, and a number of London classical churches seem to
have taken up this theme. The spire of Nicholas Hawksmoor's
Christ Church, Spitalfields, originally had twelve small windows
surmounted by urns.[222] The second stage of the tower of
Christchurch, Newgate Street, has a cornice topped by twelve
urns. Solid stone urns or pine-apples were set up on cornices
where they had an additional dynamic engineering function.

---

218 *Quaest. Rom.*14.

219 *Parentalia* was the title chosen by Christopher Wren, Jr., for the work
    that contained his father's writings (London, 1750).

220 Virgil, *Aenid*, V, 59-60.

221 Gordon J. Laing, *Survivals of Roman Religion*, Harrap, London, 1931,
    80.

222 Original drawing reproduced in Hart, op. cit., fig. 215, p. 156.

They are a ubiquitous feature of London classical church steeples. During his renovation work at Windsor, Sir Christopher
Wren removed the Royal Beasts from the buttresses of the
Royal Chapel and replaced them with stone pine-apples (the
beasts were put back again later). In place of the proposed
statue of Queen Anne over the portico of St Mary-le-Strand
(1714-1717), after her death James Gibbs placed a monumental urn.

Following the custom of acknowledging the spiritual powers
of the four directions, many urns and circular altars bear four
cherubim or other orientated 'grotesque' faces. The churchyard
urns of St Andrew-by-the-Wardrobe, probably 1694, and the
tower urns of St Bride, Fleet Street (1703) each have four such
cherubim. The south side of St Paul's Cathedral has four-faced
garlanded circular altars surmounted by near-spherical urns.
Almost free-form urns surmount St Alfege, Greenwich. They
resemble the four-faced urns at Stowe, designed by Sir John
Vanbrugh after 1719 for his Temple of Sleep (demolished)
and now flanking the Oxford Bridge there. The designs of
many of these urns reflect contemporary silver and glassware,
especially covered bowls, which have gadrooning or wrythen
decoration, intended to enliven light and shade, and emphasise
the modelled form of the vessel.

The Cosmic Egg

The egg is an element in classical architecture. It is the form
of the omphalos that marks the navel of the earth, a conceptual centre-point that mediates between the underworld, this
world and the upperworld. It also appears in egg-and-dart
mouldings in the Ionic and Composite columns and in profile
in the classical moulding called the ovolo. The Caryatides on
the Erechtheum in Athens have headdresses composed of
egg-and-dart garlands. The egg was recognized as such by the
craftsmen who worked on the classical churches in London
after the Great Fire. A churchwardens' account for St Olave,

Jewry, tells of a payment to Richard Cleere, joiner, for carving "lace, folding, leaves, eggs, beads and festoon".[223]

But in the seventeenth century, the symbolism of the egg was much more than ornamental. As the progenitor of the independent organism, the egg is a symbol of coming-into-being. The Greek alchemical text, the *Anonymus*, expressing ideas current in the third and fourth centuries CE, places the origin of the four elements in this primordial Cosmic Egg of the Philosophers, or the seed of Pythagoras. The author followed the Orphic coming-into-being symbolism expressed in dramatic form in Aristophanes' play, *The Birds*. In the state before time existed, Aristophanes wrote, when there was only chaos and night:

> At length, in the dreary chaotical closet
> Of Erebus old, was a secret deposit;
> By night the Primaeval in secrecy laid
> A Mystical Egg, that in silence and shade
> Was brooded and hatched.[224]

The symbolism of this ovum philosophorum or philosophers' egg is evident in the works of medieval and renaissance philosophers of the Hermetic science. The alchemist Nicolas Flamel (c.1330-c.1417) wrote of it in *His Exposition of the Hieroglyphical Figures*,[225] describing it as the vessel in which the Philosophers' Stone is created. It appears in numerous alchemical works of the sixteenth and seventeenth century. It is on the title page of John Dee's[226] *Monas hieroglyphica* (1564), which shows his

223 Cobb, op. cit., 47.

224 Lethaby, op. cit, 263.

225 Nicolas Flamel, *His Exposition of the Hieroglyphical Figures* (trans. Eirenaeus Orandus, London, 1624), in Linden, Stanton J. (ed.), *The Alchemy Reader*, Cambridge, Cambridge University Press, 2003, 132.

226 John Dee, 1527-1606.

'monas' or 'hieroglyphic monad'[227] sigil enclosed within an egg-shaped cartouche. Eggs are depicted as the finials on either side of the engraving that makes a classical architectural setting for the text. The Gate of Honour at Gonville and Caius College, Cambridge, designed by Dr Caius[228] and built in 1575, has obelisks at the four corners topped by cosmic eggs. The finial is also a cosmic egg, once topped by a dove-and-serpent weather vane.

The primordial egg appears in Salomon Trismosin's late sixteenth century *Splendor Solis* and in an illustration by Matthäus Merian in Michael Maier's alchemical work *Atalanta fugiens* (1617);[229] *Emblema VIII* shows a philosopher wielding a sword. He is about to strike a large egg standing upon a low table. The motto says, "Take the egg and cut it with a fiery sword".[230] By smashing the egg, a new form will be

The alchemical emblem of the cosmic egg, Emblema VIII from Michael Maier's Atalanta fugiens.

227 Gettings, Fred, *Dictionary of Occult, Hermetic and Alchemical Signs*, London, Routledge & Kegan Paul, 1981, 175.

228 Master 1559-1573, Willis & Clark, op. cit., 1, 177-179.

229 Michael Maier, *Atalanta fugiens*, Frankfurt, 1617, Emblema VIII.

230 Ibid. 41.

released into existence. This is the true meaning of 'invention', the revealing of that which hitherto was hidden in the workings of the cosmos. Heinrich Jamsthaler's 1625 hermetic work, *Viatorum Spagyricum* has the 'egg of nature' containing the seven traditional 'planets' (the Moon, Mercury, Venus, the Sun, Mars, Jupiter and Saturn), a dragon, a circle or sphere containing a triangle and square, and a human figure with both a man and woman's head, holding a pair of compasses and a set square (later adopted as the symbol of freemasonry). Like the urn and other 'hermetically' enclosed receptacles, the egg can symbolize the alchemical vessel within which transmutation is effected.

In 1650, Thomas Vaughan likened the egg to the philosopher's stone or elixir: "I am the egg of Nature known only to the wise such as are pious and modest, who make of me a little world. Ordained I was by the Almighty God for men, but – though many desire me – I am given only to few that they may relieve the poor with my treasures and not set their minds on gold that perisheth".[231] The emblem book *Ova Paschialia Sacra Emblemata*, published in 1672 at Ingolstadt, deals with the spiritual oneness of the cosmic egg and the symbolic Easter egg. The Mundane Egg is also an important element in Thomas Burnet's *Sacred Theory of the Earth* (1684-1690), which may have later influenced William Blake.[232]

In the seventeenth century, the primordial egg in its own right appeared as an architectural emblem on churches in the Netherlands. Two finials on the east front of the octagonal Oostkerk in Middelburg (1648-1667), designed by Bartholomaeus Drijfhout and Pieter Post, are cosmic eggs,

231 Thomas Vaughan, Coelum Terrae, originally published as Eugenius Philalethes: *Magia Adamica…* London, 1650.

232 William Blake, *Milton a Poem*, eds. and introduction Robert N. Essick & Joseph Viscomi, The William Blake Trust/Tate Gallery, London, 1998, 29.

garlanded like the *omphalos* of Delphi. The porch of the Nieuwe Kerk in The Hague (1649-1656), designed by the architects Pieter Noorwits and Barthold van Bassen, also has garlanded eggs, a little different in form. An unbuilt plan by Nicholas Hawksmoor for All Souls' College in Oxford[233] has cosmic egg finials. Robert Hooke, like Hawksmoor an associate of Sir

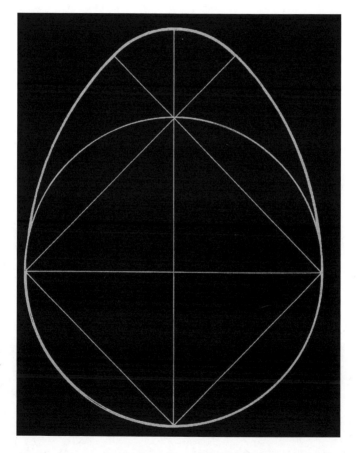

The geometry of the Cosmic Egg.

233 Preserved at Worcester College, Oxford.

Christopher Wren, had a drawing of the Nieuwe Kerk,[234] and
this may be the source of Hawksmoor's design. Like the Dutch
forerunners in Middelburg and The Hague, his cosmic eggs
are garlanded. According to Kerry Downes, this symbolizes
the breaking of the bonds of death at the Last Judgement.[235]
An egg-form garlanded urn is shown in an eighteenth century
engraving of St Luke's, Old Street by T. Lester. It is the central
feature of the churchyard boundary, crowning the central pier
supporting the iron railings. Similar egg forms exist on the
cornice of a fine eighteenth century house, Little Trinity, in
Jesus Lane, Cambridge, circa 1725.[236] As with the oval, there
are various geometric methods of creating the egg form. The
simplest method is based upon an equilateral triangle from
whose two basal angles equal arcs are drawn.

The cosmic egg appeared later in the works of the London
mystic William Blake as the 'mundane shell', where it signifies the outer limit of the physical universe. Blake's spiritual
sources are plural and personally interpreted, but his use of the
egg symbol is within the traditional understanding. His 1793
engraving *The Gates of Paradise* shows a winged *putto* emerging
from a breaking egg. In *Milton a Poem*, his diagram of the 'Four
Zoas' overlaps the cardinally-directed spheres of Urthona,
Luvah, Tharmas and Urizen, and encompasses Adam and
Satan.[237] The 'fires of Los' also burn within this 'mundane
shell'. In the late nineteenth century, the philosopher-architect
William Richard Lethaby (1857–1931) published *Architecture,
Mysticism and Myth*, a work that was influential upon the Arts
and Crafts Movement, describing and explaining the elements
of the eternal tradition in architecture. In chapter XII, 'The

234 Margaret Whinney, *Wren*, Thames & Hudson, London, 1971, 64.

235 Kerry Downes, *Hawksmoor*. London, 1970, 78.

236 Royal Commision on Historic Monuments, *City of Cambridge*, 2 vols.,
   London, 1959, 2, 349.

237 Blake, in Essick & Viscomi, op.cit., 29.

Symbol of Creation', he describes the symbolism of the Cosmic Egg as the progenitor of existence: "From desire and vapour procceeded primitive matter. It was a muddy water – black, icy, profound – encompassing insensible monsters, incoherent parts of forms to be born. Then matter condensed and became an egg. It broke; one half formed the earth and the other half the firmament. The sun, the moon, the winds and the clouds appeared, and a crash of thunder awakened the sentient animals".[238]

William Richard Lethaby notes that the egg, as a symbol of creation, is associated with funeral rites, and perhaps rebirth or resurrection. He notes Alfred Butler's comment "marble eggs are said to have been discovered in some early martyrs' tombs at Rome, and that in all Christian lands eggs are associated with Easter-time, some think that the egg was regarded as emblematic of the Resurrection".[239] Lethaby notes also an antique Pagan connexion between the egg and the dead. He states that "in a tomb at Bologna an Etruscan was exhumed with an egg in his hands"[240] and quotes Dognée that "they affected the ovoid form of funeral vases".[241] Egg symbolism reappeared in architecture at the end of the nineteenth century in the Arts and Crafts movement as the result of Lethaby's researches. The Passmore Edwards Settlement, Tavistock Place, London, built 1897-1898 (now Mary Ward House, a Grade I listed building) was designed by two up-and-coming architects, Dunbar Smith, (1866-1933) and Cecil Brewer (1871-1918). Their competition-winning design for the settlement, published in 1895, was an influence on Charles Rennie Mackintosh for his Glasgow School of Art (designed 1896). Their mentor was none other

---

238 Lethaby, op.cit., 263.

239 Alfred Joshua Butler, *Coptic Churches of Egypt*, The Clarendon Press, Oxford, 1884, quoted by Lethaby, op.cit, 257.

240 Lethaby, op. cit., 267.

241 Ibid.

than William Richard Lethaby, who designed a symbolic fire-
place inside and some other symbolic features. He was clearly
influential in the choice of cosmic egg finials for the main
entrance.

The Obelisk

The obelisk originated in ancient Egypt as a solar symbol,[242]
and was used in some form by the Etruscans in funeral monuments, the most celebrated of which was the tomb of Porsenna
at Clusium in Italy. Although described as pyramids, these may
have been cones, as in the tomb or Aruns at Albano.[243] In
seventeenth century England, architects certainly believed that
they were pyramids. In imperial times, Egyptian obelisks were
taken as trophies to Rome and set up at important locations.[244]
In the renaissance, they were moved to new locations as foci
of straight streets, Christianized with a metal cross at the apex
of the crowning pyramidion. Various apical structures became
acceptable on renaissance obelisks, the cosmic egg being a
frequent choice. The Gate of Honour at Gonville and Caius
College, Cambridge, has obelisks topped by cosmic eggs.

Interest in pyramids and obelisks appeared in Britain in
renaissance times, where they were used on tombs and festal
designs. In 1646, John Greaves's *Pyramidographia: or a Description
of the Pyramids in Egypt* appeared, illustrating also his impression
of Porsenna's non-Egyptian multi-pyramidal tomb. Porsenna's
tomb was one of the ancient structures that Sir Christopher
Wren attempted to reconstruct from ancient accounts. He
described the tomb as a form of Tyrian architecture. An early
scheme for the Monument, before the present column was

---

242 Said to symbolize the rays of the sun, e.g. Robert Macoy: *A General
    History, Cyclopedia and Dictionary of Freemasonry*, Masonic Publishing
    Company, New York, n.d. c. 1890, 270.

243 Fergusson, op. cit., 300.

244 Sebastiano Serlio, Book III, LXII, claimed that the St Peter's obelisk
    had the ashes of Caius Caesar deposited in its apex.

decided upon, was for an obelisk supporting a phoenix.[245]

When classical architecture was recovered from obscurity, obelisks became the functional answer to Gothic pinnacles, serving the same stabilizing purpose in engineering terms. Obelisks were chosen as suitable parapet structures for St Olave, Jewry; All Hallows, Bread Street; and St Mary Somerset. Several City church spires attributed to Wren can also be viewed as obelisks, especially that of the now-demolished church of St Michael, Queenhythe. Hawksmoor's church of St Anne, Limehouse was to have had two pyramids on cubic towers at the east end flanking an aedicule housing a statue of Queen Anne.[246] Neither the aedicule nor the pyramids were constructed. A pyramid tomb at the west end of the churchyard is said to be one of the unused roof-line pyramids. But perhaps they were not intended to be read as pyramids at all, but the masonic form known as the broached thurnel, a cubic stone with a pyramidal top, a symbol of perfection.

Façade of the octagonal Oostkerk in Middelburg, Zeeland, the Netherlands (1648-1667), with a carving of a human skeleton over the door and with garlanded cosmic eggs surmounting the cornice.

London was not rebuilt on right lines, and so obelisks did

245 Kerry Downes, *The Architecture of Wren*, Redhedge, Over Wallop, 1988, 66.

246 Shown in an engraving by Jan Kip, 1714.

not appear in the streets as characteristic structures at focal points as had been planned. The closest were the two small obelisks set up at either end of the western entrance steps of St George, Hanover Square,[247] which carried lamps. They remain

A Roman obelisk erected on later base, Arles, France.

247 Built 1712-1724.

today in altered form, without the lamps. What might have been can be seen in Ripon, Yorkshire, where, in 1702, an obelisk was set up in the centre of the market place on the site of the former market cross. It was designed by Nicholas Hawksmoor "according to the most exact antient symetry".[248] Eighty feet tall, it has a finial composed of a fleur-de-lys combined with a cosmic egg, above which is a sunburst topped by a weather-vane in the form of the Wakeman's horn, which is blown every night to the four directions.[249] This is a warding ceremony performed "every night at nyne of the clock at the four corners of the crosse in the market stead" (Archibishop of York, 1598). Around 1724, Hawksmoor drew up a design for a memorial obelisk at Blenheim Palace, the drawing of which still exists.[250] The Ripon obelisk is another instance of foursquare orienta-

St Olave Jewry with obelisk finials. Engraving from 1833.

---

248 Darke, op.cit., 225.

249 Ibid., 226. See also George C. Williamson, *Curious Survivals*, Herbert Jenkins, London, 1925, 137-138; F.J. Drake-Carnell, *Old English Customs and Ceremonies*, Batsford, London, 1938, 72, figs. 65, 79.

250 Preserved in the Bodleian Library in Oxford. Hart, op.cit., 87, fig. 119.

tion to the cardinal directions, in this case, associated with a
particular ancient custom. Hawksmoor later used the obelisk
form in his and John James's design for the church of St Luke,
Old Street. Finished in 1733, has an imposing obelisk atop its
tower in the usual place of spires and steeples.

The Pine-Apple

As a classical emblem, the so-called pine-apple represents the
cone of the pine tree, not the tropical fruit. In older usage, the
word "apple" is not so specific, meaning a fruit, as in an oak
apple (gall), the French and Dutch words for potato – earth
apple – *pomme de terre* and *aardappel*, and the East Anglian dialect
word 'deal apple' for a pine cone. It is a symbol of fecundity
and regeneration, healing and conviviality,[251] an embodiment of
sacred number manifested in the Fibonacci Series, related to the
Golden Section, as is the geometry of the egg. The pine tree is
associated with the gods Osiris and Attis, who was personified
as the spirit of the tree. It is sacred to the goddess Cybele, and is
depicted on religious artefacts with the musicial instruments of
her cultus, the bell, cistrum and tambour, hanging in its branches,
as on a third century CE Roman stone altar preserved in the
Fitzwilliam Museum in Cambridge.[252] The wand of Dionysos is
the thyrsus, a stave tipped with the pine-apple. The pine-cone is
the emblem of the Swabian goddess Zisa, and numerous large
stone ones survive from Roman times at Augsburg in Bavaria.
The Swabian holy city of Zizarim, locus of the goddess's shrine,
became the Roman city of Augusta Vindelicorum, the present-
day Augsburg. The *Stadtpyr* cone remains the emblem of the
city, and the goddess with her cone appears as a weather vane
on St Peter-am-Perlach church, (on the Site of the holy hill
of the goddess), in a classical plaque on the early seventeenth

---

251 Arnold Whittick, *Symbols: Signs and the Meaning and Uses in Design*,
    London, 1971, 296.

252 Fitzwilliam Museum catalogue number GR.5.1938.

century Hercules fountain, and as the red-clad foundress of the city in a painting in the *Rathaus*.[253]

The pine cone appears in carved stone garlands and swags on Roman altars and tomb-shrines among other fruits of the Earth. As an emblem of healing, it is a minor attribute of Aesculapius, for the seed of the Stone Pine was an ingredient of ancient medicines. In northern Europe, the pine is viewed as the tree of illumination, both on the outer level as the light-bringing flaming torch, and on the inner level as understanding.[254] In architecture, it is primarily a symbol of fecundity and regeneration. It surmounted Etruscan tombs, urns and pillars.[255] Hadrian's mausoleum in Rome was surmounted by a gilt bronze pine-cone (later removed and replaced by an image of the Archangel Michael), and a Carolingian cone of bronze is preserved in the atrium of Aachen Cathedral, the omphalos of the Holy Roman Empire.

The tropical pineapple was

The isolated tower of St Mary Somerset (1686–1694), surmounted by obelisks on summit.

253 Nigel Pennick, 'The Goddess Zisa', *Tyr*, Vol. 1, 2002, 107-109.

254 E.g., Nigel Pennick, *The Complete Illustrated Guide To Runes*, Element, London, 1999, 52.

255 G. Dennis, *The Cities and Cemeteries of Etruria*, 2 vols., London, 1848, ii, 103, 157, 492.

first grown in England in the reign of King Charles II, and a
painting was made of the royal gardener, John Rose, present-
ing the first one to the king.[256] Perhaps at that point, the two
distinct forms, the pine-apple (cone) and pineapple (tropical
fruit) were merged into a single emblem. London architects of
the post-Great Fire period used the pine-apple freely. It appears
as finials to gate pillars, towers, cupolas and domes, and on top
of urns. In some contexts, they were used in conjunction with

*Roman pine-apples, the symbol of the Goddess Zisa and the present-
day city emblem, the* Stadtpyr, *at Augsburg, Bavaria, Germany.*

---

256 Reproduced in Arthur Bryant, *Restoration England*, Collins, London,
    1960, opposite p. 112.

urns, for example the tower parapet of St Edmund King and Martyr is topped by urns at the four corners and pine-apples in the centre of each side. The urns have tall, spire-like lids, each topped with a cosmic egg finial. Garlanded urns flank the tower at a lower level. St Mildred, Bread Street, destroyed in an air raid in 1941, had an urn on the apex of the street façade, flanked by lower pine-apples. Pine-apples also mark the corners of the façade of St Martin-within-Ludgate, which had no other urns, eggs or pine-apples, and the corners of the tower of the now demolished St Michael, Queenhythe. The western towers of St Paul's Cathedral are topped with gilded pine-apples, and the later sevenfold altar of the Saxon gods at Stowe had a central garlanded urn topped by a pine-apple.

The Death's Head

Skulls, an emblem of mortality, are naturally prevalent in the London classical churches, which were located in earlier burial grounds or had churchyards provided for burials when built new. The death's-head was a common image of tombstones of the period, sometimes paired with winged hour-glasses, symbolizing the transience of life. Human remains were not an uncommon sight in London then. Skulls and bones were unearthed continuously during rebuilding; from churchyards to be built upon where the churches were not to be rebuilt, mass burials from the 1665 plague, and the remains of those who died in the Great Fire. St Nicholas, Deptford, had prominent skull carvings, and skulls impaled on iron spikes at St Olave, Hart Street. At that time, the real human heads of executed rebels could be seen impaled on iron spikes on top of Temple Bar. St Katherine Cree had a carving of a recumbent skeleton in the pediment.

There are no truly macabre stone swags or garlands depicting human bones, like those on the earlier Oostkerk in Middelburg, Zeeland, which also has such a skeleton *in situ* and winged hourglasses with one bird's and one bat's wing, showing that time flies continuously whether it is day or night. Skulls were a notable feature of All Hallows in Lombard Street (demolished and the tower re-erected at Twickenham). Just such a church skull is depicted in the fourth of William Hogarth's painting cycle *The Election – Chairing the Members* (1754). Led by a fiddler and accompanied by brawling men, the just-elected Member of Parliament, held aloft on a chair by his supporters, is mocked by a black boy sitting on a pier at a churchyard gate. The boy holds a pair of spectacles in front of the eyes of a stone skull, horrifying the newly-elected MP with this macabre *memento mori*.

The Mystic Spiral

Spiralling, or wrythen decoration, is part of the repertoire of seventeenth and eighteenth century blacksmiths, glasshouse gaffers and master wood-turners. Many of the wooden balustrades, altar rails and pulpit details in post-Great Fire churches have spiral elements. At St Mary Abchurch, the carved wooden font cover by William Emmett is suspended from the ceiling by a spiral that serves as a screw to lift the cover so that the font can be used for baptism. The spiral also appeared in the London churches in the form of spiral columns, of which only St Mary Woolnoth now has an example.

Traditionally, spiral columns are connected with both Jewish and early Christian places of worship. They supported the ciborium in the original St Peter's church in Rome, built by the first Christian emperor, Constantine. The Roman legendarium told how they were brought thence from Jerusalem by Constantine, having come originally from the Holy of Holies in the Jewish temple at Jerusalem, built on the orders of King Solomon.[257] Spiral columns were used occasionally as special features, denoting especially sacred places within medieval

---

257 Charles Avery & David Finn, *Bernini: Genius of the Baroque*, London, 1997, 95.

churches. The tenth century crypt of the Anglo-Saxon church of St Wystan at Repton in Derbyshire, England[258] has spiral columns that surrounded the royal tomb-shrine of the Mercian kings Aethelbald and Wiglaf (740s CE). Gothic spiral columns support ciboria in Regensburg Cathedral, Germany. Among the most notable geometric masterworks of the Expert Roman Masters are spiral columns inlaid with geometric mosaic. An early example is the twelfth century Easter candlestick in the basilica of San Clemente in Rome. This is in the form of a column with a complex spiral, inlaid with geometric mosaic. It is topped by a Corinthian capital supporting the candleholder, an urnlike form topped by a classical egg-and-dart frieze.

The most sacred altar of western Christendom, at St Peter's in Rome, has always been guarded by spiral columns. The original Constantinian columns, which were taken from a pre-Christian building, were removed when Gianlorenzo Bernini (1598-1680) designed the new baldacchino of St Peter's in continuity with his Constantinian forerunners (1624-1627).[259] Bernini re-used eight of the original twelve Constantinian marble columns, once adorned with silver, to flank the four reliquary aedicules high up on the inner piers of the crossing, facing the baldaccino.[260] As classical spiral columns, they are in four parts, alternately fluted and ornamented. Bernini's are in three sections, with only the lower third ornamented with fluting. The classical spiral columns are ornamented with vine branches, whereas for the baldaccino Bernini used olive leaves, apparently made from real ones reproduced through a lost wax process. They are topped by composite capitals.

The origin of the spiral column in Pagan temples seems to have worried some commentators, and attempts were made to demonstrate their origin in ancient Israelite building.

258 G.H. Cook, *The English Mediaeval Parish Church*, London, 1961, 125.
259 Avery & Finn, op. cit. 95-100.
260 James Lees-Milne, *St Peter's*, London, 1967, 253-254.

Juan Batista Villalpando (1552-1608) described 'Solomonic' columns in his influential exegesis of the Biblical book of Ezekiel, *In Ezechielem Explanationes*. These, however, are not spiral, but have parallel fluting and capitals composed of lily leaves and pomegranate seeds.[261] After the reformation and counter-reformation, apologists claimed that all classical art and architecture had originated with the Biblical Jews. John Milton's *Paradise Regained* has an instance of this theory: "Our Hebrew songs ... That rather Greece from us these arts derived".[262] So, uneasy with the real origin of classical architecture in Pagan temples, certain architects pretended that all five classical orders originated in the Solomonic temple.[263] This religious re-working of history appeared again in architectural circles in the late twentieth century, in a text by the classical architect Quinlan Terry called *The Origin of the Orders* (1982).[264] This essay won the £5000 European Prize from the Philippe Rothier Foundation in 1982.

However, despite Villalpando's description of straight fluted columns, spiral columns began to be associated with the Temple in Jerusalem, and to be called Solomónicas. Generally, they are in four parts, like the pre-Christian columns now in the aedicules in St Peter's. Paintings by Raphael and Giulio Romano of the Solomonic temple depict it with spiral columns. However, Giulio Romano used fluted spiral columns in combination with heavy rustication in a secular structure, the Cortile delle Cavallerizza at Mantua (1538-1539). The 1515

261 Juan Bautista Villalpando, *In Ezechielem Explanationes*, Rome, 1693-1604, 420.

262 John Milton, *Paradise Regained*, London, 1671, Book IV, 336-339; also see William Blake, preface to *Milton*, c. 1804, (which contains the poem now known as *Jerusalem*).

263 E.g., John Wood, *The Origin of Building, or, the Plagiarism of the Heathens Detected*, London, 1754.

264 Quinlan Terry, 'The Origin of the Orders', *Archives d'Architecture Moderne*, 26, 1984.

Raphael cartoon of Jesus at the Gate Beautiful of the Jerusalem Temple was brought to England by Sir Francis Crane in 1623. It depicts four-section spiral columns. In 1634, in Inigo Jones's

Ancient Jewish priests in the Jerusalem temple, with spiral 'Solomonic' columns as visualized in a Biblical engraving by John Sturt, London, 1721.

banqueting house in Whitehall, Peter Paul Rubens painted an allegory of King James I as Solomon. The painting shows the king enthroned between four spiral columns with Ionic capitals. Three years later, John Jackson (1602-1663) made spiral columns as part of the porch of St Mary's church in Oxford. In eighteenth century England, such spiral columns were not called after Solomon, but rather 'garlanded columns'. John Sturt's 1721 engraving reproduced here of a biblical text from *The Gospel according to St Matthew* shows priests in a setting with garlanded columns, so it is clear that nevertheless they were associated with the Jewish temples (in this case, the Temple of Herod).

The geometrical principles for drawing and making spiral columns were published by Andrea Pozzo (1642-1709) in 1693[265] and under the rubric of the Corinthian order by Guarino Guarini (1624-1683) published posthumously in 1737.[266] Actual spiral and garlanded columns were made in a number of variants in terms of a number of divisions, fluting and types of capital. Rococo architects in southern Germany made spiral columns to flank aedicules and side altars as well as several notable baldacchini at high altars. Spiral columns survive at the Abbeys of Aldersbach, Michelsfeld, Osterhofen and Weltenburg; St Nikolaus at Bernbeuren and two Munich churches: St Anna-am-Lehel and St Johann-Nepomuk. The spiral columns vary in complexity from simple spirals at Aldersbach to full three-section garlanded ones at Michelsfeld. Three-section spiral columns designed by Nicholas Hawksmoor and made in 1727 support the carved wooden reredos of the church of St Mary Woolnoth. The lower third is spirally fluted and terminates in a golden crown. Above this, a non-fluted section with a gilded garland rises to another crown, which

265 Andrea Pozzo, *Perspectiva pictorum et architectorum*, 2 vols, Rome, 1693-1700. English edition, Perspective, London, 1707, fig. LII.

266 Guarino Guarini, *Architettura civile*, Turin, 1737, Treatise III, pl. 7.

delimits the centre section. The third, upper, section is the same as the centre section, and all is topped with a gilded capital. The north column (left as viewed) is a sunwise spiral, and the south one counter-sunwise.

The diverse symbolic and emblematical references in these London churches make them the epitome of sacred art, for they can be read and understood on many levels. Later literalism, first with neo-classical academic copies of actual ancient buildings, and then the Gothic revival, also literalistic copying of earlier buildings, removed much of the creativity from subsequent church building. The Arts and Crafts movement reinvigorated symbolism for a while, but the rise of modernism in the twentieth century removed almost all symbolism from Christian sacred architecture, leaving it impoverished.

CHAPTER 7

TOWERS AND STEEPLES

> Carpenter, mason, glazier,
> Each according to his craft,
> There one sets, another cuts,
> This one hits, this one bats, this strikes;
> He of the axe, he of the hammer,
> He of the mallet and of the chisel.

Matthew Paris, *The Story of St Edward, the King* (c. 1245).

Characteristic Structures

Individually designed towers and steeples visible from afar were an integral part of how the new churches character-ized each place. Apart from the examples mentioned above, they were located among secular buildings in the old city street plan, and not on Wrenian avenues. In his 1711 letter of recommendations, Wren wrote of "handsome Spires, or Lanterns, rising in good Proportion above the neighbouring Houses (of which I have given several examples in the City of different forms)".[267] In 1728, James Gibbs commented, "Steeples are indeed of a Gothic Extraction but they have their Beauties when their Parts are well disposed, and when the Plan of the several Degrees and Orders of which they are compos'd gradually diminish, and pass from one Form to another without confusion, and when every Part has the Appearance of a proper Bearing".[268] The limitless scope for creative design can still be seen in those that remain. Their individual authorship is a matter of continuing debate. Various commentators ascribe them to Wren alone, in asso-

---

267 Wren, op. cit., *Parentalia*, 319.

268 James Gibbs, *A Book of Architecture containing Designs of Buildings and Ornaments*, London, 1728, VIII.

ciation with or by Dickinson, Hooke, Oliver, Woodroffe or Hawksmoor.[269]

Based largely upon Ad Quadratum geometry, they create wonderful interplays of light, shadow and profile, ever-changing with the weather and the time of day, appearing in multiple perspectives across the cityscape. Both creating and expressing place-identity, they are masterpieces of sacred geometry and classical proportion. Ad Quadratum gives a basically octagonal cross-section to the upper portions of a square tower, sometimes as an octagonal cornice on an otherwise circular columniated structure (as at Wren's St Mary-le-Bow, Cheapside, 1680). Like all the classical churches of the period, they are masterpieces of non-verbal communication that can be experienced on multiple levels.

Several first-century CE Roman tombs may have been the inspiration for the basic form of these towers. Among them are the Tomb of the Julii at Saint-Rémy in southern France, the Conocchia at Capua, and several similar structures in Tunisia and Syria. The numerous ancient monuments, tombs and mausolea along the Appian Way out of Rome were examined in minute detail by Italian and other architects, and were well known to all classical scholars. Some of them were illustrated in published works of the seventeenth century,[270] and others may have come to the notice of architects through private drawings made by travellers. Because a church is orientated, ideally towards the four cardinal directions, each face of the octagon faces one of the eight winds described by Vitruvius and given by him as the recommendation for the orientation of city streets.[271]

269 See e.g. A. Geraghty, 'Nicholas Hawksmoor and the Wren city church steeples', *The Georgian Group Journal*, Volume 10 (2000), 1-14.

270 E.g. Jacob Spon, *Recherches curieuses d'antiquité*, Paris, 1683.

271 Marcus Vitruvius Pollo, *The Ten Books of Architecture*, Book I, vi, 2-13.

Towers of the Winds

The Tower of the Winds at Athens, designed by the
Macedonian architect Andronikos of Cyrrhus around 50
BCE, and mentioned by Vitruvius, is the epitome of this tradition. On its eight sides are the personifications of the corresponding winds. In former times, a vane in the form of a

Street view of St Mary le Bow (1680).

triton holding a pointer indicated which wind was blowing. The custom of naming the eight directions or winds exists in northern Europe as well, but with other names,[272] and it is the basis of the compass rose used by mariners. Hawksmoor makes a direct reference to this building in his unbuilt design for Worcester College in Oxford.[273] Later University buildings in both Oxford and Cambridge are based on Andronikos's tower.[274] The diminishing stages of the steeple of St Bride's in Fleet Street have been viewed as deriving from a fanciful woodcut of the Athenian tower in Cesare Caesariano's 1521 edition of Vitruvius.[275]

In his erudite *The Anatomy of Melancholy* (1660), Robert Burton (1576-1640), writing under the pseudonym Democritus Junior, systematically described the causes of what would now be called mental illness. His section titled *Digression of Air*[276] gives an insight into the many ideas, theories, and superstitions circulating in his time about the effect of the air and the winds on human health and well-being. It contains information on the location of the "artificial site of houses" with regard to the terrain, the orientation of windows: "A clear air cheers up the spirits, exhilarates the mind; a thick, black, misty, tempestuous, contracts, overthrows".[277] According to this seventeenth century esoteric outlook,[278] the winds could be viewed as spirits operating under powers delegated them by the four archan-

---

272 See e.g. Reuter, op.cit., 6-7.

273 Downes, *Hawksmoor*, op. cit., 151.

274 E.g. the Maitland Robinson Library, Downing College, Cambridge, by Quinlan Terry, 1992.

275 Folio XXIV, v.

276 Part II, Section II, Member III.

277 Robert Burton, *The Anatomy of Melancholy*, 3 vols, G. Bell, London, 1926, II, II, III, 76.

278 E.g. the works of Robert Fludd, *Philosophia Sacra* and *Medicina Catholica*.

gels who stand at the four cardinal directions. The individual winds are ruled by planetary powers, and affect the health and well-being of those subject to them.

Robert Fludd's symbolic illustration of *The Fortress of Health* shows good angels at the four cardinal points of a fortress guarding a praying man. The angels ward off small demons of disease riding on the wind, sent from four great demonic powers seated at the four cardinal directions.[279] In the north is the great demon Egyn, in the east, Oriens, in the south, Amaymon, and in the west, Paymon. The illnesses carried on the four winds from the great demons have the corresponding direction-quality. Diseases of the north are cold and sad; those of the east, hot, seething, fevers; from the south come corrupt air and pestilence; and from the west, dropsy and mental affliction. As with Fludd's orientated diagrams of spiritual virtues, the meaning of each wind was far more than just the coming weather to those who followed Hermetic philosophy. Four-faced urns on classical churches may be seen in the light of these beliefs.

The effect of the wind on buildings has always been recognized, and traditional buildings are designed to cope with the prevailing wind, being orientated to mitigate the worst effects of the wintry blast. The tall brick chimneys of Tudor and Jacobean buildings are designed with cluster and spiral forms that interact with the wind to produce an up-draught that takes the smoke away from the house. Their geometric design is quite different from their Gothic forerunners, and can be seen as a foretaste of the later post-Great Fire steeples, which also had to cope with winter winds coming off the river, but with a different purpose.

In the days before the noise of machines was ever-present, the sound of the wind often indicated its direction to people who knew their locality well. In medieval times on church

279 See Jocelyn Godwin, *Robert Fludd: Hermetic philosopher and surveyor of two worlds,* Thames & Hudson, London, 1979, ill. 62, p. 56.

steeples there were even whistling weathercocks whose note
indicated wind speed and change of direction. One still exists
in Devon at Ottery St Mary, and another was once on St Mary
Major in Exeter in the same county.[280] Now both city and country is ever under the pall of noise coming from road vehicles
and aircraft; industrial, farming and gardening machinery.[281]
The acoustic environment of former times can no longer be
experienced. Henry Vaughan (1622-1695), in his poem *The
Revival*, tells us:

> Hark! How his winds have chang'd their note!
> And with warm whispers call thee out.
> The frosts are past, the storms are gone,
> And backward life at last comes on.[282]

Even in the nineteenth century, sound was included as
an important element of weather-forecasting. Numerous
instances are given in Richard Inwards's *Weather Lore* (1893). He
quotes Lord Francis Bacon that "the ringing of bells is heard at
greater distance before rain; but before wind it is heard more
unequally, the sound coming and going, as we hear it when
the wind is blowing perceptibly".[283] No longer can a Londoner
hear the wind blowing through the pillars of a church steeple,
and the sound of Bow Bells is blotted out by the never-ending
roar of traffic, building works and other mechanical sounds.

Weather Vanes

As literal towers of the winds, nearly every steeple is (or
was) topped by a wind-vane whose design complements the

---

280 Philip and Patricia Mockridge, *Weathervanes of Great Britain*, Hale,
London 1990, 35, 57; Nicholas Orme, *Exeter Cathedral as it was 1050-
1550*, Devon Books, Exeter, 1986, 53.

281 See Nigel Pennick, *Celtic Sacred Landscapes*, London, 1997, 51 for the
former moorland sounds created by rocking stones.

282 W.S. Scott, *The Fantasticks*, 159.

283 Richard Inwards, *Weather Lore* (1893), Pryor, Whitstable, 1999, 105.

The steeple of St Anne, Soho.

tower. In a maritime nation, the direction of the wind had far more meaning than it has now in the mechanized twenty-first century. Traditional weathercocks were few. They adorned St Dunstan's-in-the-East and St Stephen, Coleman Street, both destroyed by enemy action in 1940, as well as the pre-fire survivors, St Catherine Cree and St Ethelburga, Bishopsgate, where they were combined with vanes. The magnificent London dragon on St Mary-le-Bow is the largest, eight feet in length. It was designed in 1680 by a mason, Edward Pearce, who carved a model in wood for the coppersmith Robert Bird to make. It is an instance of a craftsman doing work outside his demarcated field, a sign of the skills shortage of the time. The dragon was gilded, along with the ball beneath it, and the four flaming urns on the four corners of the tower, by Thomas Lane, painter.[284]

Vanes in the form of a comet were set up at St Mary Aldermanbury and St Mary-le-Strand. Another comet vane topped the church of St John Horselydown, designed by Nicholas Hawksmoor and John James (1727), which was bombed in World War II and demolished as late as 1970. In 1931, Cecil Parker described it as "one of those queer eighteenth-century churches which seem to have been the especial feature of that rather pagan era".[285] A comet was also planned for James Gibbs's second London church, St Martin-in-the-Fields, but it was not installed. Some weather-vanes reflect the attributes of the saint to whom the church is dedicated, such as the grid-iron on St Lawrence, Jewry and the key on St Peter, Cornhill.[286] The letters B, B and M formed the vane of St Mildred, Bread Street (destroyed 1941). The church of St Anne and St Agnes had the letter A with what is described by

---

284 Cobb, op. cit., 49.

285 Charles G. Harper, *Queer Things About London*, Cecil Palmer, London, 1931, 238-239.

286 Cobb, op. cit., 64-65.

Cobb as "what appears to be a griffin's head",[287] but which may well be the lion's head crest from Sir Christopher Wren's coat of arms. Both St Michael Queenhythe (demolished 1876) and St Mildred Poultry (demolished 1872) had vanes in the form of ships.

Each vane is a unique piece of craftsmanship in metal, designed precisely with "justness of proportion" to the steeple on which it denotes wind-direction. Wind vanes are more than ornaments, for, in the days when the average person knew his or her locality intimately, one could tell by the sky and the direction of the wind what the weather would be. That is why they are sometimes called 'weather vanes'. The direction was easily determined by eye by comparison with the vane's angle to the various facets of the familiar steeple. Apart from St Paul's Cathedral, whose dome stood high above them, and the monumental column commemorating the Great Fire, these were the tallest structures in the city. St Paul's is not surmounted by a vane, but an orb and cross. Its two flanking towers at the west end have pine-apple finials without vanes. The height of the cathedral, 365 feet, and its symbolic function as sacred omphalos[288] of the city, the immovable central point, make a windvane inappropriate. The church of St Mary Magdalen, Old Fish Street (demolished 1890) also had no vane, but an urn as the finial, and St Benet Fink (demolished 1844), a cross.

Towers, Steeples, Obelisks and Spires of 'Wren' Churches

Forerunners of the London church steeples can be found in several sources: the Tower of the Winds at Athens, descriptions of the Pharos at Alexandria, ancient Roman tower-tombs, a published design by Leon Battista Alberti,[289] designs for façade-flanking church towers by Sebastiano Serlio and

287 Cobb, op. cit., 65.

288 Navel or centre-point.

289 Alberti, op.cit., Book VIII, V, 'Of Towers and their Ornaments'.

Antonio de Sangallo the Younger (1485-1546), and also classical continuations of Gothic towers.[290] Unbuilt designs by John
Webb (1611-1672), who was the only student of 'Vitruvius

*London Dragon weather-vane of St Mary le Bow. The London
Dragon is a symbol of protection, and is always shown with crosses
beneath the wings.*

---

290 E.g. Thomas H. von der Dunk, ' Hoe Klassiek is de Gothiek?
    Jacob van Campen en de Toren van de Nieuwe Kerk te Amsterdam',
    Vijfentachtigste Jaarboek van Het Genootschap Amstelodamum, 1993, 49-90.

Britannicus', Inigo Jones (1573-1652) include multi-storeyed classical steeples. In 1613 Jones had visited Parma in Italy at the time when Simone Moschino was designing the tower of San Sepolcro church there. One of Webb's drawings, preserved in Worcester College, Oxford, is a church with two flanking towers, the seeming forerunner of Wren's St Mary-le-Bow steeple.

The transmission of the classical tower from renaissance Italy to seventeenth century London is not a simple copying of published works; built classical towers that pre-date the London ones stand at Parma in Italy and in the Netherlands, e.g. the Montalbaanstoren and Zuidertoren, Westerkerk and Ouderkerk in Amsterdam. Most of the towers and steeples on the London churches were built some years after the completion of the main building, and sometimes to a

Vane formerly on St John Horselydown, drawing by Charles G. Harper, 1923.

The PHAROS of PTOLOMY, a Magnificient Tower at the Port of Alexandria as a Guide to Vessels

An artist's impression of the Pharos at Alexandria, from William Granger, The Wonderful Museum, *Vol. III, London, 1805.*

design by a different architect. In addition to the many built designs that survive, and those built but now destroyed, there are a number of surviving projects by several architects of the day that were never translated into stone and metal. The first outstanding tower was designed by Sir Christopher Wren, who also designed the body of the church. After St Paul's, the tower of St Mary le Bow was the tallest church in the city of London. Finished in 1680, it was also the earliest tower to be completed. Though emulated later, the design was an original.

The church's design was based upon the Basilica of Maxentius and Constantine in Rome, which Wren believed to have been the Temple of Peace, and during construction a crypt made of Roman bricks was discovered (actually constructed in the tenth century). The steeple that rises above the square-section orientated tower is a basic exercise in eightfold geometry, derived, it seems, from Antonio da Sangallo the Younger's unbuilt project for St Peter's, Rome, with twin towers on the east façade, still extant as a wooden model. By way of engravings,

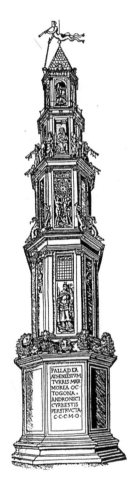

Caesariano's theoretical reconstruction of the Tower of the Winds at Athens (1521).

it may have influenced Wren's design of the steeple of St Mary-le-Bow. The lower part of the steeple is an eight-columned circular upper colonnaded Corinthian structure topped by an octagonal cornice. On the four corners of the tower flanking this 'tempietto' are urns on 'bows'. A version of them was used later by Wren on the twin towers on the western end of St Paul's.

Reconstruction of the Tower of the Winds, Athens, Greece.

*Alberti's theoretical design for a classical tower was the starting-point
for all classical towers and steeples built subsequently.*

*A forerunner of the London steeples, the tower of San Sepolcro, Parma,
Italy, designed by Simone Moschino and finished in 1616. Inigo Jones
visited Parma in 1613 when the tower was being planned. Shortly
afterwards, Pier Francisco Battistelli designed a funeral monument to
Ranuccio I of Parma. Published as an engraving, it was a multi-stage
Classical tower, another forerunner of the later steeples designed by
John Webb, Sir Christopher Wren and his followers.*

An unbuilt steeple design by John Webb, Inigo Jones's assistant and successor.

The St Mary's 'tempietto' is topped by flying buttresses or 'bows' that support an octagonal columniated upper stage. These bows resemble a cupola in profile, and Sangallo had proposed this structure in his St Peter's tower design. On top of the columniated stage of St Mary's is a four-sided pedestal flanked by urns that carries an obelisk surmounted by the gilded ball and dragon. Its magnificence comes from the proportions used rather than the subtly complex geometry displayed by some of the later steeples, and Wren's west towers of St Paul's Cathedral. Thirty years later, Hawksmoor made a similar design for the steeple of All Saints' church in Oxford, built by Henry Aldrich between 1713 and 1720 and now the library of Lincoln College.

When the burnt churches were rebuilt, except for St Mary-le-Bow, several years passed before steeples were added to complete the buildings. Before they were started, an earth tremor rocked the city on the eighth of September 1692.[291] It is unknown what damage the new churches sustained. The spires of St Augustine, Watling Street, and St Margaret Lothbury were completed in 1694 and 1699 respectively. But the vast majority of steeples were built in the next century, in the years between 1701 and 1726. The damage wrought during construction by the catastrophic hurricane of the twenty-seventh of November 1703 is also unknown. This hurricane "unroofed many houses and churches, blew down several chimnies and the spires of many steeples … the leads of some churches were rolled up like scrolls of parchment …".[292] The classical church steeples in London date from after the hurricane, and perhaps their new designs were in response to it. The year 1717, the year that the freemasons organized themselves into the Grand Lodge, saw the completion and topping-out of four

291 John Timbs, *The Romance of London*, Warne, London & New York, n.d., c. 1887, 286.

292 *The Tablet of Memory*, op. cit., 57.

A Dutch forerunner of the London steeples, the Westerkerk in Amsterdam.

steeples at St Stephen Walbrook, St Michael Paternoster Royal, St James Garlickhythe, and St Mary-le-Strand. This marked the formal end of the reconstruction of churches destroyed in the Great Fire.

The new steeples took various forms. St Mary Aldermary in Bow Lane was reconstructed in the Gothic manner upon the remains of the 1518 church burnt out in the Great Fire. The upper part of the tower was designed by Wren's assistant, William Dickinson, and built between 1701 and 1704.[293] Restoration in 2004 revealed reinforcements to the stone in the shape of long wrought-iron cramps more than a yard in length, probably made by an anchorsmith. These were made secure by being set in lead and reinforced by oyster shells embedded in the mortar. St Mary's followed on from another Gothic steeple, at St Dunstan-in-the-East, built 1697-1699. This is a spire on flying buttresses or 'bows' inspired by that of the burnt Gothic church of St Mary-le-Bow.

The classical tower of St Bride, Fleet Street, was built between 1701 and 1703. It has a square tower with pilasters and engaged columns at the angles. This supports four octagonal storeys of diminishing size. According to oral lore, it served as the model for the traditional wedding cake. It is composed of a series of four octagonal stages, diminishing in width, and topped by an octagonal pyramid. Like St Mary-le-Bow, the tower has a central spiral staircase. Apart from St Paul's Cathedral, St Bride's is the tallest of Wren's churches, at 235 feet high, ten feet taller than St Mary-le-Bow.

The tower of St Magnus the Martyr, Lower Thames Street, which was completed in 1705, is a classical square structure topped with an octagon, cupola and spire.[294] The steeple form is probably derived from the tower and cupolas of the

293 H.M. Colvin, 'The Church of St Mary Aldermary and its rebuilding after the Great Fire of London', *Architectural History*, 24, 1981, 24-31.

294 B.F.L. Clarke, *Parish Churches of London*, London, 1966, 30-31.

St Mary-le-Bow, elevation and cross-sections.

Steeple of St Mary le Bow.

church of St Carolus Borromeus in Antwerp, Belgium, which
was designed by the Jesuit architect Pieter Huyssens and built
between 1615 and 1623. Huyssens previously designed the
Jesuit church in Maastricht, and Wren actually had a drawing
of the Antwerp church in his office (sold as part of the Bute
collection at Sotheby's on the twenty-third of May 1951, as lot
10/32). St Vedast, Foster Lane, has a unique baroque spire, built
1709-1712. Based upon a square tower, it has a lower concave
stage and an upper convex one, topped by an obelisk.

The steeples of St Michael, Paternoster Royal and St James
Garlickhythe (in College Hill and Garlick Hill respectively)
resemble one another. St Michael's steeple, built by the mason
Edward Strong Jr., is of square plan with Ionic columns, whilst
St James's, built by the same man, has an octagonal basis. Like
the tower of St Stephen Walbrook, built at the same time (1713-
1717), they are both ascribed to Nicholas Hawksmoor, as the
ornate style of the urns on St James's steeple indicate. The last
tower added to a Wren church was designed by James Gibbs,
architect of the church nearest to it, nearby St Mary-le-Strand
(1714-1717). His steeple completed Wren's new church of St
Clement Dane's (1680-1682), the medieval forerunner of which
had not been burnt in the Great Fire, but was in a bad state
of repair and needed reconstruction. It has three stages, each
composed of a different classical order: Ionic, Corinthian and
Composite. It was built between 1719 and 1720 by the mason
William Townesend.[295]

The Geometry of Towers and Steeples by James Gibbs

James Gibbs was the designer of four London church steeples, St Mary-le-Strand (1714–1717); St Clement Danes (1719-
1720); the Oxford Chapel in Marylebone, now called St Peter,
Vere Street, built for Edward Harley, Earl of Oxford between

295 Geoffrey Beard, *The Work of Christopher Wren*, Bloomsbury, London,
    1982, 76.

Left – tower of the church of St Carolus Borromeus in Antwerp, Belgium (1621) (left) compared with the tower of St Magnus, London Bridge (right). The design of the latter may have been influenced by the former.

Tower and steeple of St Bride, Fleet Street, from Ludgate Circus.

1721 and 1724, and his most famous church, St Martin-in-the-Fields (1721-1726). His 1725 rebuild of All Saints' church in Derby, now the cathedral, retained its original medieval tower. Gibbs's London steeples are the finished examples of a whole series of steeple designs that were not built. In addition to his London churches and All Saints', Derby, Gibbs designed St Nicholas West church in Aberdeen, together with churches at Patshull, Staffordshire and Shipbourne, Kent. In his *A Book of Architecture containing Designs of Buildings and Ornaments*, published in London in 1728, Gibbs published seven different designs for the steeple of

The relationship between the steeple of St Vedast and St Mary le Bow.

*The steeple of St Augustine, Watling Street (1695–1696, reconstructed
after World War II).*

St Martin-in-the-Fields. One, similar to that actually built, is shown on his second round church design.[296] Six others,[297] which also remain unbuilt, are designed according to the same geometrical system, and all are identical in height, according to the width to length to height proportions of the built church. In addition to the St Martin's towers, drawings survive of alternative towers for St Mary-le-Strand and an unbuilt project for St George, Bloomsbury.[298] This latter tower would have been a baroque masterpiece with alternating convex and concave stages, topped by an openwork crown and weather vane.

St Mary-le-Strand, a church splendidly situated on an 'insular site' in the middle of The Strand, has a tower that rises above a two-stage western façade. The lower part of the façade has a semicircular porch capped with a low cupola and a prominent urn. The upper part of the façade is topped by a pediment that overlaps the balustrade with urns that top out the church walls. Rising above this pediment, the tower has a square section with recessed corners. From a lower clock stage rises the bell stage with engaged Ionic columns on the face, and freestanding ones at the four corners. The churches of this period are notable as the first to be designed to accommodate clock-faces. The clock stage supports an entablature

ST MICHAEL'S CROOKED LANE

St Michael's Crooked Lane (demolished 1831) an early 19th century engraving.

---

296 Ibid., plate XIII.

297 Ibid., plates XXIX & XXX.

298 See Paul Jeffery, 'Unbuilt Gibbs: A Fresh Look at His Designs for the 1711 Act Church Commissioners', *The Georgian Group Journal*, 1994, 11-19.

Tower of St Bene't, Paul's Wharf, 1677–1683.

and cornice with four urns. The section above this is an exercise in self-similarity, first proposed by Alberti in his ideal tower of the late fifteenth century, the form of the lower stage on a smaller scale. And the stage above that repeats the motifs, though in the form of an irregular octagon with its wider faces cardinally orientated, and the pilaster faces at 45 degrees. A

Steeple of St Edmund, and related Wren steeple designs. An acrylic transfer print on canvas by Nigel Pennick.

Tower of St Vedast, Foster Lane, showing interacting curved surfaces.

smaller stage above this is topped by a square-section cupola, which supports the gilded sphere and comet wind-vane. The proportions are best understood from the four circular openings that stand one above the other, alternating with the round heads of the arches and the horizontal cornices, giving an alternate rhythm of round and straight as one's eye moves up the tower.

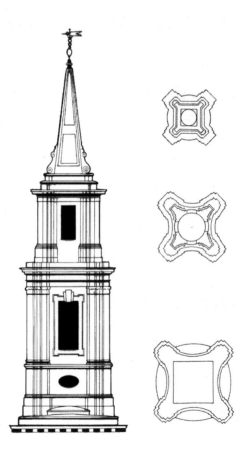

Drawing of St Vedast's steeple and cross-sections.

The tower of Christchurch, Newgate Street, which stands north of St Paul's Cathedral. The church was destroyed in the Blitz and only some of the walls remain.

Gibbs's steeple for Wren's St Clement Danes complements that of the nearby St Mary-le-Strand. The two steeples can be seen together today from a vantage point on the Strand's southern side, and in the nineteenth century *The Strand Magazine* used the two steeples seen from the north side of the Strand as its cover illustration. Rising from a square-section tower with four urns at the corners, the mid-stage of St Clement's is an irregular octagnal tempietto with arched cardinal faces and 45 degree angled Ionic corner pilasters. It is topped by an entablature and cornice of the same shape with eight urns at

The steeple of St Martin-within-Ludgate whose form stands as a foil to the towers and dome of St Paul's Cathedral when seen from Ludgate to the west. This church stands on the site of the reputed burial-place of the ancient Celtic kings of Britain.

St Dunstan-in-the-East has a gothic steeple with a spire on arches, one of the few churches reconstructed in the gothic style after the 1666 Great Fire of London. The church was left as a ruin after the Blitz of 1940–41.

Cupola of St Peter-upon-Cornhill. The church stands on a site reputed to be that of the earliest Roman Christian church in London.

the angles. Above this, the tower becomes a regular figure, with eight curving sides defined by exscribed circles. The corner pilasters also follow these curved surfaces, and the cornice has sharp spiky angles. This cornice, too, is topped by eight urns. A narrower, regular octagonal tempietto stands on top of this section. It has an octagonal cornice supporting a ribbed stone

St Paul's Cathedral viewed from the north.

cupola with a small, solid octagonal lantern topped by a cupola that supports the gilded apical ball and wind-vane. St Peter, Vere Street, has a minor steeple, unlike the magnificent ones along the Strand.

The design of the steeple of St Martin-in-the-Fields, topped out in 1726, amply demonstrates James Gibbs's mastery of geometry and proportion with its dynamic contrast between curves and straight lines. The lowest section of the tower,

The dome of St Paul's Cathedral, 365 feet high to the top of the cross which surmounts it.

where it rises above the roof-line is square in plan. Its sides measure one-third of the width of the façade, or one-sixth the length of the church. This is determined by the helikon diagram. The ground-plan of the tower thus occupies one

South-west tower of St Paul's Cathedral.

eighteenth of the church's area, located at the central point of the western half of the double-square church, demonstrating James Gibbs's understanding of the principles of "justness of proportion".

The basic geometric diagram determines the arrangement of the features of the tower at every level. There are seven distinct

The relationship between the steeple of St James Garlickhythe to the dome of St Paul's and other steeples.

stages of the tower. The supporting structure is part of the back wall of the portico, punctuated only by the main entrance and a circle-and-cross shaped atrium. This circle and cross is the theme for the inner forms of the tower above, with the four arms of the cross pointing towards the cardinal directions in every case. Above the entrance, the tower is square in cross-section and emerges above the roof-line. Within this section is the bellringers' chamber, a rectilinear shape based upon an inner square crossed by two longer rectangles. The next stage is the belfry, which has arched openings, inset corners and eight Ionic pilasters. The four corners above are surmounted by spirally-fluted urns. Higher up comes the section housing the clock mechanism and four clock faces. Internally, it is geometrically a circle and cross.

Above this the tower is octagonal, first with a 'tempietto' with applied Corinthian pillars; it has round-headed openings with prominent keystones, surmounted by a cornice of sixteenfold geometry supporting eight urns. Above this stage is a smaller octagon with four circular apertures and an incurving cornice. Its internal form is again the circle and the cross. This stage supports an octagonal obelisk or spire, made of stone like the rest of the tower. Three oval apertures diminishing in size towards the top punctuate each of the faces of the spire. The summit of the obelisk-spire is an octagonal pyramid with incurving sides. The apex of the steeple has a wrought-iron finial with a ball and flag-shaped wind vane topped by a small crown and knob. This wind-vane was originally designed by Gibbs to be in the form of a comet, like that on St Mary-le-Strand, but the present flag-vane was made instead.

The tower's plan is designed according to an eight- and sixteenfold radial geometry. This is the sixteenfold-fold system used by Gibbs at St Clement Danes and later at the Radcliffe Camera (Library) in Oxford, built 1737-1748. The

Steeple of St Mary-le-Strand designed by James Gibbs and built 1714.

West end and steeple of St Peter, Vere Street, originally called the Vere Street Chapel. One of James Gibbs's lesser-known buildings.

cross-section of each stage is related to all of the others through the ruling geometric scheme This is a development of the basic medieval system of Ad Quadratum or *acht-uhr*, in which the square is divided up by successive squares whose corners spring from the middle of a larger square, or squares turned at 45 degrees to make an octogram.[299] The space of

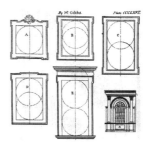

Batty Langley's illustration of the James Gibbs's geometrical construction of windows. Batty Langley, Ancient Masonry, *1736.*

'Serliana' or 'Venetian windows' at the east end of St Peter, Vere Street, a favourite theme of James Gibbs.

299 See Pennick, *Sacred Geometry*, op. cit., 110-111; Nigel Pennick & Professor Marinus Gout, *Sacrale Geometrie: Verborgen Lijnen in de Bouwkunst*, Uitgeverij Synthese, The Hague 2004, 129.

the cross-sectional square of the lower part of the tower is subdivided by a smaller square inside it at 45 degrees as in Ad Quadratum. From a circle inscribed in this inner square, in a ratio of 13:8, a smaller circle is drawn inside it from the same centre. Eight further circles of the same smaller radius are drawn on the eight axes of the two squares,, touching the

Gilded geometrical ceiling of St Mary-le-Strand.

inner circle. Features of the various stages of the tower, including the pillars and cornices, are defined by this diagram, their size and position determined by intersections of lines and circles. In this way, each part of the tower relates geometrically and proportionally to each other part, and, in turn, to the entire building. In this way, Gibbs designed St Martin's as the epitome of eurythmy. The overall ratio of width to length to height of St Martin's is 4:8:9, whole number proportions determinable by the helikon diagram. In classical terms, the ratio 4:8 is the duple ratio (2:1) and 8:9 the epogdoic ratio. The ratio of the façade height to the tower is 2:7; 2 being the height of the top of the entablature, and 7 being the remainder above it. The tower occupies one eighteenth of the ground area; the main body of the church twelve eighteenths (two thirds) and the portico three eighteenths.

The Geometry of Towers and Steeples by James, Archer, Hawksmoor, Dance, Flitcroft and Carr

The church of St George, Hanover Square, designed by the master of perspective geometry, John James, was built between 1712 and in 1724. St George's has a tower that rises from the main part of the building behind a hexastyle portico. The tower's location behind the portico is the same as that later used by Gibbs at St Martin-in-the-Fields (which has been the butt of architectural critics who do not recognize that James's church was the first to use this layout) and many colonial churches afterwards. But unlike Gibbs's spire at St Martin's, it is a more typically baroque form. The lower part of James's tower is square in section. Above this 'clock stage' is an unequal octagon surrounded by four coupled pairs of Ionic pillars. These support a cornice with eight urns directly above the pillars. From this stage, the unequal octagon rises to another cornice, which supports a stone cupola topped by a square-section lantern with a pyramidal apex, from which rises the staff of the weather vane.

James's other individual steeple is at St Alfege in Greenwich; it was completed in 1730. Rising from an older square tower reconstructed by Nicholas Hawksmoor, the clock stage is a concave-convex eightfold structure that gives space for the four garlanded urns that stand at each corner of the tower. Eight smaller urns top this stage. Above it it is a circular

The steeple of St Clement Dane's, designed by James Gibbs, built 1719–20.

A steeple designed by James Gibbs for his unexecuted design of St George, Bloomsbury. Many designs which were not used for buildings nevertheless exerted an influence on designs that did get built, hence they are part of the corpus of designs of the buildings that do exist.

tempietto with eight engaged Ionic pillars. Between them are round-headed windows below circular ones. The tempietto is topped by a circular cornice, which supports an octagonal section itself surmounted by eight more urns. Above this is a stone cupola divided into eight sections by ridges, on top of which is an octagonal base that supports the stone spire, metal ball and wind-vane.

The cupola of St George, Hanover Square.

James was also joint designer, with Hawksmoor, of the unique spires of St Luke, Old Street and St John, Horselydown, both completed in 1733. St Luke's has a square-section tower that supports a smaller square clock stage, which is proportioned as a plinth for the fluted obelisk that is the steeple. It is topped by a wind-vane. Although no longer used for worship, having been seriously damaged in the blitz and at one time scheduled for demolition, it was fortunately not demolished and continues its function as a sacred landmark to this day. In a description of an obelisk to be built at Blenheim Palace, Hawksmoor notes, "on the apex may be placed a star",[300] and a similar form was actually used at St John Horselydown, now demolished, which, was another unique design. It had a lower square section tower that supported a smaller clock stage whose dimensions were defined geometrically by the Ad Quadratum square-within-the-square. Like the corresponding stage at St Luke's, this was the conceptual plinth of an Ionic column. This fluted column was perspectivized with a pronounced taper, giving it the appearance of being much taller than it actually was, perhaps reflecting James's admiration for Pozzo's geometric masterworks in Rome. Above the Ionic capital was a Hawksmoorian circular altar-like section with a conical cap, that supported a tall iron staff topped with a comet weather-vane. Like all London towers blitzed in World War II, the tower stood although the church was burnt out. It was a great loss to London when it was needlessly demolished in 1970.

Thomas Archer's built designs have towers that are basically circular in cross-section. The single tower of St Paul's, Deptford (1712-1730) rises above a semicircular Tuscan portico, which supports an entablature and balustrade. Above this, a circular drum supports a round tempietto which has four prominent

---

300 Nicholas Hawksmoor, 'Explanation of the Obelisk', in Kerry Downes, *Hawksmoor*, London, 1959, Appendix B, 262-264.

pilasters at the intercardinal corners. Between the pilasters, standing on the roof of the drum, are four egg-shaped urns. The pilasters are topped by urns. This lower circular storey

The steeple of St Alfege, Greenwich.

supports a narrower circular stage with eight buttress-pilasters. Above this, an even smaller circular stage is also eightfold, with scrolled pilasters. This supports another drum, from which rises an obelisk-spire.

The four identical towers at the four conceptual corners of Archer's church of St John the Evangelist, Smith Square (1714-1728), are unique monumentally baroque structures. Arising from each corner of the two opposite identical pedimented facades on the northern and southern sides, they are circular in cross-section with eight curved Corinthian pilasters apiece. The towers rise from square bases, and are flanked at the four corners by Corinthian columns on high circular plinths. They are topped by four-sided incurving roofs surmounted by prominent pine-apples. This church was burnt in the Blitz, and although reconstructed, it is now used as a concert hall.

Apart from All Saint's, in Oxford, the towers of the London churches designed by Nicholas Hawksmoor are quite different from those of Wren's churches, and those designed by James Gibbs, Thomas Archer and John James alone. Hawksmoor's Christ Church, Spitalfields (1714) has a relatively conventional steeple whose Gothic roots are apparent, though re-worked in a unique and new classical form and

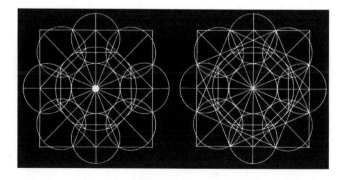

St Martin-in-the-Fields steeple plan geometry.

visible from afar along a 'right line'. Christ Church has an imposing Serlian tetrastyle portico from which rises a version of a Roman triumphal arch supporting two diminishing storeys. The whole is surmounted by an obelisk-spire, whose present form is not the original. It was altered in the nineteenth century to a more Gothic appearance. Hawksmoor's original spire design, as built, had three windows, one above the next, on each cardinal face; the two lower ones were plain rectangles, and the upper one was rectangular with a semicircular cutout in the top edge. All were surmounted by urns, the lower two capped with knobs, and the uppermost flaming. Above an apical gilded sphere, the wind-vane is flag-form and its finial is a fleur-de-lys.

Hawksmoor's churches, St Anne's at Limehouse (1712–1724), and St George-in-the-East (1715–1723) near the Radcliffe Highway, have related tower designs. During this period, Hawksmoor designed several steeples for 'Wren' churches, which can be seen to be related to St Anne's and St George-in-the-East by way of the geometry of their regular or irregular octagonal upper sections. The main western tower of St George-in-the-East is surmounted by a 'lantern' or tempietto composed of eight square engaged columns or pilasters linked by curving sections of wall. The pillars are built across the angles, giving the prismatic lantern a sixteenfold geometry. Each of the eight is surmounted by a fluted and swagged Roman altar, a favourite theme of Hawksmoor that he also used at St Alfege and St John, Horselydown. It appears that Hawksmoor made this design for the upper part of the tower of St Alfege, Greenwich, as depicted in an engraving of 1714 by Jan Kip. But John James's design was used instead. At this St George's, there are four subsidiary towers with cupolas corresponding with the outer corners of an internal square. These are the closest in form to Andronikos's Tower of the Winds of any London church.

At Limehouse, St Anne's western entrance is geometrically Ad Triangulum with a tower whose facade is across the centre of the semicircular domed porch. An intermediate design by Hawksmoor for the tower of St Anne, but not used, topped it with a small version of the Tower of the Winds.[301] The tower as built is square in basic section with two heavily-projecting pilasters or buttresses on both the north and south sides. Above these buttresses rises the clock stage, which is actually a continuation of the square section with the semicircular arches above the belfry opening. On top is the openwork 'lantern', an Ad Quadratum structure with a complex interplay of octagonal geometry. To-day it has a tall flagmast topped with a ribbed gilded globe and a flag-form vane.

The old medieval church of St Mary Woolnoth, in Lombard Street in the City of London, was patched up after the Great Fire, but then completely rebuilt to Hawksmoor's design between 1719 and 1727. Its façade is seemingly a re-working of an engraving in the 1691 work *Li cinque libri di architettura* by Giovanni Battista Montano (1534-1621). Here, Montano illustrates an antique Roman sepulchre, which has a square rusticated lower section surmounted by three diminishing storeys. St Mary's (1719–1727) reflects this design, having coupled twin towers that give a solid, monumental, almost full-width façade, unlike the more common narrower western steeple. The London *legendarium* tells that the church stands on the site of the ancient Temple of Concord, and the two equal turrets of St Mary's are a fine symbol of concord. The 'Bloomsbury Wonder', the tower of St George, Bloomsbury (1720–1730), is described in the next chapter. It is a unique stepped pyramidal form based upon a paper reconstruction of one of the Seven Wonders of the World – the Mausoleum at Halicarnassus, whose design Hawksmoor drew for Sir Christopher Wren, who had worked out the dimensions from ancient writings.

---

301 Downes 1970 op. cit., fig 107.

Steeple of Christ Church Spitalfields.

Christ Church Spitalfields west front.

Another of Wren's paper reconstructions, the Temple of Diana at Ephesus, was drawn by Henry Flitcroft (1697-1769). His major London church is St Giles-in-the-Fields, rebuilt on the site of an earlier church and hospital between 1731 and

Gothic tower of St Michael, Cornhill, designed by Nicholas Hawksmoor.

St John, Smith Square, pediment and two towers. This symmetrical church with four identical round corner towers was burnt out in the Blitz, 1940–41 and subsequently deconsecrated and converted into a concert-hall.

St John, Smith Square, street view.

The steeple of St Anne, Limehouse, designed by Nicholas Hawksmoor, viewed from the south-east.

*Steeple of St Luke, Old Street, in the form of an obelisk, designed by
Nicholas Hawksmoor and John James, built 1727-1733.*

1734. His name is proudly inscribed on the west end. The tower and steeple are in the current of James Gibbs. Flitcroft's other church, St Olave, Tooley Street, (1737-1739), was demolished in 1929. St John, Hampstead (1745-1747) by John Sanderson may be a version of Flitcroft's rejected design for the site. St Giles's tower is square in cross-section, topped by a heavy cornice, the four corners that support onion-shaped urns. An octagonal clock stage above this has a curving cornice accommodating the four cardinal clock faces. Above the clock stage, an octagonal tempietto with engaged Ionic columns supports a prominent sixteenfold cornice. This supports a balustrade with urns on the eight square corner pillars. Within this balustrade rises an octagonal section topped by an octagonal entablature. Above this is the eleven-section octagonal spire, whose proportional diminutions are perspectivized. This is topped by a golden ball and wind-vane.

St George the Martyr in Southwark was built on an insular site between 1734 and 1736. Its architect was John Price. Its tower follows the square-octagon pattern, and is relatively simple when compared with the previously-described designs. From a square tower rise three octagonal stages, successively smaller in cross-section. These lead to an irregularly octagonal spire with a flat top that supports a golden ball and vane. St Leonard's, Shoreditch was built between 1736 and 1740, and is much richer in treatment. Designed by George Dance the Elder (1695-1768), it was another rebuild on an existing church site. It is notable for its tall steeple and spire, which rises from the main body of the church behind the portico in the manner pioneered by John James and James Gibbs at their respective churches of St George, Hanover Square, and St Martin-in-the-Fields. Its podium was originally approached by ten steps, but the churchyard pavement level was raised in 1766,[302] and this has damaged the proportional system. The

---

302 Young & Young, op. cit., 135.

St George-in-the-East, designed by Nicholas Hawksmoor. The church was burnt in the Blitz of 1940–41 and a smaller, modernist chucrh exists within the walls of the original one, which still stand.

One of the twin towers of All Souls' College, Oxford, designed by Nicholas Hawksmoor with gothic ornament, but recognizably in the same style as the steeple of St Anne, Limehouse.

The steeple of St George the Martyr, Southwark (1734–1736).

lower section of the tower, which is the clock stage, is square in section with recessed corners. Above this rises the belfry stage, which is also square but with engaged Ionic columns. Above this is a circular tempietto with eight pillars connected to the central drum by arches that together support an octagonal entablature with a stone cupola. On top of this is a cylindrical section with engaged columns that supports a circular cornice. Above this rises a square section with recessed corners that supports an obelisk-spire, square in section with recessed corners. Surmounting the obelisk was a gilded globe with a series of baroque elements leading to the weather vane. This is missing now, and the spire ends with a metal spike.

The last church built in this strictly Roman Classical geometric current is St James, Clerkenwell, designed by James Carr and built between 1780 and 1792 on an earlier church site. It has a steeple, in the tradition of Gibbs and Flitcroft, rising from two square storeys to three octagonal ones topped with an eight-sided obelisk spire, gilded sphere and weather vane. The square section is topped by a balustrade and four rather neoclassical urns. Like the steeples of St Clement Danes and St Giles-in-the-fields, the octagonal stage has successive cornices that follow the sixteenfold geometry of the pilasters and give an emphatic outline when viewed from below.

CHAPTER 8

MASTERWORKS OF A SUPERIOR ORDER

> No person can in this life reach the point at which he is
> excused from outward works.
>
> **Meister Eckhart.**

Tradition, Continuity and Innovation

Although every London church of the era was built according to sacred geometry and classical proportions, and founded
with customary rites and ceremonies, there is not space to
describe each one individually. St Paul's Cathedral is, without
doubt, the major London church of this period, and my work
on it will appear in a subsequent publication. This chapter
is a selection of the more notable examples of the work of
three architects: Wren, Hawksmoor and Gibbs. The principles
embodied in these churches reveal the character of the others
not described here. They all embody structure and symbol in
a masterly way, emulating a superior order that emanates from
the creative intelligence that is the source of all. This commo-
nality of purpose is the thread that links them all.

The London architects of this era understood and
acknowledged continuity. Many new churches were built on
the sites of earlier ones, themselves having replaced, it was
believed, Pagan temples of the ancient Britons and Romans.
These architects acknowledged pluralistic sources in Pagan,
Jewish and Christian spiritual traditions, and understood
their basic principles well enough to create unified ensem-
bles. Inscriptions in Hebrew, Greek and Latin acknowledge
these multiple sources of spirituality, whilst mathematical,
mythic, emblematic, symbolic, astrological and craft traditions also have their often unobtrusive places. Clearly, these
structures expressed something of the aspirations of their

builders, and possess a soul of their own.[303]

In their studies of ancient architecture, these architects sought the inner realities of the ancients' buildings, rather than just making good-to-look-at slavish copies. Architecture

The steeple of St Giles-in-the-Fields (1731–1734).

303 See M.H. Baillie Scott, *Houses and Gardens*, George Newnes, London, 1906.

aims at eternity, and timeless true principles were employed, not only in construction, but also in the spiritual qualities that remain apparent to this day in their enduring chapels, churches, monuments and mausolea. Projects that were not built are also significant expressions of the spirit and are equally part of an architect's corpus of work. We are fortunate that many

St James, Clerkenwell, designed by James Carr, built 1780–1792.

design drawings of Sir Christopher Wren, Sir John Vanbrugh, Nicholas Hawksmoor and James Gibbs are preserved. The continued existence of a plan means that it can be built, perhaps centuries later. In the 1990s, Inigo Jones's early seventeenth century theatre design achieved physical reality as an adjunct to the rebuilt Shakespeare's Globe in Southwark. Further from this, *The House for an Art Lover* by Charles Rennie Mackintosh, designed in 1901, was built at Bellahouston Park in Glasgow (1988-1995). The continued existence of drawings of the Frauenkirche in Dresden, destroyed in 1945, meant that it could be rebuilt in the twenty-first century according to the original plans. Perhaps at some time yet to come, some of the London architects' as-yet unbuilt schemes may take physical form.

St Stephen's Walbrook and Wrenian Proportion

St Stephen's, now the Lord Mayor's church, is one of Sir Christopher Wren's finest designs. Francis Penrose commented that this church "has often been spoken of as Sir Christopher Wren's masterpiece", though he thought the unbuilt design of St Paul's Cathedral surpasses it.[304] Kerry Downes notes that the 1428 church replaced after the Great Fire by Wren's building itself had replaced an early church built on the site of a Roman temple of Mithras.[305] Rebuilding to Wren's design began with the rites and ceremonies of foundation, which took place on the seventeenth of December, 1672. The stones were laid in the east by the Lord Mayor, Sir Robert Hanson; Sir Thomas Chitchley, a descendent of the founder of the 1428 church acknowledged continuity, and the other stone-layers were the Lieutenant of the Tower, six officials of the Grocers' Company

304 Penrose, op. cit., 243.

305 Kerry Downes, *A Thousand years of the Church of St Stephen Walbrook*, church leaflet n.d. (c. 2000) 2.

and two churchwardens.[306] Building the main body of the church took until 1679, but it was not deemed fully finished until 1687.[307] The steeple was not completed until 1717, one of the last of the Great Fire replacements to receive one.

The dedication of St Stephen is associated with the circular form, as early round churches dedicated to San Stefano exist in Bologna and Rome. San Sefano Rotundo in Rome is a circular structure seventy-nine feet in diameter, with a drum supported by twenty-two columns. In Wren's time, San Stefano was believed to have been a Roman temple of Faunus, converted to a church.[308] The central space of San Stefano Rotondo is enclosed by an ambulatory which opens out into four deep spaces on the four main axes. This is the broad form that St Stephen's Walbrook takes. Whilst the dedication of Wren's church reflects the round form of the Roman one, the external form of its dome is patterned on Gianlorenzo Bernini's Santa Maria dell'Assunta church at Ariccia, near Rome (1664). The dome has the same form, only the lantern of St Stephen's is smaller in proportion.

Francis Penrose comments that "it may safely be said that in no other building has so much been made of a plain oblong space and sixteen columns. The secret lies entrely in the arrangement of the plan and the harmony of the propor-tions…".[309] Wren described it so: "In the centre of the church is a spacious cupola and a lantern in the middle of that. Over the rest of the church the roof is flat supported by Corinthian

---

306 Cobb, op. cit., 51, Vestry minutes X 112.

307 Ibid., 50.

308 Francesco Borsi (trans. Rudolf G. Carpanini), *Leon Battista Alberti: The Complete Works*, Electa, Milan, 1986, 35. The theory was disputed by R. Krautheimer, 'Santo Stefano Rotondo a Roma e la chiese del San Sepolcro a Gerusalemme', *Rivista Archeologica Cristiana*, 12, 1935, 51–102.

309 Penrose, op.cit., 244-245.

columns and pilasters".[310] The architect covered the space with a coffered dome, ultimately inspired by the Pantheon in Rome, but made of plaster over a timber frame, not site-cast concrete as in Hadrian's first century CE temple. The dome

Arched façade of St Mary Woolnoth.

310 Sir Christopher Wren, *Parentalia* quoted by Penrose, ibid., 243.

is divided into four zones. Eight structural ribs rise from sixteen coffers, ornamented with rosettes, which form the lowest zone. Next come eight sections finely plastered with oval garlands with central rosettes. The next zone has sixteen coffers with rosettes, and finally the zone leading to the oculus and cupola has eight sections, also with rosettes. Unlike the Pantheon, whose oculus is open to the aether, St Stephen's has an eight-windowed lantern

St Stephen, Walbrook, whose medieval predecessor stood on the site of the Roman Temple of Mithras. Engraving from 1833.

St Anne, Limehouse, cryptoporticus.

topped by a baroque copper-clad cupola that supports two gilded spheres and a wind-vane.

The dimensions given in *Parentalia* are inaccurate, as shown by the accurate nineteenth century survey by John Clayton.[311] Wrenian proportions detected by Penrose at St Stephen's

St Stephen's Walbrook (1672–1679) is one of seven churches with domes designed by Sir Christopher Wren; an external view.

311 John Clayton, *The Works of Sir Christopher Wren*, London, 1849.

are: 2:7; 5:8; 7:5; 1:10; 7:8; 7:9; 5:9; 3:7, as well as the more
complex ratios 7:15; 7:18; 7:20; 9:14.[312] "It is certainly interesting to find in St Stephen's, Walbrook", wrote Penrose, "so
many accurate proportions in terms of low numbers".[313] He
noted that "although the arrangement of the columns under
the cupola is apparently octagonal, the proportion between
the openings is as the numbers 7 to 10 and not as 7 to 9·8992,
which would have made the octagon exact. The former
proportion appears to have been preferred on account of the
closer harmony of the numbers".[314]

Wren also used ratios with the number seven in St Paul's
Cathedral to determine the heights of columns and pilasters. One of his earliest designs, St Benet Fink (1670–1681,
demolished in 1846) had a most ingenious oval geometry
that incorporated two sections of 14-sided regular polygons,
geometrically related to one another, numerically a 2:7 ratio.
Wren's writings are few, but some church design recommendations survive in a letter to a friend published in *Parentalia*.[315]
The only London church he designed that was not on old
foundations was St James, Westminster (Piccadilly), which
he mentions in the letter. This appears to be nearest to the
Wrenian ideal, and the letter gives optimal dimensions: "the
new church should be at least 60 feet broad, and 90 feet long,
beside a chancel at one end, and a belfry and portico at the
other", a 2:3 ratio. St James's has a 2:3:4 system of proportion, and it is properly orientated. Internally, St James was
lavishly furnished and ornamented, befitting its location in an
upper-class district. But it never had a magnificent tower and
steeple to compare with some of the other churches built at
the same time.

312 Penrose, op.cit., 246-247.

313 Ibid., 247.

314 Ibid., 247.

315 Wren, op. cit., 318-321.

The Bloomsbury Wonder: St George's, Bloomsbury

Nicholas Hawksmoor's church of St George, Bloomsbury is unique among London churches, for it has a tower based upon one of the ancient Seven Wonders of the World. It is one of the churches built as the result of an Act of Parliament of 1711 that proposed to build fifty new churches in and around the Cities of London and Westminster (Statute at Large, IX Anne, c.22). A Commission was set up to locate, plan and build them with funding derived from a tax on coal, just as the rebuilding of the City churches after the Great Fire had been. The Bloomsbury Wonder was built between 1720 and 1724, though it was not consecrated until the twenty-eighth of January, 1730.[316] When the building was finished in 1724, a new parish was created from part of the old County of Middlesex parish of St Giles-in-the-Fields. St George's was erected on an open space in Bloomsbury

The concrete dome of the Pantheon in Rome, built c.125 CE, served as the model for the coffering of many renaissance and Baroque domes.

316 St George's Church, Bloomsbury, *Yearbook* 1953/54, 1.

known as 'Lady Russell's ground'. This controversial piece of land was a rectangle with its long dimension north-south. In 1711 Hawksmoor made a site plan, and competing designs were prepared by him as well as James Gibbs and John Vanbrugh. Gibbs's design of a church for what was probably this site is preserved.[317] In May 1715 Vanbrugh's design was chosen. But it had an altar to the north instead of the ritually correct east,

An internal view of the dome of St Stephen, Walbrook, restored after damage in the Blitz, 1940–41.

317 Paul Jeffery, 'Unbuilt Gibbs...", *The Georgian Group Journal*, 1994, 14-17, figs. 6, 7 & 8.

because, according to the architect, the site meant that it "cannot conveniently be built any other way".[318]

However, the prospect of an altar in the north was against the stated objective of the Commissioners to locate altars in their proper orientation according to ancient Christian tradition. After the Great Fire, St Edmund's church had been built north-south, but this was no longer considered acceptable. The design was never used, and Vanbrugh was particularly unfortunate in that none of his church designs were ever built, a significant loss to London's potential heritage. Alternative plans for the church continued to be produced, because it took five years of negotiation before the ground could be purchased from the owner,

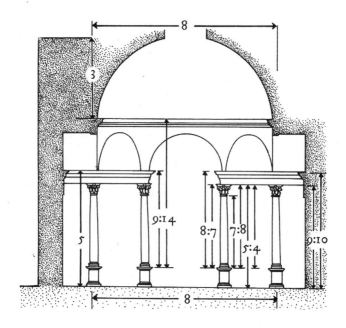

Whole-number proportions define the dimensions of the interior of St Stephen, Walbrook, drawing after Francis Penrose.

318 Lambeth Palace Library manuscripts 2690, 17 May 1715.

Lady Rachel Russell. In the interim, Hawksmoor proposed an oval design so that the altar could be in its liturgically correct location in the east. It would have had two identical cupolas over the north and south ends, not the single tower later built, and a façade similar in form to that of his church of St Alfege, Greenwich, but using different proportions. Geometrically, it is not an oval laid out by the usual techniques employed by Sebastiano Serlio and Francisco Borromini.

Hawksmoor's sacred geometry for the location is apparent from this first plan for a church on the Bloomsbury site. The rectangular portion of its plan is defined by a circle with an inscribed hexagram, a six-pointed 'star' composed of two interpenetrating equilateral triangles. In Jewish tradition this is the *Magen David*, 'the Shield of David'. Alchemically, it signifies the union of the four elements as the quintessence, the source of all. The outer walls of this part of the church are delineated by the east-west rectangle produced by joining adjacent angles of the triangles. Semicircles are drawn from the intersection-points of a cross drawn between the half-way points of the rectangle's sides. Semicircles drawn inwards to the east and west define the dimensions of the east-west walls and main pillars, whilst semicircles in the north and south drawn outwards define the inner part of transept ends. From these foci, larger semicircles define the outer walls of the transepts and the centre-lines of the twenty columns (the number of external columns on the Mausoleum at Halicarnassus). These would have served as porticos for entrances in the north and south. The largest outer semicircles spring from the line of the inside north-south walls.

But, like so many, this plan never got off the drawing board. Instead, Hawksmoor's present design of a more conventional cross-axial building was agreed upon, perhaps because of its ingenious solution to the orientation problem, allowing the proper location of the altar in the east. First sketched out in

1711, when the ground was surveyed,[319] it has a double axis, correctly located foursquare with the axes running terrestrial north-south and east-west respectively. As William Lethaby later noted: "The perfect temple should stand at the centre of the world, a microcosm of the universe fabric, its walls built four square with the walls of heaven".[320] The church is entered by a hexastyle portico to the south, but has a round eastern apse that reflects the tower to the west. The main axis of the church is north-south, as in Vanbrugh's design, and the roof ridge is, too, reflecting the pediment of the portico. This gives the impression of a double pediment, something resembling that of the Pantheon in Rome, but it is not visible from the street.

Comparison of the towers and steeples of St Michael Paternoster Royal (left) and St Stephen, Walbrook (right), designed by Nicholas Hawksmoor and completed in 1717.

319 Lambeth Palace Library manuscripts 2750, 20, 21.

320 Lethaby, op. cit., 53.

If the church is viewed traditionally as an east-west structure, it resembles a drawing preserved in the Lambeth Palace library that Hawksmoor made for a project for a 'Basilica after the Primitive Christians'. 'Primitive Christians' meant 'from the purest times of Christianity' (seen as the fourth century), rather than the modern pejorative usage of unlearned or unsophisticated. This basilica is on a site plan made in November 1711 for a surveyed location in Bethnal Green, on land that

Sacred Geometry diagram of St George, Bloomsbury.

was never purchased.[321] This church was to be set within its own temenos and orientated properly "east and west", with a rounded apse to the east. This plan is very close to the central portion of St George's Bloomsbury as built with its east and west terminations. St George's tower is at the western end, opposite the apse, the traditional location for a tower.

Entrances were provided on the north side as well as the south, but these are long disused by churchgoers. The main entrance as built faces the street on the south side. Approached by steps, it is an imposing Corinthian hexastyle portico. Whilst it has elements of the Temple of Bacchus at Baalbek, built under the reign of Antoninus Pius (138-161 CE), that temple is an octastyle, with eight, not six, pillars like the church. This Temple of Bacchus was illustrated by Jean Marot in a series of engravings in 1660, and by Jacob Spon & George Wheler in their *Voyage d'Italie, de Dalmatie, de Grèce, et du Levant faix aux années 1675 et 1676*, published in London in 1682.[322] So William Stukely was wrong when he noted in his diary[323] that Hawksmoor's portico was based in style and dimensions on that temple. The Baalbek temples were subsequently seriously damaged by an earthquake in 1759.

The tower is a version of Wren's reconstruction of the Tomb of Mausolus, the Mausoleum, as drawn for the master by Hawksmoor himself. Like the drawing, the portico of St George's has six columns, and the façade of each side of the upper section, equivalent to the pteron of the Mausoleum, four. It also resembles closely, but in greatly enlarged form, the tomb of C. Julius Samsigeranos at Homs in Syria, built in 78-79

321 Kerry Downes, *Hawksmoor*, Thames & Hudson, London 1969, 100.

322 Jacob Spon & George Wheler, *Voyage d'Italie, de Dalmatie, de Grèce, et du Levant faix aux années 1675 et 1676*, 2 vols., Lyon, 1678; Amsterdam, 1679; London, 1682.

323 William Stukely, *The family Memoirs of Rev. William Stukely, M.D.*, vol. 3, 9, in *Surtees Society Publications*, vol. 80, 1887. Noted the seventeenth of February 1750.

CE.[324] A wooden model was made of St George's proposed tower in 1723,[325] so it appears to have been built in 1724. Rising from a base on the southwestern side of the church, the tower is square in form, using Ad Quadratum geometry for its plan, whose width is related to the central space geometry. The section that rises above the roof-line has four rectangular corner columns which serve as buttresses, set at forty-five degrees from the square. Each face of the section above this is a pedimented tetrastyle temple front with Corinthian columns. At each corner is another Corinthian column, making twenty in all. Thus in his design for St George's Hawksmoor retained the four-column faces of the upper part of the Mausoleum, whilst allowing for structural necessities and reflecting the twenty outer pillars of the Mausoleum's lower storey. The entire church of St George has forty-eight columns: eight in the portico, sixteen in the interior, and twenty-four on the tower.

Above the pedimented section of the tower is a lightly stepped pyramid. Hawksmoor's drawing of the Mausoleum divides this pyramid into eight ascending sections; however the St George's pyramid has nineteen. Partly-stepped steeples had been used before on two City churches: St Mary Magdalene, Old Fish Street, whose steeple was built 1683-1687; and St Michael, Queenhythe, a steeple built in 1685-1687. St Mary's had an octagonal stepped portion that rose above the parapet to support a lantern, whilst St Michael's was square in section, like St George's. The pyramidal section of St Michael's supported a pedestal with an obelisk-spire. Both churches have been demolished, St Michael's in 1876 and St Mary's in 1890.

The architectonics of the inner part of the church of St George correspond with Hawksmoor's design for a 'Basilica

---

324 Roberto Marta, *Archittura Romana*, Edizione Kappa, Rome, 1990, 177, fig. 539.

325 Downes, 137.

after the Primitive Christians'. It is, like the earlier rejected oval design, based upon Ad Triangulum sacred geometry. The outer length of the church east-west, including the tower and the apse, is defined by a circle with an inscribed rectangle that marks the limit of the two bays cut off by double columns

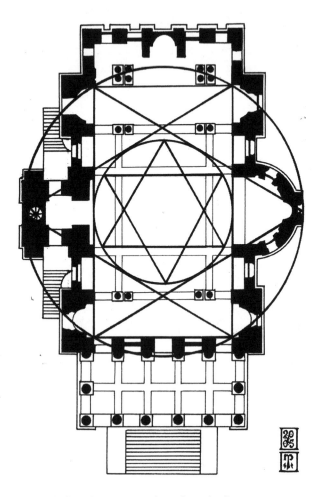

Geometrical plan of St George, Bloomsbury, built 1720-1730.

immediately to the north and south of the central space. This rectangle is the product of a hexagram based on the large circle. Within the hexagon defined by the large hexagram is inscribed another, smaller circle. Within this is inscribed another hexagram, orientated at right angles to the larger one. This defines the width of the coving in the central space of the church and the dimensions of the basal plan of the tower. Extensions of the south-facing triangle define the location of the centres of the outer pillars of the portico.

According to Pliny, "on the summit [of the Mausoleum – N.P.] is a marble quadriga, made by Pythis".[326] The quadriga, a charioteer in a chariot drawn by four horses, represents Helios. Here, apparently, King Mausolus was apotheosized as the sun god. St George's finial is not a quadriga, but a statue of King George I in antique costume that stands on a garlanded circular altar atop the pyramidal tower. Hawksmoor had previously designed four round altars with carved cherubim and swags for the east portico front of his St Alfege church in Greenwich (1712-1714). At St George's, carved crowns and swags were accompanied by large stone lions and unicorns climbing up the pyramid, removed as "very doubtful ornaments" by G.E. Street in 1871.[327] The most recent reconstruction in 2006 saw the lions and unicorns restored; the unicorns resplendent with gilded metal horns that were ceremonially paraded around the block before being erected.

St George's tower is depicted by William Hogarth (1697-1764) in his satirical engraving, *Gin Lane* ("Publish'd according to Act of Parliamt Feb. 1, 1751. Price 1s."), which contrasts the horrors of drunken debauchery in the notorious slums of St Giles's (sometimes called 'Satan's Kitchen' or 'Seven Dials') with the sacred tower of St George's in the distance.

---

326 Pliny, *Natural History*, 36.4.31.

327 Downes, 138; St George's Church, Bloomsbury, *Yearbook* 1953/54, 1.

It shows the heraldic beasts well. Verses to appear with the engraving were written by the Reverend James Townley. The church tower also appears in the background of a watercolour by George Scharf (1788-1860) showing the laying of the foundations of a new British Museum gallery in 1845.[328] The gallery was being built to exhibit the 'Lycian Marbles' brought to London from Asia Minor by Charles Fellows. Unfortunately Scharf did not depict the beasts, choosing to obscure them by a piece of scaffolding. By a strange coincidence, in 1857 the remaining sculpture from the ruins of the real Mausoleum at Bodrum in Turkey was brought to the British Museum and can be seen there to-day, a few minutes' walk from Hawksmoor's masterpiece.

On The Square: the London Temple of Concord, St Mary Woolnoth

An example of the complex symbolism, geometry and an understanding of the legendary nature of the place on which it stands is the church of St Mary Woolnoth. Located at the corner of Lombard Street and King William Street in the City of London, this church was also designed by Hawksmoor and constructed between 1719 and 1727. St Mary Woolnoth is widely known as the spiritual home of the hymn and later 'gospel song', *Amazing Grace*, written as one of the *Olney Hymns* by repented slave-ship seaman turned evangelist John Newton, vicar of St Mary's 1780-1807. Nicholas Hawksmoor's building replaced a fifteenth century church that had been repaired after the Great Fire, but which, by the early 1700s, had to be demolished.

A key factor in St Mary's design comes by way of the London legendarium. It is the understanding that there was once a temple of Concord upon this site. In 1716, Hawksmoor had found Roman temple remains beneath the old church during its

---

328 Peter Jackson: *George Scharf's London: Sketches and Watercolours of a Changing City, 1820-50*. John Murray, London 1987, 101.

Steeple of 'The Bloomsbury Wonder', St George, Bloomsbury, with lion and unicorn restored in 2006. This steeple is Nicholas Hawksmoor's rendition of the Mausoleum at Halicarnassus, one of the ancient Seven Wonders of the World. By chance, over 100 years after the church was built, fragments of the sculptures from the real Mausoleum were brought from Halicarnassus to the nearby British Museum. They remain there, a ten-minute walk away from the church.

demolition,[329] and in 1839, George Godwin the Elder referred to this when he wrote of "the belief that a temple, probably that which was dedicated to Concord, at one time occupied the site".[330] Matthew of Westminster ascribes the foundation of this temple of Concord to the ancient British king, Dunvallo Molmutius. It was Molmutius who "established the Molmutine laws, which to this day are celebrated among the English [1307 – N.P.]. Moreover, he enacted that the temples of the gods and their cities should have such dignity, that whatever fugitive or criminal took refuge in them, he might be allowed to depart unhurt through the midst of his enemies".[331] The right of sanctuary at certain holy places, such as Beverley Minster, Westminster Abbey and St Martin's-le-Grand in the City of London, was only abolished in 1623. St Martin's was an enclave of Westminster Abbey within the City of London, a religious college said to have been founded by Wythred, King of Kent, in 700 CE.[332] It was thus outside the jurisdiction of the City authorities. When the college and its church were demolished in 1548, a tavern was built on the site, which continued to have a lawless reputation. Later, the General Post Office took its place.

Molmutius was recognized as the epitome of good governance, having suppressed crime successfully so that "no one dared do violence to his fellows".[333] "When he had maintained the kingdom forty years in peace he died, and was buried in the city Trinovantum, near the temple of Concord, which he himself had built, for the purpose of giving confir-

---

329 Du Prey, op. cit., 107.

330 George Godwin & John Britton, *The Churches of London*..., vols., London, 1839, 2, p.2 of section on St Mary Woolnoth.

331 Matthew of Westminster, op.cit., Book V, Ch. II.

332 John Thomas Smith, op. cit., 322.

333 Gaufridus, op. cit., ii, 17.

mation to his laws".[334] According to the chronology worked out by Matthew's translator, C.D. Yonge, this was around 460 BCE. Concord was thus the symbol of the Molmutine Laws. The London legendarium goes on to tell that the original Christian church was founded by a Saxon called Wulfnoth on the temple site.

Several commentators have noted that the body of the church takes the general form of a cube, with its close associations with Pythagorean, Judaic and Masonic symbolism, though they have not explained why this particular church should take this form.[335] Neither the 5th century BCE Greek Doric 'Temple of Concordia' at Agrigento in Sicily nor its Roman counterpart in Rome is cubic in form. The Agrigento 'Temple of Concordia' is a later attribution, as the original dedication is unknown. It was converted into a church in 597 CE.

In the thirteenth century, Pierre de Roissy wrote, "Squared stones signify the squareness of the virtues of the saints. These are Temperance, Justice, Fortitude and Prudence".[336] These four Cardinal Virtues, with their origin in Classical Pagan philosophy, were, before the rise of amoral modernist theories of politics, known to be essential to the harmonious functioning

Nineteenth century engraving of St George, Bloomsbury.

334 Matthew of Westminster, op.cit., Book V, Ch. II.

335 Du Prey, op.cit.,106; Hart, op. cit., 98.

336 Cited by Bernard E. Jones, op. cit., 410.

of society. Thus the cube is the symbolic embodiment of virtue, perfectly appropriate for a church of the Lord Mayor of London, whose rule should ideally be conducted according to the four Cardinal Virtues and the rule of law taught by its founder, Molmutius. The cubic stone or 'perfect ashlar' is a central symbol in speculative freemasonry, expressing this virtuous meaning. The rule of Concord is an essential necessity for a peaceful and prosperous city. The tower that forms the west front of St Mary Woolnoth is a unique structure, composed of the unification of two parallel elements side by side. This is a perfect symbol of concord.

St Mary's and the other churches founded or rebuilt after the 1711 Act of Parliament were constructed at exactly the period when philosophical or speculative freemasonry was emerging, culminating in the emergence of the first Grand Lodge in London on the twenty-fourth of June, 1717, when

St Mary Woolnoth, a church in cubic form that stands on the reputed site of the ancient Temple of Concord. Engraving from 1833.

four already-existing freemasons' lodges banded together. Just before this, a political, sectarian, version of freemasonry, the Orange Lodges, had emerged in support of the Protestant cause when in 1688 the Dutch prince William of Orange overthrew the last Roman Catholic monarch of Britain, King James II. Grand Lodge freemasonry, unlike that of the Orangemen, was and is non-sectarian, being deist in philosophy. At that time, speculative freemasonry was set up as something distinct from the functional operative craftsmen's guild of free masons.

As the fifteenth century German master mason Matthäus Roriczer explained, the work of operative free masonry is "not for private glory, but altogether for general benefit",[337] and this principle was applied to the new speculative freemasonry. The moral philosophy inherent in the spiritual arts and crafts

An engraving by Giovanni Battista Montano (1534–1621) of an antique Roman mausoleum near Rome, from Li cinque libri di architettura *(1691) (left) compared with the façade of St Mary Woolnoth (1719–1727) (right).*

337 Papworth, John W., *Roriczer on Pinnacles*. London, Architectural Publications Society, 1848-1853, the first English translation of the original text by Roriczer given by Heideloff, C., *Die Bauhuette des Mittelalters in Deutschland*, Nuremberg, 1844.

means that the worker is ever aware that the work has a wider dimension than the materialistic pursuit of profit or fame. The work is "not for himself, but for the public good", as the epitaph of Sir Christopher Wren in St Paul's Cathedral tells us. This public spirit of personal improvement and the public good was taken into the principles of what became known as 'speculative freemasonry'. In Britain during the seventeenth century there emerged a new kind of organization that used the language and symbols of the practical art of building. Whether it emerged from the building guilds or not has been exhaustively investigated and hotly disputed. No unquestionable evidence has emerged that it did.[338] Whatever its origins, and they are poorly documented, it had a spiritual and social dimension as a 'speculative' society with an ethical and esoteric purpose. In the early twenty-first century, the history of the origins and activities of the British geomancy/earth mysteries movement in the 1960s and 1970s have already been presented in different, incomplete, versions,[339] questioning the possibility of a historically-definitive interpretation of the origin of any movement or institution.

Masonic historians have shown that the symbolism and ritual of freemasonry developed rapidly between 1717 and 1730. Samuel Pritchard's seminal publication, *Masonry Dissected* (1730), demonstrates that there had been much recent development in ceremonial and esoteric ritual.[340] It has also been demonstrated that the claim that Sir Christopher Wren was a freemasonic Grand Master is a fabrication.[341] Masonic

338 For an overview of the origin of freemasonry, see John Hamill, *The Craft: A History of English Freemasonry*, Crucible, Wellingborough, 1986, 19-40. For an earlier viewpoint, see Henry Sadler, *Masonic Facts and Fictions*, London, 1887.

339 See Bob Trubshaw, *Sacred Places. Prehistory and Popular Imagination*, Heart of Albion, Wymesword, 2005, 91-92.

340 Bernard E.Jones, op. cit., 165.

341 By James Anderson, 1738. Hamill, op.cit., 17.

researchers of the 'authentic school'[342] have shown that the symbolism and ritual of freemasonry was not fixed at the beginning, but developed considerably during the first fifteen years of the Grand Lodge, finally taking on a form that set the later standard.

The axis of St Mary Woolnoth is orientated twenty-eight degrees south of east, which is likely to have a significant meaning, as orientation was strictly observed by the architects who followed Wren, as demonstrated by the difficulties over the design of St George's Bloomsbury. Hawksmoor used a ten-foot module in the design of St Mary Woolnoth, just as Wren had recognised the ten-foot module in his paper reconstruction of the Mausoleum that was drawn up by Hawksmoor. Unfortunately, the tradition that the church is on the site of the temple of Concord cannot now be verified archaeologically by modern scientific methods. Fragments of pottery and "bones and tusks of sacrificial animals" were found by the builders in Hawksmoor's day.[343] Hawksmoor's crypt and whatever lay beneath that were destroyed between 1897 and 1900 by the City and South London underground railway.[344] The engineering works included the construction of an underground ticket hall where the crypt had been, sinking lift shafts down to the station platforms and running tunnels deep beneath the street. It is now part of Bank tube station, and the church's supports are steel girders. The bones of the dead buried there were exhumed and reburied in a cemetery at Ilford. The work led to an acrimonious legal dispute for compensation that went through the courts all the way to the

---

342 For definition of the 'authentic' and 'non-authentic' schools, see Hamill, op. cit., 22.

343 John Britton & Augustus Pugin, *Illustrations of Public Buildings of London…* 2 vols., London, 1825-1828, I, 91.

344 M.A.C. Horne, *The Northern Line*, Douglas Rose, Finchley, 1987, 10-11.

House of Lords.[345] But the works for the new underground railway did enable Alfred C. Bossom to make accurate measured drawings of the church.

The wooden fittings of the church, which are still there, include a pulpit with esoteric diagrams and an altarpiece with garlanded (spiral) columns. In 1707 John James, later to design St George's, Hanover Square and to be Hawksmoor's co-worker, published his English translation of Andrea Pozzo's treatise on perspective, which included the geometry of this type of column.[346] Hawksmoor placed crowns on his columns, which, if he was aware of the Molmutius legend, may refer to Holinshed's description of Molmutius: "bicause he was the first that bare a Crowne here in Britaine, after the opinion of some he is named the first King of Britaine".[347] Like several other surviving post-fire pulpits, that of St Mary Woolnoth has symbolic designs set out in high-quality marquetry. They are part of the emblematic tradition of esoteric diagrams current at that time, used by deistic mystics and freemasons. St Mary's pulpit includes a diagram that closely resembles Robert Fludd's emblem of the Ethereal Sphere,[348] the second day of creation in Judaeo-Christian cosmology. This emblematizes the unperishable Quintessence or Spiritus. The awesome darkness of the sun witnessed at its total eclipse at London on the twenty-second of April 1715 must also still have been a potent memory.

If the planners had had their way, London's temple of Concord would have been destroyed, for between 1840 and 1920, five attempts were mounted to have the church

345 Mike Horne & Bob Bayman, *The Northern Line: An Illustrated History*, Capital Transport, London, 1999, 14-17.

346 Andrea Pozzo (trans. John James): *Perspectiva pictorum et architectorum*, London, 1707, Fig. LII.

347 Holinshed, op. cit., III, 16.

348 Robert Fludd, op. cit., I, a, 58.

demolished.[349] But, as the Lord Mayor's church, and perhaps recognized also as a necessary temple of the Virtues, the building remained, and was fortunate to escape the aerial bombardment in World War II that devastated so much else in London.

St Martin-in-the-Fields: James Gibbs and the Symmetry of Order

The site of St Martin-in-the-Fields appears to have possessed a chapel as early as the twelfth century.[350] It is referred to in a document of 1222 as "the church and burial place of St Martin".[351] In the sixteenth century, as the city of Westminster was expanding in population, it was made into a parish church, taking a portion of the parish of St Margaret, Westminster.[352] Rebuilt in 1543, and extended in 1607,[353] the old church finally had a tower with a cupola designed by Sir Christopher Wren.[354] The accretional building was demolished finally in 1721 for the construction of the present church. The Architect, James Gibbs (1682-1754) was born near Aberdeen, and, as a Scots Roman Catholic, had a different training from the other architects working in London at that period. He was educated in Scotland and Holland,[355] and then worked in Rome in the office of Carlo Fontana (1634-1714), an architect who had collaborated with the masters of the Roman Baroque of the previous generation, Pietro de Cortona (1596-1669) and Carlo Rainaldi (1611-1691).

---

349 Elizabeth Young & Wayland Young, *London's Churches*, Grafton, London, 1986, 169.

350 Ibid., 146.

351 Paul Devereux and Ian Thomson, *The Ley Hunter's Companion*, Thames & Hudson, London, 1979, 96.

352 Young & Young, op. cit., 146.

353 John Thomas Smith, op. cit., 78.

354 Ibid., 147.

355 Sacheverell Sitwell, *British Architects and Craftsmen*, Batsford, London, 1948, 107.

Fontana was a leading architect in the Rome of his time, elected head of the Academia de San Luca, 1686, 1692-1700. This academy was the guild to which all artists and architects

Three of the twelve Corinthian pillars that support St Mary Woolnoth.

in Rome belonged. The guild church, Santi Lucae Martina, was Cortona's masterpiece, built between 1635 and 1650. This was a reconstruction of a church built in the sixth century on the ruins of the Senate Secretariat of ancient Rome. S. Luca (St. Luke) is the patron saint of artists. Fontana assisted Pietro de Cortona (aka Pietro Berrettini) in the design of Santa Maria delle Pace in Rome in 1655. Some of Cortona's work shows influences of the ancient Roman temple of the goddess Fortuna at Praeneste (Palastrina). With Rainaldi, Fontana designed the church of Santa Maria del Miracoli for Pope Alexander VII (1658). Its tetrastyle portico, somewhat of an innovation at the time, may be the inspiration for Gibbs's design for St Martin. Fontana was a master of the sacred art of geometry who designed an oval church to be erected inside the Flavian Amphitheatre (the Colosseum) as a memorial to the Christians who died there at the hands of gladiators or the teeth and claws of wild beasts. It remained an unbuilt project, though the design survives. His most notable church is San Marcello on the Via del Corso in Rome (1682-1683).

As Fontana's one-time assistant, Gibbs had first-hand experience of the best and most innovative building design of the time. On his return to Great Britain in 1709, Gibbs was effectively the only modern Roman architect in the country, possessing a working knowledge of both ancient Roman buildings and contemporary design. Unlike his British colleagues, who had to study published works by the continental masters, or reports brought back by those who travelled, Gibbs had lived in Rome, seen and studied antique and modern buildings, and worked in the mileu of Roman classical forms in their Baroque interpretation as the assistant of one of the leading architects at the Academia de San Luca. Thus he had a unique understanding of the Roman tradition. His precise use of canonical eurythmy (beauty and fitness in a work produced by width suited to length and length suited to height[356]) distinguishes his two built London churches and

---

356 Marcus Vitruvius Pollio, *De Architectura*, I, 2, 3.

one steeple from those of Wren and his followers. The word 'eurhythmy' was appropriated in the early twentieth century by Rudolf Steiner in a quite different meaning as the name of his "new art of movement".[357] But this should not destroy its original Vitruvian meaning.

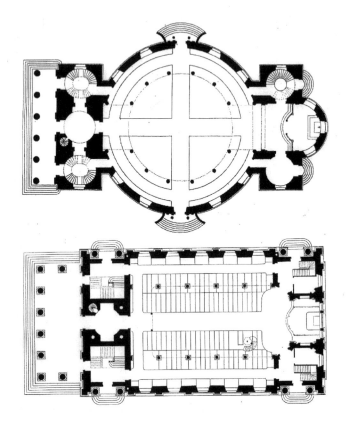

James Gibbs's plans for St Martin-in-the-Fields. The circular church (top) was rejected on grounds of cost, and the present one (below) actually constructed. After James Gibbs, 1728.

The west end and steeple of St Martin-in-the-Fields, drawing by the author, 1984.

Gibbs's two original designs for the new St Martin-in-the-Fields were for circular churches, perhaps based upon a 1693 design by Andrea Pozzo.[358] The round version would have had a portico to the west and an apse, containing the altar, to the east. It is orientated properly according to Christian tradition, with an eastward altar. Both churches, together with the chapel built by Gibbs in London, have ritually-correct orientations. As well as his built churches, Gibbs designed a number of others that were considered by the Commissioners in competition with alternative designs by other architects, among them being Thomas Archer, William Dickinson, Nicholas Hawksmoor, John James and Sir John Vanbrugh. One was a church with a northern altar, intended to be built on the problematic north-south site in Bloomsbury. The new St Martin's was built on the site of the former ritually-correct medieval church, so the orientation was never in doubt. The foundation stone of the new church was laid on the nineteenth of March, 1721[359] "with full religious and masonic rites".[360]

The steeple of St Martin-in-the-Fields.

The original wooden model of St Martin's made

---

358 David Watkin, *English Architecture*, Thames & Hudson, London, 2001, 122.

359 James Gibbs, *A Book of Architecture*, op. cit., IV.

360 J. McMaster, *A Short History of St Martin's in the Fields*, London, 1916, 75. For church foundation-stone rites and ceremonies and electional astrology see Pennick, Beginnings, 67-84, 257-261.

to Gibbs's design still exists in perfect condition. Until the nineteenth century, it was customary to make models of projected buildings. In the eighteenth century, as before, the word 'model' actually meant an original design, *later* used as a guide for the full-size building, not the reverse it now means, a small replica of something that already exists. A series of seventeen

Ornamented geometric coffering of the portico ceiling at St Martin-in-the-Fields.

models of church designs for the 1711 Commission were preserved in Westminster Abbey until around 1854, when they were sent to South Kensington. Apart from a damaged (and repaired) model of Gibbs's other London church, St Mary-le-Strand, their fate is unknown, although it is possible that they were destroyed in the 1940s in the Blitz.[361] But Flitcroft's model of St Giles-in-the-Fields, made in the early 1730s, was not among these and is preserved in the church itself.

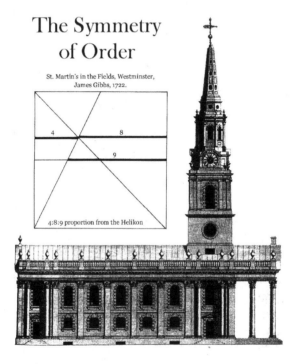

The Symmetry of Order (James Gibbs): the proportions of width, length and height of St Martin-in-the-Fields, 4:8:9 are defined by the Helikon diagram.

---

361 Paul Jeffery, 'The Commissioners' Models for the Fifty New Churches: Problems of identity and attribution', *The Georgian Group Journal*, 1995, 81-96.

St Martin's: The Proportional System

St Martin's is constructed according to Vitruvian principles of order, symmetry and eurythmy, creating a building in which the measurements, number and geometry of each component are interrelated and thus harmoniously reflected in the whole ensemble. The platform or podium, on which the church is built in

St Martin-in-the-Fields steeple, elevation and sections at various stages.

the manner of ancient Greek and Roman temples, is a double square in form. Excepting the sides of the Corinthian hexastyle portico, the outer walls come to the edge of the platform, which is approached by steps on the south, west and north sides. The façade is thus half as wide as the length of the building. On the façade, the cornice is half the height of a square whose height is the width of the church. The angle of the pediment is constructed according to Gibbs's published method.[362] The façade conforms to a geometrical system that governs the entire building, demonstrating Gibbs's "justness of Proportion" and emphasising the unity of parts and overall regularity of rhythms of the building that gives the work its phenomenally subtle unity. The same "symmetry of order"[363] defines the façades of his University Senate House in Cambridge, which is based on the same double-square geometric plan. It is exactly contemporary with St Martin's, having four foundation stones laid on the twenty-second of June, 1722.

St Martin-in-the-Field plan of steeple with its ruling geometry overlaid.

Through sacred geometry, timeless universal spiritual principles can be brought into physical presence, for "Architecture aims at Eternity".[364] Each part of St Martin's tower relates geometrically and proportionally to each other part, and, in turn, to the entire building. In this way, James Gibbs designed the church as the epitome of eurythmy. The overall ratio of

362 James Gibbs, *Rules for Drawing the Several Parts of Architecture*, London, 1732, XXVII, 2.

363 Gibbs, *A Book of Architecture*, Introduction, ii.

364 Wren, op. cit., 351.

width to length to height of St Martin's is 4:8:9, whole number proportions determinable by the helikon diagram. In classical terms, the ratio 4:8 is the duple ratio (2:1) and 8:9 the epogdoic ratio. The ratio of the façade height to the tower is 2:7; two units being the height of the top of the entablature, and seven being the remainder above it. The tower occupies one eighteenth of the ground area; the main body of the church twelve eighteenths (two thirds) and the portico three eighteenths.

Through Gibbs's book of 1728, the design of St Martin-in-the-Fields was very influential in the western colonies of the British Empire, being emulated in many parts of eastern North America and the West Indies. King's Chapel in Boston, Massachusetts by Peter Harrison,[365] and the churches of St Michael and St Philip in Charleston, South Carolina, are the most notable. Most of these churches were inevitably less well designed and built than St Martin's. Until 1826, St Martin's faced onto a narrow lane, on the opposite side of which, a little to the north, was the separate parish burial ground, called St Martin's Churchyard. It appears on John Rocque's accurate map of London,

An exterior bay on the south side of St Martin-in-the-Fields that shows the proportional arrangement of pilaster, windows and cornice. The window-surrounds are typical of Gibbs.

365 John Coolidge, 'Peter Harrison's first design for King's Chapel, Boston', *De Artibus Opuscula*, XL, 1961, 64-75.

published in 1747. A parish workhouse was built later on part
of this graveyard. Rocque's map appears to show much wider
steps than currently rise to the church podium, also giving
access to an alley called Lancaster Court that ran along the
south side of the church and then southeast to the Strand.
Around the church and graveyard was a slum area, 'rooker-
ies' known as 'The Bermudas'.[366] In that year the buildings
opposite and around it were demolished.[367] Duncannon Street
replaced the insanitary Lancaster Court. The construction of
Trafalgar Square and the National Gallery transformed the
area, and gave St Martin's the splendid setting it has today.

*South wall exterior of Nicholas Hawksmoor's Christ Church
Spitalfields showing arcaded arrangement with round windows above
that illuminate the gallery within.*

---

366 Professor T.G. Bonney, *Cathedrals, Abbeys and Churches in England and
    Wales*, Cassell, London, 1891, Vol.I, 314.

367 John Thomas Smith, op. cit, 78.

St Martin-in-the-Fields became a major London landmark when the buildings near it were demolished and Trafalgar Square was constructed, shown in this engraving from 1890.

The northern one of the twin towers at the west end of Westminster Abbey, designed by Nicholas Hawksmoor and constructed in 1733.

Later 18th century churches include St John, Wapping, the only part of the church not destroyed in the Blitz of 1940–41 being the tower and cupola.

St Botolph, Bishopsgate.

A series of Classical churches was constructed in London in the early 19th century, mostly under the influence of neoclassicism. St Marylebone church, designed by Thomas Hardwick and constructed in 1813. This church is orientated north-south with the altar to the south.

All Saint's Marylebone, designed by Sir John Soane and built 1828 as part of a series of churches to commemmorate Napoleon's defeat in 1815. This is orientated north-south with the altar in the north. It is no longer consecrated as a church.

In the seventeenth century, the myths, legends and stories told by writers such as Matthew of Westminster and Raphael Holinshed were everyday currency, known by every learned Briton and an integral part of their identity. William Blake saw all myths as recurrent, attaching themselves to particular individuals whilst having a more archaic, primal, origin (e.g. "The stories of Arthur are the Acts of Albion applied to a Prince of the Fifth Century"). Of course, they may not be taken literally, though some do in angry opposition to the world, but absence of historical veracity does not mean that they are of no value. On the contrary, the principles expressed in the myths are eternal, referring to 'the way of the world', the way things happen and the processes of development, rather than any particular definitive event in the past that gave rise to them.

The principles and practical uses described in this book are inspired by the world-view of European Traditional Spirituality. The inspiration of and reference to the local legendarium by the architects who rebuilt the city after the Great Fire cannot be discounted as meaningless, worthless or irrelevant. Sneering at tradition is a modern and post-modern projection of present-day devalued materialist and literalist beliefs back upon another era whose people had a different world-view, that of the Eternal Tradition. To use modern or post-modern one-dimensional critical techniques upon past understandings is anachronistic. But, too often, they are used as a tool by those who have the ulterior agenda, of destroying tradition and continuity, and supplanting them with their particular regime.

The rebuilding of London's temples after the Great Fire shows that the spiritual dimension of making, the Spiritual Arts and Crafts, are ever-present in the creation of effective holy spaces and sacred artefacts. Making things in this honourable

way is a two-way process, both of personal spiritual development and an outward manifestation of the power of the
cosmos present in all being. The Spiritual Arts and Crafts seek
to realize spiritual ideals materially through a process that itself
is the craftsperson's spiritual journey. The architects, artists
and craftspeople who built the new London temples certainly
brought spiritual principles into a physical form that continues
to resonate three centuries later.

Subsequently, in the early nineteenth century, although classi-
cal-style churches continued to be built, the influence of Greek
neoclassicism took their design in a different direction. The
designs of Sir John Soane and others who built the 'Waterloo
Churches' in celebration of the defeat of Napoleon have their
own special qualities, but are considerably removed from the
monumental influence of Sir Christopher Wren. But every
London church of the time is an expression of this venerable
spiritual tradition. The architects and craftsmen whose work we
can still experience in the twenty-first century had the task of
fusing symbol and form, which the language of Classical architecture enabled them to do. By working within tradition, they
were able to express both the contemporary sanctity of these
buildings, the continuity of the sacred place, and their cultural
meaning within the legendarium. By following tradition, their
work was part of that cyclic renewal that is characteristic of
the way of Nature. Living in an age when tradition has become
the exception rather than the norm, we can see that progress is
no longer equated with a renewal of the Eternal Tradition, but
with constant change and the destruction of the old with its
replacement by something completely unrelated, which itself
will not last long before something else replaces it. For most of
the twentieth century, 'the shock of the new' was a recommendation for the New Brutalism and other fashionable political
movements that aimed to destroy tradition forever. The disas-
trous results are well-known. But timeless principles cannot be

abolished, only ignored. To so ignore them, however, leads to spiritual impoverishment, as can be seen. The spiritual buildings of post-Great Fire London were genuinely reflective of their present time, whilst expressing true principles in continuity with their predecessors. Tradition allows constant renewal without breaking continuity, whilst allowing creative freedom in its contemporary re-statement. Rather than being a historical reminiscence or a nostalgic reflection on times past, it is a call to action in the present.

The contemporary setting of the city churches: the steeple of St Nicholas Cole Abbey reflected in the glass curtain wall of a modern office building.

BIBLIOGRAPHY

Act of Parliament, *Statute at Large*, IX Anne, c.22, 1711

Ackermann, J.S., 'Ars sine Scientia nihil est', Gothic Theory of Architecture at the 'Cathedral of Milan', *The Art Bulletin.* Vol. XXXI No. 1, 1949, 84-111

Anon., *The Tablet of Memory*, J. Bew, London, 1774

Anon., *Yearbook 1953/54*, St George's Church, Bloomsbury, London, 1954

Alberti, Leon Battista, trans. Giacomo Leoni: *The Ten Books of Architecture (De re aedificatoria)*, London, 1755

Ashmole, Elias (ed. C.H. Josten), *Elias Ashmole (1617-1692), His Autobiographical and Historical Notes*, London, 1966

William Atkins, *A History of St George, Hanover Square*, London, 1976

Avery, Charles & David Finn, *Bernini: Genius of the Baroque*, London, 1997

Baillie Scott & Mackay Hugh, *Houses and Gardens*, George Newnes, London, 1906

Barchusen, Johann Conrad, *Elementa chemiae*, Leiden, 1718

Barocchi, P. (ed.), *Scritti d'arte del Cinquecento*, Milan 1971

Barozzi di Vignola, Jacopo, *Le due regole della prospettiva pratica*, Rome, 1633

Bath, Michael, 'Recent Developments in Emblem Studies', *De Zevientiende Eeuw,* 6-2 (1990), 91-96

Battisti, E., *Brunelleschi, the Complete Works*, London, 1981

Bauchhenss, Gerhard, *Jupitergigantensäulen*, Aalen, 1976

Beard, Geoffrey, *The Work of Christopher Wren*, Bloomsbury, London, 1982

Behm, Jacob (Jakob Boehme), trans. H.B., *Four Tables of Divine Revelation*, London, 1654

Bennett, J.A. & Brown, Olivia, *The Compleat Surveyor*, Whipple

Museum of Science, Cambridge, 1982

Bibiena, Giuseppe Galli, *Architteurae Prospettive*, Vienna, 1740

Biermann, Veronica; Grönert, Alexander; Jobst, Christoph & Stewering, Roswitha, *Architectural Theory From the Renaissance to the Present*, Taschen, London, 2003

Blake, William, *Milton a Poem*, Eds. and intro. Robert N. Essick & Joseph Viscomi, The William Blake Trust/Tate Gallery, London, 1998

Bonney, Professor T.G., *Cathedrals, Abbeys and Churches in England and Wales*, 2 vols., Cassell, London, 1891

Bordino, Giovanni, *De Rebus Praeclare Gestis a Sixto V Pont. Max*, Rome, 1588

Borsi, Francesco (trans. Rudolf G. Carpanini), *Leon Battista Alberti: The Complete Works*, Electa, Milan, 1986

Britton, John & Pugin, Augustus, *Illustrations of Public Buildings of London...* 2 vols., London, 1825-1828

Brolin, Brent C., *Architectural Ornament, Bansihment and Return*, New York, 2000

Brown, Terry, *English Martial Arts*, Anglo-Saxon Books, Hockwold-cum-Wilton, 1997

Browne, Sir Thomas, *Hydrotaphia, in Religio Medici and Other Essays*, E. Grant Richards, London, n.d

Bryant, Arthur, *Restoration England*, Collins, London, 1960

Bucher, F., *Architector: the Lodge Books and Sketchbooks of Medieval Architects*, New York, Abaris, 1979

Burton, Robert, *The Anatomy of Melancholy*, 3 vols, G. Bell, London, 1926

Bussagli, Marco, *Rome: Art and Architecture*, Königswinter, 2000

Butler, Alfred Joshua, *Coptic Churches of Egypt*, The Clarendon Press, Oxford, 1884

Campbell, Colen, *Vitruvius Britannicus*, London, 1715

Castañeda, Joseph, *Compendio de los Diez Libros de Arquitectura de Vitruvio* ... Madrid, 1761

Cataneo, Pietro, *I quattro primi libri di Architettura*, Venice, 1554

Cats, Jacob, *Silenus Alcibiadis, sive Proteus* and *Spiegel van den ouden ened nieuwen tijdt*, Middelburg, 1618

Cesariano, Cesare, *Di Lucio Vitruvio Pollione de Architectura*, Como, 1521

Clarke, B.F.L., *Parish Churches of London*, London, 1966

Clayton, John, *The Works of Sir Christopher Wren*, London, 1849

Cobb, Gerald, *The Old Churches of London*, Batsford, London, 1948

Colonna, Francesco, trans.& ed. Jocelyn Godwin, *Hypnerotomachia Poliphili*, Thames & Hudson, London, 2003

Colvin, H.M., 'The Church of St Mary Aldermary and its rebuilding after the Great Fire of London', *Architectural History*, 24, 1981, 24-31

Cook, G.H., *The English Mediaeval Parish Church*, London, 1961

Coolidge, John, 'Peter Harrison's first design for King's Chapel, Boston', *De Artibus Opuscula*, XL, 1961, 64-75

Cornford, F. (trans), *Plato's Cosmology: The Timaeus of Plato translated with a running commentary*, London, Routledge & Kegan Paul, 1937

Critchlow, Keith, *Order in Space*, London, Thames & Hudson, 1969

Crowe, Norman, *Nature and the Idea of a Man-Made World*, M.I.T. Press, Cambridge, Mass., 1995

Crossley, F.H., *English Church design 1040 to 1540 A.D*, London, Batsford, 1948

Darke, Jo, *The Monument Guide to England and Wales*, Macdonald, London, 1991

Defoe, Daniel, *A Journal of the Plague Year*, London, 1721

de Leenheer, Jan, *Theatrum Stultorum*, Brussels, 1669

della Porta, Giambatista, *Magia naturalis*, 2 vols., Venice, 1558 de Bazel, K.P.C., 'Onze tijd en het werk van M. de Klerk', *Wendingen*, 2, 2, 1919, 3-12

de Lobkowitz, Juan Caramuel, *Architectura civil recta, y obliqua*, 3 vols., Vigevano, 1678

de l'Orme, Philibert, *Le premier tome de l'architecture*, Paris, 1567

De Vries, Vredeman, *Architectura*, Antwerp, 1577

Dennis, G., *The Cities and Cemeteries of Etruria*, 2 vols., London, 1848

Devereux, Paul and Ian Thomson, *The Ley Hunter's Companion*, Thames & Hudson, London, 1979

Dietterlin, Wendel, *Architectura von Ausstheilung, Symmetria und Proportion der Fünff Seulen*, Nuremberg, 1598

Dölger, Franz Josef, 'Zur Symbolic der altchristlichen Taufhauses: Das Oktagon und die Symbolik der Achtzahl', *Antike und Christentum*, Münster, 1933

Doré, Gustave and Jerrold, Blanchard, *London: A Pilgrimage*, London, 1872

Downes, Kerry, *Hawksmoor*, London, Zwemmer, 1979

Downes, Kerry, *Hawksmoor*, London, Thames & Hudson, 1970

Downes, Kerry, *The Architecture of Wren*, Redhedge, Over Wallop, 1988

Downes, Kerry, *A Thousand years of the Church of St Stephen Walbrook*, St Stephen Walbrook, London, N.d. (c. 2000)

du Prey, Pierre de la Ruffinière, *Hawksmoor's London Churches, Architecture and Theology*, University of Chicago Press, Chicago, 2000

Davies, J.H.V., 'Nicholas Hawksmoor', *Royal Institute of British Architects Journal*, Vol.69, No.10, October 1962

Diels, H., *Die Fragmente der Vorsokratiker*, Berlin, 1934

Drake-Carnell, F.J., *Old English Customs and Ceremonies*, Batsford, London, 1938

Dryden, John, *On the Pythagorean Philosophy*

Durandus, Guilielmus (William Durand), trans. Neale, J.M. & Webb, B., *Rationale Divinorum Officiorum*, London 1843

Endell, August, 'Originalität und Tradition', *Deutsche Kunst und Dekoration*, 9, 1901-1902, 289-296

Evelyn, John (ed. E.S. de Beer), *Diary and Correspondence*, London, 1894

Fabri, Ria, 'Perspectiefjes in het spel 'Optische Spielereien' in Antwerpse kunstkasten uit de zeventiende eeuw', *De Zeventiende Eeuw*, 15 (1999), 109–117

Faral, E., *Les Arts Poétiques du XIIe et du XIIIe Siècle*, Paris, 1924

Fergusson, James, *A History of Architecture in All Countries*, John Murray, London, 1893

Fernee, Ben, *Geomantic Survivals in York*, Northern Earth Mysteries, York, 1985

Flamel, Nicolas, trans. Eirenaeus Orandus, *His Exposition of the Hieroglyphical Figures*, London, 1624

Flemming, W., *Die Begründung der modernen Aesthetik und Kunstwissenschaft durch L.B. Alberti*, Berlin/Leipzig, 1916

Fludd, Robert, *Utriusque Cosmi Maioris scilicet et Minoris Metaphysica, Physica atque Technica Historia*, 2 vols., Johann Theodor de Bry, Oppenheim, 1617

Frankl, Paul, 'The Secret of the Medieval Masons', *The Art Bulletin*, XXVII, 1945, 46-64

Freeman, Rosemary, *English Emblem Books*, London, 1948

Gadol, J., *Leon Battista Alberti: Universal Man of the Early Renaissance*, Chicago/London, 1969

Gaudí, Antoni, 'Originality III', in Maria Antonietta Crippa, *Living Gaudí*, Rizzoli, New York, 2002

Geraghty, A., 'Nicholas Hawksmoor and the Wren city church steeples', *The Georgian Group Journal*, Volume 10 (2000), 1-14

Gettings, Fred, *Dictionary of Occult, Hermetic and Alchemical Signs*, Routledge & Kegan Paul, London, 1981

Giorgi, Francesco, *De Harmonia Mundi totius*, Venice, 1525

Gibbs, James, *A Book of Architecture containing Designs of Buildings and Ornaments*, London 1728

Gibbs, James, *Rules for Drawing the Several Parts of Architecture*, London, 1732

Glass, Dorothy F., *Studies on Cosmatesque Pavements*, BAR International Series 82, Oxford, 1980

Gombrich, E.H., *The Sense of Order: A Study in the Psychology of Decorative Art*, Phaidon Press, London, 1979

Götz, Wolfgang, *Zentralbau und Zentralbautendenz in der gotischen Architektur*, Berlin, 1968

Götze, Heinz, *Castel Del Monte: Geometric Marvel of the Middle Ages*, Prestel, Munich – New York, 1998

Godwin, George & Britton, John, *The Churches of London* ... 2 vols., London, 1839

Godwin, Jocelyn, *Robert Fludd: Hermetic philosopher and surveyor of two worlds*, Thames & Hudson, London, 1979

Gout, M., Wilhelmus van Nassouwe, *The Mausoleum of Prince William of Orange in the New Church in Delft*, Rijswijk, Quantes, n.d., c. 1990

Ghyka, Matila, *Le Nombre d'or*, 3 vols, Gallimard, Paris, 1931

Ghyka, Matila, *Esthétique des proportions dans la Nature et dans les Arts*, Gallimard, Paris, 1933

Groves, Derham, *Feng-Shui and Western Building Ceremonies*, Graham Brash, Singapore, 1991

Guarini, Guarino, *Architettura civile*, Turin, 1737

Hamill, John, *The Craft: A History of English Freemasonry*, Crucible, Wellingborough, 1986

Hammond, J.H., *The Camera Obscura, A Chronicle*, Bristol, 1981

Hancox, Joy, *The Byrom Collection: Renaissance Thought, The Royal Society and the Building of the Globe Theatre*, Jonathan Cape, London, 1992

Harper, Charles G., *Queer Things About London*, Cecil Palmer, London, 1931

Harris, John; Orgel, Stephen, & Strong, Roy, *The King's Arcadia: Inigo Jones and the Stuart Court*, Arts Council of Great Britain, London, 1973

Hart, V, & Hicks, P. (trans), *Sebastiano Serlio: On Architecture*, Yale University Press, New Haven, 1996

Hart, Vaughan, *Nicholas Hawksmoor*, Yale University Press, New Haven & London, 2002

Harvey, John, *Gothic England: A Survey of National Culture*, London, Batsford, 1947

Heath, T.L., *Euclid: The Thirteen Books of the Elements*, Cambridge University Press, Cambridge, 1926

Heilbron, J.L., *The Sun in the Church: Cathedrals as Solar Observatories*, Harvard University Press, Cambridge, Mass./London, 1999

Helliesen, Sidsel, 'Thronus Iustitiae, A Series of Pictures of Justice by Joachim Witwael', *Oud Holland*, 91, 1977, 232-266

Herrick, Robert, *The Poems of Robert Herrick*, Grant Richards, London, 1902

Hersey, G.L., *Pythagorean Palaces: Magic and Architecture in the Italian Renaissance*, Cornell University Press, Ithaca, N.Y., 1976

Hitchcock, Henry-Russell, *Rococo Architecture in Southern Germany*, London, Phaidon, 1968

Hogarth, William, *The Analysis of Beauty*, London, 1753

Hogg, Ian V., *Fortress: A History of Military Defence*, Macmillan, London, 1975

Holden, Alan, *Shapes, Space and Symmetry*, New York, Dover, 1971

Hooft, P.C., *Emblemata Amatoria*, W. Lansz, Amsterdam, 1611

Hopton, Arthur, *Baculum geodaeticum*, London, 1610

Horne, M.A.C., *The Northern Line*, Douglas Rose, Finchley, 1987

Horne, Mike & Bayman, Bob, *The Northern Line: An Illustrated History*, Capital Transport, London, 1999

Hughes, T. Harold & Lamborn, E.A.G., *Towns and Town-planning Ancient & Modern*, Oxford, Clarendon Press, 1923

Hutton, Edward, *The Cosmati*, Routledge & Kegan Paul, London, 1950

Hutton, Ronald, *The Stations of the Sun*, Oxford University Press, Oxford, 1996

Icher, François (trans. Zielonka, Anthony), *Building the Great Cathedrals*, Harry N. Abrams, New York, 1998

Icher, François (trans. Goodman, John), *The Artisans and Guilds of France*, Harry N. Abrams, New York, 2000

Inwards, Richard, *Weather Lore* (c. 1893), Pryor, Whitstable, 1999

Jackson, Peter, *George Scharf's London: Sketches and Watercolours of a Changing City*, 1820-50, John Murray, London 1987

Jardine, Lisa, *On A Grander Scale: The Outstanding Life of Sir Christopher Wren*, HarperCollins, London 2002

Jeffery, Paul, 'Thomas Archer's Deptford rectory; a reconstruction', *The Georgian Group Journal*, 1993, 32–42

Jeffery, Paul, 'Unbuilt Gibbs: A Fresh Look at His Designs for the 1711 Act Church Commissioners', *The Georgian Group Journal*, 1994, 11–19

Jeffery, Paul, 'The Commissioners' Models for the Fifty New Churches: Problems of identity and attribution', *The Georgian Group Journal*, 1995, 81–96

Johnson, Walter, *Byways in British Archaeology*, University Press, Cambridge, 1912

Jones, Bernard E., *Freemasons' Guide and Compendium*, Harrap, London, 1963

Jones, Prudence: 'Geomancy – Origins of the Word from the Oxford English Dictionary', *Ancient Mysteries* 16, 1980, 3–11

Jones, Prudence, & Pennick, Nigel, *A History of Pagan Europe*, Routledge, London, 1995

Jonson, Ben (W. Gifford, ed.), *The Works of Ben Jonson*, 9 vols, London, 1816

Kauffman, S., & Knox, G, *Fantastic and Ornamental Drawings*, Portsmouth College of Art and Design, Portsmouth 1969

Kell, J. T., *Practical Astronomy during the Seventeenth Century: A Study of Almanac-makers in America and England*, Ph.D. thesis, Harvard, 1977

Kern, Otto, *Orphicorum Fragmenta*, Berlin, 1922

Kieser, Franciscus, *Cabala chymica*, Mühlhausen, 1606

Kircher, Athanasius, *Obeliscus Pamphilius*, Rome, 1650

Kircher, Athanasius, *Musurgia universalis*, Rome, 1650

Kircher, Athanasius, *Ars magna lucis*, Rome, 1665

Kostof, Spiro, *A History of Architecture: Settings and Rituals*, Oxford University Press, Oxford, 1985

Krautheimer, R., 'Santo Stefano Rotondo a Roma e la chiese del San Sepolcro a Gerusalemme', *Rivista Archeologica Cristiana*, 12, 1935, 51–102

Kruft, Hanno-Walter, *A History of Architectural Theory from Vitruvius to the Present*, Princeton Architectural Press, New York, 1994

Kuhn, J.R., 'Measured appearances: Documentation and Design in Early Perspective Drawing', *Journal of the Warburg and Courtauld Institutes*, LIII, 1990, 114–132

Gordon J. Laing, *Survivals of Roman Religion*, Harrap, London, 1931

Landewehr, John, *Emblem Books in the Low Countries, 1554–1949*, Haentjens, Dekker & Gumbert, Utrecht, 1970

Langley, Batty, *Ancient Masonry,* London, 1736

Lauweriks, Johannes Ludovicus Mathieu, 'Het Titanische in de Kunst', *Wendingen* 2 Nr. 4, 1919

Lawlor, Robert, *Sacred Geometry: Philosophy and Practice*, Thames & Hudson, London, 1982

Leapman, Michael, *Inigo: The Troubled Life of Inigo Jones, Architect of the English Renaissance*, Headline, London 2004

Leeman, F.W.G., *Alciatus' Emblemata: Denkbeelden en voorbeelden*, Bauma, Gronigen, 1984

Lees-Milne, James, *St Peter's*, Hamish Hamilton, London, 1967

Lethaby, W.R., *Architecture, Mysticism and Myth*, London, 1892

Lethaby, W.R., *Westminster Abbey, and the King's Craftsmen*, London, 1906

Lethaby, W.R., *Londinium: Architecture and the Crafts.* (1923), Benjamin Blom, New York, 1972

Linden, Stanton J. (ed.), *The Alchemy Reader*, Cambridge, Cambridge University Press, 2003

Lister, Raymond, *Great Works of Craftsmanship*, G. Bell & Sons, London, 1967

Loftie, W.J., *A Brief Account of Westminster Abbey*, Seeley, London, 1894

Leybourn, William, *Dialling*, London, 1682

Maass, Michael, & Berger, Klaus W. (eds.), *Planstädte der Neuzeit vom 16. bis 18. Jahrhundert*, G. Braun, Karlsruhe, 1990

Macdonald, William L., *The Pantheon: Design, Meaning, and Progeny*, Harvard University Press, Cambridge, Mass., 1976

Macdonald, William L. & Pinto, John A., *Hadrian's Villa and Its Legacy*, Yale University Press, New Haven & London, 1995

MacDonnell, Joseph, *Jesuit Geometers: A Study of Fifty-six Prominent Jesuit Geometers During the First Two Centuries of Jesuit History*, The Institute of Jesuit Sources & The Vatican Observatory, St Louis/Vatican City, 1989

Macoy, Robert, *A General History, Cyclopedia and Dictionary of Freemasonry*, Masonic Publishing Company, New York, n.d. c. 1890

Mackmurdo, Arthur Heygate, *Wren's City Churches*, London, 1883

Maier, Michael, *Atalanta fugiens*, Oppenheim, 1618

March, Lionel, *Architectonics of Humanism: Essays on Number in Architecture*, Academy Editions, London, 1998

Marta, Roberto, *Architettura romana*, Edizione Kappa, Rome, 1990

Martin, Jean, *Architecture ou Art de bien bastir*, Paris, 1547

Matthews, John & Potter, Chesca (eds.), *The Aquarian Guide to Legendary London*, Aquarian Press, Wellingborough, 1990

Matthew of Westminster, trans. C.D. Yonge, *The Flowers of History*, Henry G. Bohn, London, 1853

McFadzean, Patrick, *Astrological Geomancy, An Introduction*, Limited edition of 40, Northern Earth Mysteries, York, 1985

McMaster, J., *A Short History of St Martin's in the Fields*, London, 1916

Milton, John, *Paradise Regained*, London, 1671

Milton, John, *The Poetical Works of John Milton*, Routledge, London, n.d., c. 1880

Mockridge, Philip & Patricia, *Weathervanes of Great Britain*, Hale, London, 1990

Monemutensis, Gaufridus (Geoffrey of Monmouth), *History of the Kings of Britain*

Mowl, Tim, & Earnshaw, Brian, *John Wood: Architect of Obsession*, Millstream Books, Bath, 1988

Müller, Werner, *Grundlagen gotischer Bautechnik*, Munich, 1990

Nobel, John V. & de Solla Price, Derek J., 'The Water Clock in the Tower of the Winds', *The American Journal of Archaeology*, 1968, 345-355

Norberg-Schulz, Christian, *Genius Loci: Towards a Phenomenology of Architecture*, Rizzoli, New York, 1980

Nussbaum, Norbert, *German Gothic Church Architecture*, Yale University Press, New Haven/London, 2000

Obrist, Hermann, 'Die Zukunft unserer Architektur: Ein Kapitel über das Persönliche und das Schöpferische', *Dekorative Kunst*, 4, 1901, 329-349

Ottenheym, K.A., 'Mathematische uitgangspunten van de Hollandse bouwkunst in de 17de eeuw', *De zeventiende eeuw*, 7, 1, 1991, 17-35

Orme, Nicholas, *Exeter Cathedral as it was 1050-1550*, Devon Books, Exeter, 1986

Palladio, Andrea, *I Quattro Libri dell'Architettura*, Venice, 1570

Papworth, John W., *Roriczer on Pinnacles*, Architectural Publications Society, London, 1848–1853

Pennick, Nigel, *The Mysteries of King's College Chapel*, Cokaygne Press, Cambridge, 1974

Pennick, Nigel, 'Glastonbury Abbey', in Roberts, Anthony (ed.), *Glastonbury: Ancient Avalon: New Jerusalem*, Zodiac House, London, 1976

Pennick, Nigel, *The Ancient Science of Geomancy*, Thames & Hudson, London, 1979

Pennick, Nigel, *Sacred Geometry*, Thorsons, Wellingborough, 1980

Pennick, Nigel, *The Cosmic Axis*, Runestaff-Old England, Cambridge, 1985

Pennick, Nigel, 'Parametric Diagrams'(sic), in Joy Hancox, *The Byrom Collection, Renaissance Thought, The Royal Society and the Building of the Globe Theatre*, Jonathan Cape, London, 1992, 'Appendix One', 291–292

Pennick, Nigel, *Celtic Sacred Landscapes*, Thames & Hudson, London, 1997

Pennick, Nigel, *Beginnings: Geomancy, Builders' Rites and Electional*

Astrology in the European Tradition, Capall Bann, Chieveley, 1999

Pennick, Nigel, *The Complete Illustrated Guide To Runes*, Element, London, 1999

Pennick, Nigel, *Masterworks: The Arts and Crafts of Traditional Buildings in Northern Europe*, Heart of Albion Press, Wymeswold 2002

Pennick, Nigel, 'The Goddess Zisa', *Tyr*, Vol. 1, 2002, 107–109

Pennick, Nigel, *On The Spiritual Arts and Crafts*, Old England House, Cambridge 2004

Pennick, Nigel, *The Bloomsbury Wonder*, Spiritual Land, Cambridge, 2005

Pennick, Nigel, *The Mysteries of St Martin's: Sacred Geometry and the Symmetry of Order*, Spiritual Land, Cambridge, 2005

Pennick, Nigel, *New Troy Resurgent: Continuity and Renewal through the Eternal Tradition*, Spiritual Land, Cambridge, 2005

Pennick, Nigel, *The Eldritch World*, Lear Books, Earl Shilton, 2006

Pennick, Nigel, *The Spiritual Arts and Crafts*, Spiritual Arts & Crafts Publishing, Cambridge, 2006

Pennick, Nigel, *The Ideal Tower* (2009), The Society of Esoteric Endeavour, Hinckley, n.d.

Pennick, Nigel, *Secrets of King's College Chapel*, Aeon, London, 2012

Pennick, Nigel & Paul Devereux, *Lines on the Landscape*, Robert Hale, London, 1989

Pennick, Nigel & Helen Field, *Muses and Fates*, Capall Bann, Milverton, 2004

Pennick, Nigel & Professor M. Gout, *Sacrale Geometrie: Verborgen Lijnen in de Bouwkunst*, Uitgeverij Synthese, The Hague, 2004

Penrose, Francis C., 'St Stephen's Walbook', *Royal Institute of British Architects Transactions* N.S. VI, 1890

Penrose, Francis, *Principles of Athenian Architecture*

Perrault, Claude, *Ordonnances des Cinq Espèces de Colonne*, Paris, 1676

Petronotis, Argyres, *Bauritzlinien und andere Aufschnürungen am Unterbau griechischer Bauwerke in der Archaik und Klassik: Eine Studie zur Baukunst und technik der Hellenen*, privately published, Munich, 1968

N. Petter, *Onderrichtinge der Vooreffelicke Worstel-Kunst*, Amsterdam, 1674

Pleij, Herman (trans. Diane Webb), *Dreaming of Cockaigne: Medieval Fantasies of the Perfect Life*, Columbia University Press, New York, 2001

Power, Cyril E., *English Mediaeval Architecture*, 3 vols., London, 1923

Pozzo, Andrea, *Perspectiva pictorum et architectorum*, 2 vols, Rome, 1693–1700

Praz, Mario, *Studies in Seventeenth Century Imagery*, London, 1939

Quiller-Couch, A.T., ed., *Early English Lyrics*, Clarendon Press, Oxford, n.d. c. 1910

Reuter, Otto Sigfrid (1936), trans., Behrend, Michael, *Skylore of the North*, The Library of the European Tradition, Cambridge, 1999

Ridgway, Christopher, & Williams, Robert (eds.), *Sir John Vanbrugh and Landscape Architecture in Baroque England*, Sutton, Stroud, 2004

Ripa, Cesare, *Baroque and Rococo Pictorial Images, the 1758–60 Hertel Edition of Ripa's Iconologia*, Dover Publications, New York, 1971

Roberts, Anthony, *Geomancy: A Synthonal Re-appraisal*, Zodiac House, Westhay, 1981

Robinson, H.W. & Adams, W., *The Diary of Robert Hooke, 1672–80*, London, 1935

Robinson, John Martin, *Temples of delight: Stowe Landscape Gardens*,

The National Trust/Pitkin, London/Andover, 1990

Robson, V.E., *Electional Astrology*, New York, 1972

Rock, D., *The Church of Our Fathers*, London, 1903

Roriczer, Matthäus, *Das Büchlein von der Fialen Gerechtigkeit*, Regensburg, 1486

Rosin, P.L., 'On Serlio's construction of ovals', *Mathematical Intelligencer*, Vol. 23, 1, 2001, 58-69

Royal Commission on Historic Monuments, *City of Cambridge*, 2 vols., London, 1959

Rykwert, J., *The Dancing Column: On Order in Architecture*, The MIT Press, Cambridge, Mass/London, 1996

Sadler, Henry, *Masonic Facts and Fictions*, London, 1887

Sartori, Paul, 'Ueber das Bauopfer', *Zeitschrift für Ethnologie*, 30, 1898, 1–54

Serlio, Sebastiano, *Tutte l'opere d'architettura et prospettiva*, Venice, 1619

Scamozzi, Vincenzo, *L'idea della architettura universale*, Venice, 1615

Schestag, Franz (ed.), *The Triumph of Maximilian I*, Adolf Holzhausen, Vienna, 1883–1884

Scott, W.S., *The Fantasticks: Donne, Herbert, Crashaw, Vaughan*, John Westhouse, London, 1945

Sekler, Eduard F. *Wren and His Place in European Architecture*, Macmillan, New York 1956

Shelby, L.R., *John Rogers: Tudor Military Engineer*, Clarendon Press, Oxford, 1967

Shelby, L.R., *Gothic Design Techniques: The Fifteenth Century Design Booklets of Mathes Roriczer and Hanns Schmuttermeyer*, London/Amsterdam, 1977

Shute, John, *The First and Chief Groundes of Architecture*, London, 1563

Siegloch, Magdalene, *How the New Art of Eurythmy Began*, Temple Lodge, London, 1997

Sitwell, Sacheverell, *British Architects and Craftsmen*, Batsford, London, 1948

Skinner, F.G., *Weights and Measures*, Her Majesty's Stationery Office, London, 1967

Smith, John Thomas, *The Streets of London*, Richard Bentley, London, 1861

Smith, Jonathan Z., *To Take Place: Toward Theory in Ritual*, University of Chicago Press, Chicago, 1987

Soo, Lydia M., *Wren's 'tracts' on Architecture and Other Writings*, Cambridge, Cambridge University Press, 1998

Speckle, Daniel, *Architectura Von Vestungen, Wie di zu unsern zeiten mögen erbawen werden*, Strasbourg, 1589

Speth, G.W., *Builders' Rites and Ceremonies: Two Lectures on the Folklore of Masonry*, Keble's Gazette, Margate, 1894

Spon, Jacob, *Recherches curieuses d'antiquité*, Paris, 1683

Spon, Jacob & George Wheler, *Voyage d'Italie, de Dalmatie, de Grèce, et du Levant faix aux années 1675 et 1676*, 2 vols., Lyon, 1678; Amsterdam, 1679; London, 1682

Stanley, Thomas, *The History of the Chaldaic Philosophy.*, London, 1701

Strachan, Gordon, *Chartres: Sacred Geometry, Sacred Space*, Floris, Edinburgh, 2003

Stukely, William, 'The family Memoirs of Rev. William Stukely, M.D', *Surtees Society Publications*, vol. 80, 1887

Swaan, Wim, *The Gothic Cathedral*, London, 1969

Szänto, Gregory, *Perfect Timing: The Art of Electional Astrology*, Wellingborough, 1989

Tavernor, Robert, *On Alberti and the Art of Building*, Yale University Press, New Haven/London, 1998

Taylor, A.E., *A Commentary on Plato's Timaeus*, London, 1928

Terry, Quinlan, 'The Origin of the Orders', *Archives d'Architecture Moderne*, 26, 1984

Thomas, Brian, *Geometry in Pictorial Composition*, Oriel Press, Newcastle upon Tyne, 1969

Thorpe, W. A., *English Glass*, Adam & Charles Black, London, 1949

Tickell, Thomas, *The Minor Poets: or The Works of the Most Celebrated Authors, Of whose Writings there are but small Remains*, 2 vols., Dublin, 1751

Tihon, Ferdinand, 'Notes sur les Perrons', *Bull. Inst. Arch. Liégeois* XI, 1910, 19–34

Timbs, John, *The Romance of London*, Warne, London & New York, n.d., c. 1887

Tinniswoode, Adrian, *His Invention So Fertile: A life of Christopher Wren*, Jonathan Cape, London, 2001

Tiraboschi, G., *Storia della letteratura itaiana*, 4 vols., Modena, 1772-1795

Toynbee, Jocelyn and Perkins, John Ward., *The Shrine of St Peter*, London, 1956

Thibault, Gerard, *L'Académie de l'Espeé*, Elzevier, Leyden, 1628

Trendall, A.D., *Red Figure Vases of South Italy and Sicily*, Thames & Hudson, London, 1989

Trubshaw, Bob, *Sacred Places: Prehistory and Popular Imagination*, Heart of Albion, Wymesword, 2005

Tzonis, Alexander, & Lefaivre, Liane, *Classical Architecture: The Poetics of Order*, M.I.T. Press, Cambridge, Mass., 1986

Vanbrugh, John, *Mr Van-Brugg's Proposals about Building ye New Churches* (c.1711), Bodleian Library, Bod MS Rawlinson B.376, fol. 351-352

Vaughan, Thomas, *Coelum Terrae*, London, 1650

Vagnetti, L., 'Concinnitas: Riflessioni sus significato di un termine Albertiano', *Studie decoumenti de architettura*, II, 1973

Valentine, Basil, *Artis auriferae quam chemiam vocant*, 3 vols., Basel, 1610

H. de la Fontaine Verwey, 'Gerard Thibault and his 'L'Académie de l'Espeé', *Quaerendo* VIII, Autumn 1978

Villalpando, Juan Bautista, *In Ezechielem Explanationes*, Rome, 1593–1604

Visscher, Roemer, *Sinnepoppen*, Amsterdam, 1614

Vitruvius Pollo, Marcus, trans. Morgan, Morris Hicky, *The Ten Books on Architecture*, Harvard University Press, Cambridge, Mass., 1914

von der Dunk, Thomas H., 'Hoe Klassiek is de Gothiek? Jacob van Campen en de Toren van de Nieuwe Kerk te Amsterdam', *Vijfentachtigste Jaarboek van Het Genootschap Amstelodamum*, 1993, 49–90

von Grundt, Abraham Leuthner, *Grundtliche Darstellung Der fünff Seüllen...* Prague, 1677

von Simson, Otto, 'Wirkungen des christlichen Platonismus auf die Entstehung der Gotik', in *Humanismus, Mystik und Kunst in der Welt des Mittelalters*, ed. Josef Koch, Leiden/Cologne, 1953

von Stolcenberg, D. Stolcius, *Viridarium chymicum*, Frankfurt, 1624

Waite, Arthur Edward, *The Real History of the Rosicrucians*, London, George Redway, 1887

Watkin, David, *English Architecture*, Thames & Hudson, London, 2001

Watkins, Alfred, *Early British Trackways*, Hereford & London, 1922

Watkins, Alfred, *The Old Straight Track*, Methuen, London, 1925, 124

Watson, Elizabeth See, *Achille Bocci and the Emblem Book as*

Symbolic Form, Cambridge University Press, Cambridge, 1993

Ware, Isaac, *The Complete Body of Architecture*, London, 1756

Webb, G. (ed.), 'The Letters and Drawings of Nicholas Hawksmoor Relating to the Building of the Mausoleum at Castle Howard 1726–1742', *Walpole Society*, 19, 1930–1931

Weiss, Roberto, *The Renaissance Discovery of Classical Antiquity*, Blackwell, Oxford, 1969

Westfall, C.W., 'Society, Beauty and the Humanist Architect in Alberti's *De re aedificatoria'*, *Studies in the Renaissance*, XVI, 1969, 61–79

Whinney, Margaret, *Wren*, Thames & Hudson, London, 1971

Whistler, Rex, 'Designs for the Theatre' (part 2), *The Masque* No.4, 1947

Whittick, Arnold, *Symbols: Signs and their Meaning and Uses in Design*, London, 1971

Williamson, George C., *Curious Survivals*, Herbert Jenkins, London, 1925

Willis, Robert & Clark, John Willis, *The Architectural History of the University of Cambridge*, 3 vols., Cambridge, 1886

Wittkower, Rudolf, *Architectural Principles in the Age of Humanism*, London, 1998

Wood, John, *The Origin of Building, or, the Plagiarism of the Heathens Detected*, London, 1754

Wotton, Henry, *The Elements of Architecture*, London, 1624

Wren, Christopher Jr. (ed.), *Parentalia, or, Memoirs of the Family of the Wrens*, London, 1750

Yates, Frances A., *The Art of Memory*, Routlege & Kegan Paul, London, 1966

Young, Elizabeth & Wayland, *London's Churches*, Grafton, London, 1986

APPENDIX 1

GLOSSARY OF TECHNICAL TERMS

AD QUADRATUM Geometrical scheme based upon the square and subdivisions of the square

AD TRIANGULUM Geometrical scheme based upon the equilateral triangle and its developments

AEDICULE Architectural frame of a niche or opening, with columns and entablature (q.v.)

ARCHITRAVE The lowest segment of the three parts of the entablature, also a moulding around a door or window

BEAK Complex moulding with convex geometric curve, semicircular concave undercut and oval-section lower part

BALDACCHINO Columned tabernacle covering a high altar

CAPITAL Head of a column, varying in form between the five classical orders

CARDINAL DIRECTIONS North, east, south and west. Between each are the intercardinal directions

CARDO The straight north-south road of the Etruscan Discipline, crossing the decumanus at the omphalos, or centre

CAVETTO Hollow moulding, generally a quadrant of a circle, but sometimes a more complex geometric curve

COMPOSITE Architectural order originating in Imperial Rome, combining Ionic volutes with Corinthian foliage

CORINTHIAN Athenian architectural order originating in the fifth century BCE. Acanthus-leaf capitals

CORNICE The upper segment of the entablature, also horizontal mouldings in other contexts

COSMIC EGG Symbol of the coming-into-being of the cosmos, the emanation of the material world, renewal and regeneration, and rebirth

CYMA RECTA Moulding that is concave above and convex below

CYMA REVERSA Moulding, convex above and concave below

DECUMANUS The straight east-west road of the Etruscan Discipline, crossing the cardo at the omphalos, or centre

DENTILS Regularly-spaced rectangular blocks on the underside of a cornice

DORIC Greek order with plain capitals and triglyph entablature (q.v.)

ECHINUS Moulding with four-section geometric curve, related to ovolo (q.v.)

ELECTIONAL ASTROLOGY The art of working out the optimal inceptional horoscope for a project in advance, and founding the venture at that moment (punctual time)

ENTABLATURE The section supported by the column, composed of architrave, frieze and cornice (q.v.)

FANE A Pagan sanctuary

FILLET Narrow horizontal band between curved mouldings on a base or cornice

FLUTING Parallel vertical concavities on a column or urn

FRIEZE The centre segment of the entablature. Usually a plain horizontal band, but in the Doric order it has triglyphs and metopes

FASCIA Horizontal moulding with vertical face

FOUNDATION The act of marking the beginning of a building, by ritually laying a stone with appropriate ceremonies

GADROONING A series of convex curves, such as the scalloped patterning in the lower part of a bowl or urn

GARLANDED COLUMN A spiral column with organic ornamentation

GEOMANCY The art of location of buildings etc. holistically in recognition of the site and the prevailing conditions, physical and spiritual

HELIKON Diagram noted by Ptolemy and associated with Sebastiano Serlio, the division of the square to produce whole-number ratios

HEXASTYLE Having a six-column-wide portico

INCEPTIONAL HOROSCOPE The horoscope of a project at its beginning (see electional astrology)

INTERCARDINAL DIRECTIONS The directions lying at forty-five degrees to the cardinal ones – north-east, south-east, south-west and north-east

IONIC ORDER Architectural order with voluted capitals. From Asia Minor originating mid-sixth century BCE

METOPE Square panel between triglyphs in the Doric frieze. Sometimes ornamented with emblemata

OCTASTYLE Having an eight-column-wide portico

OMPHALOS 'Navel of the World', spiritual centre-point, depicted as an egg-stone

ORDERS The forms of Classical columns and their associated ornament

ORIENTATION The alignment of a building towards the east

OVOLO Convex moulding, either a quadrant in form, or derived from a sevenfold diagonal

PEDESTAL Structure supporting a column

PILASTER Structure giving the appearance of a rectangular column built into a wall, structurally an integral part of the wall

PINE-APPLE The cone of the Pine tree, symbol of fecundity, healing and regeneration

PLINTH Supporting structure for a column, pedestal or temple

PODIUM Platform on which a temple stands

PORTICO An open ceremonial entrance to a building, leading to the main door

PTERON The upper part of the Mausoleum

PUNCTUAL TIME The exact moment for a foundation according to electional astrology

RUSTICATION Masonry with emphasised joints, producing strong textural contrasts

SCOTIA Hollow moulding with a two-centred curve

STYLOBATE Steps beneath a portico

TEMENOS The sacred enclosure around a grove, temple or church

TEMPIETTO 'Little temple', Italian term describing a small circular columniated building, in London, part of a steeple, as at St Mary-le-Bow

TETRASTYLE Having a four-columned portico

THYRSUS The wand of Dionysos, tipped with a pine-apple (q.v.)

TORUS Semicircular moulding in column bases

TRIGLYPH Element in the Doric frieze with the appearance of three raised verticals with small triangular elements (guttae) beneath

TROMPE L'OEIL A painting that 'tricks the eye' so that the viewer believes it is a real object

TUSCAN Order originating with the Etruscans, considered the most basic form of proto-Doric by renaissance writers

VESICA PISCIS 'Bladder of the fish', a geometrical form created by the interpenteration of two circles through each other's centre. It inscribes two equilateral triangles, base to base

VOLUTE Spiral

WRYTHEN DECORATION Spiral ornament made by twisting glass or metal when it is pliable

A CHRONOLOGY OF LONDON CLASSICAL CHURCH
BUILDING

There were fifty-six churches rebuilt in the City and environs in
the aftermath of the Great Fire, as well as St Paul's Cathedral.
More were built outside the City boundaries after the 1711
act. In addition to purely classical designs, significant Gothic
reconstructions and constructions are listed, for example
Hawksmoor's additions to Westminster Abbey. Few churches
ascribed to Wren are wholly his design, and this is not surpris-
ing in the context of how many designs had to be produced.
Wren was in charge of the project and he certainly author-
ized any design that was built. So the rubric 'Wren churches'
is more a matter of convenience than direct ascription. Wren
as virtually sole author is celebrated in Christopher Cockerell's
much-reproduced watercolour, *A Tribute to the Memory of Sir
Christopher Wren* (1838), and Arthur Heygate Mackmurdo's
influential book of 1883, *Wren's City Churches*.

St Paul's Cathedral, St Mary-le-Bow, St Stephen's Walbrook,
St Andrew's Holborn and St James, Piccadilly are almost totally
by Sir Christopher Wren. But not every design component in
any of these churches was necessarily by the named architect.
The associates and assistants of Wren frequently produced
their own designs for various parts, and perhaps whole
churches traditionally ascribed to Wren were not by him. In
some 'Wren' churches, the major hand in design was Robert
Hooke. Edward Woodroffe and John Oliver also may have
designed individual buildings. Events certainly affected the
buildings. No new church was begun in 1673, when England
was engaged in a naval war with Holland. Steeple design altered
radically after 1703. When Hooke died in 1703, Nicholas
Hawksmoor became a more important influence. Hawksmoor
certainly designed some steeples of 'Wren' churches, as did

William Dickinson, and later he worked in association with John James. But how much the design change came about because of Hawksmoor and how much was a response to the November 1703 hurricane is unknown.

The many individual master craftsmen who worked in the different trades also made their contributions to particular ornaments and items such as sculptural features, window grilles, doorplates, hinges, pulpits, pews and other church furniture. A number of steeples, built some years after the church body was complete, were designed by hands other than the main named architect. When a single date is given for a later steeple, that is the year of completion.

Architect: Sir Christopher Wren (1632–1723) and associates

St Benet Fink, 1670–1681. Demolished 1846.

St Dionys Backchurch, 1670–1677, tower 1685. Demolished 1878.

St Lawrence Jewry, 1670–1681.

St Mary Aldermanbury, 1670–1674. Dismantled after Blitz damage 1940 and rebuilt in Fulton, Missouri, USA, 1964–1969.

St Mary-at-Hill, 1670–1672, lantern 1695.

St Mary-le-Bow, 1670–1675, steeple 1680.

St Michael, Wood Street, 1670–1673, lantern 1687. Demolished 1897.

St Mildred, Poultry, 1670–1677. Demolished 1872.

St Olave, Old Jewry, 1670–1679. Demolished 1887. Tower remaining.

St Bride, Fleet Street, 1671–1678, steeple 1701–1703.

St George, Botolph Lane, 1671–1679. Demolished 1904.

St Magnus the Martyr, London Bridge, 1671–1676, steeple 1705–1706.

St Nicholas, Cole Abbey, 1671–1678.

St Stephen, Walbrook, 1672–1679, spire 1713–1717.

St Stephen, Coleman Street, 1674–1677. Destroyed 1940.

St Peter-upon-Cornhill, 1675–1681.

St James, Piccadilly, 1676–1684.

St James, Garlickhythe, 1676–1683, steeple 1713–1717.

St Michael, Bassishaw, 1676–1679, steeple 1708–1712. Demolished 1900.

St Michael, Queenhythe, 1676–1680, tower and spire 1685–1687. Demolished 1876.

All Hallows the Great, Thames Street, 1677–1682. Demolished 1894.

St Benet, Paul's Wharf, 1677–1683.

Christ Church, Newgate Street, 1677–1687, tower 1703–1704. Destroyed 1940. Tower remains, church left in ruins.

St Swithun, Cannon Street, 1677–1685. Destroyed 1941.

St Antholin, Budge Row, 1678–1683, spire 1686–1687. Demolished 1876.

St Mary Aldermary, 1679–1682, tower reconstructed 1701–1703.

St Augustine, Watling Street, 1680–1686, spire 1695–1696. Destroyed 1941. Church demolished, spire reconstructed.

St Clement Danes, 1680–1682, steeple James Gibbs, 1719–1720.

St Benet, Gracechurch Street, 1681–1687. Demolished 1876.

St Mary Abchurch, 1681–1686.

St Matthew, Friday Street, 1681–1686. Demolished 1885.

St Mildred, Bread Street, 1681–1687. Destroyed 1941.

St Alban, Wood Street, 1682–1687. Destroyed 1940. Tower remaining.

St Clement, Eastcheap, 1683–1687.

St Mary Magdalen, Old Fish Street, 1683–1687. Demolished 1890.

St Andrew, Holborn, 1684–1692, tower 1703–1704.

St Margaret Pattens, 1684–1687, spire 1702.

St Michael, Crooked Lane, 1684–1687, spire 1709–1714. Demolished 1831.

St Andrew-by-the-Wardrobe, 1685–1694.

All Hallows, Lombard Street, 1686–1694. Demolished 1939.

St Margaret, Lothbury, 1686–1690, spire 1699.

St Mary Somerset, 1686–1694. Demolished 1871. Tower left standing.

St Michael, Paternoster Royal, 1686–1694, steeple 1713–1717.

St Vedast, Coleman Street, 1695–1700, steeple 1709–1712.

St Christopher-le-Stocks, 1712–1714. Demolished 1781–1786.

Architect Robert Hooke (1635–1703)[368]

St Edmund, King and Martyr, 1670–1676, steeple 1706–1707.

St Bartholomew, Exchange, 1674–1681. Demolished 1841.

St Anne and St Agnes, Gresham Street, 1676–1681.

St Martin-within-Ludgate, 1677–1686.

St Peter, Cornhill, 1677–1681, steeple 1685.

Architect: William Talman (1650–1719)[369]

St Anne, Soho, 1680–1686.

Architect: John James (1672–1746)

St George, Hanover Square, 1712–1724.

Architect: Thomas Archer (1668–1743)

St Paul, Deptford, 1712–1730.

---

368 Attributions according to Adrian Tinniswoode, *His Invention So Fertile: A life of Christopher Wren,* Jonathan Cape, London, 2001, 212, 400.

369 Sometimes ascribed to Wren, but very un-Wrenian in style.

St John, Smith Square, 1714–1728.

Architect: Nicholas Hawksmoor (1661–1736)

St Anne, Limehouse, 1712–1724.

Christ Church, Spitalfields, 1714.

St Alfege, Greenwich, 1714–1718, tower John James 1730.

St George-in-the-East, 1715–1723. Roofless, interior destroyed 1941. Modernist church now occupies east end.

St Michael, Cornhill tower 1718–1724.

St Mary Woolnoth, 1719–1727.

St George, Bloomsbury, 1720–1730.

Westminster Abbey twin towers 1734–1735.

Architect: James Gibbs (1682–1754)

St Mary-le-Strand, 1714–1717.

St Peter's, Vere Street, 1721–1724.

St Martin-in-the-Fields, 1722–1726.

Architects: Nicholas Hawksmoor (1661–1736) and John James (1672–1746)

St John, Horsleydown, 1727–1733. Demolished 1970.

St Luke, Old Street, 1727–1733.

Architect: Henry Flitcroft (1697–1769)

St Giles-in-the-Fields, 1731–1734.

St Olave, Tooley Street, 1737–1739. Demolished 1929.

Architect: John Price ( )

St George the Martyr, Southwark, 1734–1736.

Architect: George Dance the Elder (1695–1768)

St Leonard's, Shoreditch, 1736–1740.

St Matthew, Bethnal Green, 1743–1746.

St Botolph, Aldgate, 1744.

Architect: John Sanderson ( )[370]

St John, Hampstead 1745–1747.

Architect: George Dance the Younger (1741–1825)

All Hallows, London Wall, 1765–1767.

Architect: James Carr (1742–1821)

St James, Clerkenwell, 1780–1792.

---

370 Possibly a modification of a design by Henry Flitcroft.

Appendix 3

St Mary-le-Bow 1680

St Anne, Soho, 1686

St Martin-within-Ludgate, 1686

St Augustine, Watling Street 1696

St Margaret, Lothbury 1699

St Bride 1703

St Margaret Pattens 1702

Christ Church Newgate Street 1704

St Paul's Cathedral west towers 1705

St Magnus 1706

St Edmund King and Martyr 1709

St Michael Bassishaw 1712

St Vedast 1712

St Michael, Crooked Lane 1714

St Stephen Walbrook 1717

St Michael Paternoster Royal 1717

St James Garlickhythe 1717

St Mary-le-Strand 1717

St Clement Danes 1720

St George-in-the-East 1723

St Anne, Limehouse 1724

St George Hanover Square 1724

St Martin-in-the-Fields 1726

St Paul's, Deptford 1730

St Alfege, Greenwich 1730

St John Horselydown 1733

St Luke, Old Street 1733

St Giles-in-the-Fields 1734

St George the Martyr, Southwark 1736

St Olave, Tooley Street, 1739

St Leonard's, Shoreditch 1740

St James, Clerkenwell 1792

About the Author

Nigel Pennick was born in 1946 in Guildford, Surrey, and spent his childhood in London and Essex. A graduate of London University, he qualified in the biological sciences, and worked in scientific research for fifteen years in Cambridge, with periods at the Université Libre de Bruxelles, Belgium and the University of Guelph, Canada. During this time he published twenty-nine scientific papers that described eight new species of marine algae. In parallel with his scientific work, he also participated in folk traditions and the scene in Cambridge, and in 1985 he became a full-time writer and lecturer on history and folklore.

In 1975, he founded the Institute of Geomantic Research, which published a journal and a number of papers on all aspects of geomancy and earth mysteries. In the late 1970s and early 80s he organized six geomantic conferences in Cambridge and nearby towns, and from the mid-1980s to the late 90s he travelled widely and gave lectures and workshops in Ireland, Holland, Germany, Switzerland, Austria and the United States as well as in Great Britain. He has also organized and participated in several spiritual tours of ancient sacred places in England, Wales and Ireland, and written books on a range of subjects, including runes, mythology, geomancy, ley lines, labyrinths, Celtic art and landscapes, traditional rites and ceremonies, folk magic and the histories of certain underground railways in London.

He is also an artist in traditional media and stained glass, and has illustrated many of his books. In 2011 a one-man show of his Visionary Steeples artwork was held at Emmanuel Church, Cambridge. He plays with The Traditional Music of Cambridgeshire Collective and participates in the traditional calendar customs of Cambridgeshire. In 2009 he restored the custom of parading the May Day Garland through Cambridge.